TARIFFS: THE CASE EXAMINED

TARIFFS:
THE CASE EXAMINED

By a Committee of Economists under the Chairmanship of
S<small>IR</small> WILLIAM BEVERIDGE, K.C.B.

LONGMANS, GREEN AND CO.
LONDON ◆ NEW YORK ◆ TORONTO
1932

LONGMANS, GREEN AND CO. LTD.

39 PATERNOSTER ROW, LONDON, E.C.4
6 OLD COURT HOUSE STREET, CALCUTTA
53 NICOL ROAD, BOMBAY
36A MOUNT ROAD, MADRAS

LONGMANS, GREEN AND CO.

55 FIFTH AVENUE, NEW YORK
221 EAST 20TH STREET, CHICAGO
88 TREMONT STREET, BOSTON
128-132 UNIVERSITY AVENUE, TORONTO

First Edition October 1931
Reprinted October 1931
Second Edition June 1932
Popular Edition June 1932

Made in Great Britain

PREFACE TO SECOND EDITION

THIS book, written for the most part before the exchange crisis which drove Britain off the gold standard in September 1931, was published on 13th October, just after the exchange crisis, but a fortnight before the General Election which followed it in October. The new conditions of the moment were dealt with, so far as possible, in an Epilogue and by an Appendix on the Gold Standard supplementing the account given in Chapter III of the machinery of International Trade.

In this new edition now published, both Epilogue and Appendix have been replaced by a chapter on "The Balance of Trade," written by Mr. F. C. Benham. This chapter is essentially a supplement both to Chapter III on "The Machinery of International Trade" and to Chapter VII on "Tariffs as Instruments of International Equilibrium." It examines on the basis of an inconvertible currency matters dealt with in those chapters on the basis of the gold standard. The other chapters in the book, though written while there was no reason to doubt the continuance of the gold standard, in Britain and elsewhere, are not in any important particular affected by assuming instead that the currency is inconvertible.

A few foot-notes have been added and a few verbal corrections made. Otherwise the book remains as in the first edition. No attempt has been made to examine or criticise the actual measures now before Parliament or already approved by it for taxing imports or establishing quota schemes. The book is issued, as it is described in the German translation that has just been published, as a text-book of the general principles of international trade, though with special reference to the position of Great Britain.

May 1932.

[v]

PREFACE

THE aim of this volume, as its title indicates, is exposition
and criticism, rather than the breaking of new ground in
science. It is addressed to general readers, as a contribution
to their judgment on a political issue of the day, rather than
to professional economists. By the nature of its subject-
matter, it is concerned both with elementary considerations
and elementary difficulties in the understanding of foreign
trade, and with intricate theorisings as to the nature and
conditions of international equilibrium. To professional
economists, accordingly, most of the book will seem a
repetition of platitudes; this will not matter, if the remainder of the book also remains intelligible to the general
reader without his having to learn a new language. In this
remaining portion the arguments for a British tariff advanced recently by one or two distinguished economists
have been examined, so far as possible, without the use of
technical terms.

The book arises out of discussions begun in November
1930 between a number of persons, all of whom are or have
been engaged academically in the study or teaching of
economics. By these other avocations the actual writing of
the book has been compressed within a few weeks of successive vacations. While it was being written, economic
troubles of all kinds crowded thick and fast on the world
and on Britain. Just after it had been finished, an exchange
crisis drove sterling off the gold standard. The bearing
of this event on the arguments and conclusions set out
in the book is discussed briefly in the Epilogue. The
account of the machinery of international trade given in
Chapter III has been supplemented in an Appendix.

The book falls into two main parts, with a conclusion.
The first part, containing Chapters I to X, is a continuous

exposition of the general issue between Free Trade and Protection in all its principal related aspects. To secure uniformity of approach and presentation it has been written by one hand, that of our Chairman, though it incorporates the work of many others. The second part has and needs less uniformity; the Chapters from XI to XVI are essays by different hands on topics which, though desirable to fill in the scope of the volume are less central to its main theme and can be discussed independently. The concluding review again has been written by our Chairman.

For the wording and detailed argument the writers named in each case are responsible. We have regarded ourselves as a Committee for discussion and mutual criticism, rather than as drafting or editing a report which each should sign with equal individual assent to every sentence and every word. There are probably in each chapter phrases which some or other of us would have altered and arguments which some one or other of us might omit or put differently. In substance what is set forth below represents our common mind, and on its main practical conclusion there is no shadow of difference between us. We have surveyed once more, in the light of to-day, the well-trodden fields of this ancient controversy. After that survey we should all think it a disaster, if the policy of Free Trade which has served Britain so well materially, as through her it has served as an inspiration to all who in any land have worked for good understanding among nations, were to-day to be sacrificed to ignorance or panic or jealousy or specious calculations of a moment's gain.

F. C. BENHAM   W. T. LAYTON
W. H. BEVERIDGE   A. PLANT
A. L. BOWLEY   L. C. ROBBINS
T. E. GREGORY   G. L. SCHWARTZ
J. R. HICKS

August 1931.

CONTENTS

[viii]

CHAPTER I

FROM 1903 TO 1931

"THE principles on which our present fiscal system was based sixty years ago seem to me to be not ultimate but derivative. They were obtained by applying certain truths, which are as universal as the truths of geometry or mechanics, to certain conditions which were transitional. If these principles are converted into dogmas the same error is made as if the rules laid down for building a bridge, when the only materials available consisted of pine logs, were regarded as sacred dogmas governing for ever the construction of bridges for purposes and under conditions of which the original builders had never dreamed, and when the materials to be used were steel or granite. The art of engineering involves an organised study and judgment of the proportions of divers considerations, tending in different directions; and no one can be certain of getting the right proportions even for the problem which he knows best. It is not by applying without question the judgments as to proportion, which were made by the great men who founded our present system, but by forming our own judgment on the facts of our own generation as they did of theirs, that we can show ourselves worthy to be their followers."[1]

With these words, in 1903, the undisputed leader of British economists began his answer to the question of "How far, and in what directions, the circumstances which formerly made Free Trade the best policy for this country have been altered." In 1931, when fiscal policy is once again the chief public issue of the day, economists making their contribution to the understanding of this issue cannot

[1] Memorandum on Fiscal Policy of International Trade (1903), § 31 ; printed in *Official Papers* by Alfred Marshall, p. 386.

take a better starting-point than Alfred Marshall's. There are in economic science immutable truths which, properly expressed, no serious economist would question. The application of these truths to practical problems does not lead all men, even of those who appreciate fully the truth, at all times to the same prescriptions for action. On the one hand, judgment as to the desirability of government action in any given sphere involves issues on which economists of equal standing may take different views; the decision may turn ultimately on their opinions of the competence of the government machinery available to execute, wisely and incorruptibly, a theoretically desirable policy. On the other hand, the material conditions both of the economic and the political problems involved may change. The practical issues of to-day must be settled, if they are to be wisely settled, with regard to the facts of to-day, not those of twenty-five or eighty-five years ago.

In what respects, relevant to fiscal policy, do conditions to-day differ materially from those which ruled in the opening years of this century? Three important changes of conditions at once suggest themselves:

The first of these is the apparent worsening of the general economic position of Britain. When fiscal policy was last the subject of general debate in this country—twenty-five to thirty years ago—all the available records showed a nearly steady growth of prosperity. For fifty years or more, up to 1900, production, trade, consumption, wages, and income per head had all been rising. The country seemed able to maintain perpetually growing numbers at a steadily rising standard of living. Those who advocated fiscal change at that time pointed, indeed, to the yet more rapid growth of other countries, or emphasised such dark spots as they could find in this bright picture. But the opening chapter of the criticism issued by Professor Pigou in 1903, of the various proposals for fiscal change then current, could be devoted to proving with a few simple figures the solid progress of the country. "The plea for urgency in finding some defence against the imminent decay of our material prosperity is not one which can be seriously sustained."[1] It would not be easy to take this line to-day, when our national income per head appears to be stationary, our exports cut down to two-thirds of the pre-War level, our average of unemployment doubled or trebled. Those who still oppose a change of fiscal policy must do so, not on the grounds of letting well alone, but on the ground that some other remedy for our ills is better, or that the fiscal measures proposed are worse than no remedy at all. There may be differences of view about the extent to which our general prosperity, as measured by indices of production or national income or trade, is really threatened. There can be none about the higher level of unemployment to-day, and the serious dislocation that this points to in our economic life.

The second change to be noted is the growth of economic nationalism. Some of the founders of Free Trade in this country were so convinced of their argument that they expected all other countries to follow the example of Britain; they looked for a speedy removal of all tariff barriers to international trade throughout the world. "I believe if you abolish the Corn Law honestly, and adopt Free Trade in its simplicity, there will not be a tariff in Europe that will not be changed in less than five years to follow your example." It looked at first as if matters would take the course thus forecast by Cobden.[2] For a generation after the repeal of the British Corn Laws, the Free Trade movement in Europe was strong; tariffs generally were lowered. Then, however, came a change. The United States after the Civil War, Germany in 1879, France in 1881 successively embarked upon a policy of Protection. Other countries followed down the same path. The multiplication of separate states since the War has meant a multiplication of tariff barriers. The movement of tariffs since 1903 has unmistakably been upwards.

How does this affect the question of fiscal policy for this country? Directly it does not affect it at all. Cobden's

[1] *The Riddle of the Tariff*, p. 9 (1903).
[2] *The Speeches of Richard Cobden*, I, p. 360, 15th January 1846.

case for Free Trade as the best policy for Britain did not depend upon the adoption of a similar policy by other countries, and is not defeated by the defeat of his expectations as to what other countries would do.[1] The uselessness of one-sided Free Trade is one of the common arguments for Protection which will be examined in due course, and in its simplest form will be disposed of simply. The protectionist policy of other countries, however, gives rise to other and less simple arguments which call for full consideration. Many people who regard tariffs as a harmful interference with business and Free Trade as the ideal, feel that the policies of other nations have made a tariff now indispensable for Britain. Only by a tariff, it seems, can we be secure against harmful forms of international trade, such as dumping from behind a tariff wall or dumping aided yet more directly by the State. Not till we have set up a tariff ourselves can we bargain successfully for the lowering of other tariffs, or make arrangements for preferential trade. "The only effective weapon against tariffs is a tariff."[2]

The third development of which note must be taken here is the growing interference by the State with individual freedom in fields other than that of foreign trade. When the fiscal policy of Free Trade was established eighty years ago it was, in the minds of many of its supporters, only one branch of a wider policy of *laisser-faire*. Cobden, Bright, and Joseph Hume fought Corn Laws and Factory Laws with equal conviction. Since their day the policy of *laisser-faire* has been abandoned or modified in one field after another. Many economic activities formerly free have become subject to restriction—by laws regulating hours and conditions of work, by minimum wage legislation, by the recognition accorded to trade unionism and collective bargaining, and latterly even by direct control of prices. This movement to State control has become markedly more rapid within the present century.

[1] Cf. Pigou, *op. cit.*, p. 29.
[2] *The Times*, Leading article, 18th December 1930.

Restriction of individual activities in one field of economic life is not, indeed, by itself, an argument for restriction in all other fields or any of them. Because a man takes to wearing a hat upon his head it does not follow that he ought to wear a hat or even gloves upon his hands. "The whole of civilised society is based on the principle that people should be allowed to do what they like until good reason is shown to the contrary. . . . A bare proof that complete *laisser-faire* is bad, impossible and inconceivable, does not carry with it a corollary that every proposal for preventing people from doing what they want to do is right."[1]

Rejection of *laisser-faire* as a general principle is not an argument for adopting an equally general opposite principle of State control. Its bearing on the tariff issue is more specific. In the first place the State is felt to be, and probably is, in fact, more competent for intervention in economic affairs than it was eighty years ago. How far the business men who support Protection would go with their Socialist allies along this line of reasoning is uncertain. But at least Britain possesses to-day, as she did not possess in 1846, a highly trained and incorruptible Civil Service, with growing practice in dealing with industrial and financial problems. In the second place, the direct argument is often used that it is irrational to compel manufacturers in this country to pay minimum wages or observe statutory conditions of work, and yet leave them exposed to the competition of manufacturers in other countries where wages are less and conditions unregulated.

These three developments—of apparent decline in prosperity, of growing economic nationalism, and of growing public interference with the economic activities of the individual—must be faced frankly by any modern inquirer into fiscal policy. Each of them will be considered incidentally in discussing the various projects for fiscal change put forward by different writers. The first of them, in its

---

[1] Cannan, *Wealth* (3rd edition), p. 250.

most prominent feature of unemployment, is sufficiently important to call for a chapter by itself.

Some things have changed since 1903. One fundamental fact which should govern all discussions of fiscal policy remains to all intents and purposes unchanged. This is our dependence on trade overseas. In 1903 Britain imported from overseas 82 per cent. of the wheat, 45 per cent. of the meat, and about 85 per cent. of the butter, as well as all the sugar needed to support her population. To-day she imports 80 per cent. of the wheat and flour, 60 per cent. of the meat, 89 per cent. of the butter and 94 per cent. of the sugar.[1] In 1903 Britain imported all the raw cotton, 68 per cent. of the wool, and 32 per cent. of the iron ore used in her industries, to say nothing of rubber, oil-seeds, and many minor raw materials; she imports still all the cotton, 77 per cent. of the wool, and 28 per cent. of the iron ore. On the side of exports the first Census of Production showed that in 1907 just over 30 per cent. of our total industrial production in that year was destined for export; in 1924 the proportion is 27 per cent. The figures for particular commodities are striking.

PERCENTAGE OF TOTAL PRODUCTION EXPORTED

	1907	1924
Cotton piece goods . . .	89	79
Wool tissues, flannels, delaines .	43	48
Tinplate	77	71
Linen piece goods . . .	51	54
Coal	37	30
Jute piece goods . . .	not given	38-40
Cutlery	50	38

Some of the figures are a little up, and some are a little down. Over all, probably, since the War at least, the

[1] In all, 60 per cent. of all our foodstuffs come from overseas. *Ministry of Agriculture Report on Agricultural Output and The Food Supplies of Great Britain.*

domestic trade of the country has gained a little on the overseas trade. Since 1920 certainly the occupations supplying goods and services to the consumer at home have grown in numbers relatively to occupations connected with export. In fundamentals the situation has not changed at all.

In the hundred years from 1830 to 1930 the real wages and other income of the working classes has been raised nearly threefold, while their number has increased fourfold. Britain as a whole has become much the most densely populated region of its size in the world at anything like its standard of living. The means to this achievement—or the price of it—has been the specialisation of its population upon activities needing little space, but exploiting to the full its natural resources for industry and its insular position for trade, *i.e.* has been the merging of itself in the economic life of the world.

The dependence of Britain upon overseas trade for prosperity is the governing fact of the situation. Any policy which neglects it can lead only to disaster. Any discussion of tariffs which is not based on understanding of the nature of international trade, of the purposes which it serves, and of the machinery by which it is carried on, is beating the air.

To the explanation of international trade the next two chapters accordingly are devoted. A fourth chapter—on the nature of tariffs—completes the introduction and clears the ground. In Chapters V to IX all the chief arguments now current for a protective tariff in Britain, that is to say, a tariff designed to keep out imports that would otherwise come in, are examined in turn. In Chapter X the clash of sectional and general interests involved in Protection is reviewed.

The four chapters that follow deal with issues other than Protection in general—with dumping and the defence against it, with agriculture as a leading case for selective Protection, with the possibilities of imperial preference, and with the case for a revenue tariff.

There follows, to bring the book up to date, an account

of tariff-making in practice, and a criticism of import boards and other devices alternative to tariffs that have been advocated for the same purpose.

In Chapter XVII the conclusions reached are summarised and the case is reviewed.

CHAPTER II

WHY do men trade? On what terms do they trade? How, in respect of terms or effects on well-being or otherwise, does trade between citizens of the same country compare with trade between citizens of different countries? In the answers to these questions lies the main theoretical argument on which the case for Free Trade for this or any other country must be based.

Why do men trade? In its simplest terms the answer is that men trade in order to gain the advantages of specialisation. While every man has many varied needs—for food, shelter, clothing, recreation, physic, and the rest—it pays each man to concentrate on doing himself what he can do best, and getting by exchange from others what they can make or do best, instead of being a farmer, a carpenter, tailor, actor, doctor in turn. By specialisation and exchange, by the shoemaker sticking to his last and the farmer to his plough, both shoemaker and farmer are enriched.

Unless, indeed, there were this prospect of enrichment on each side, there would not in a free country be specialisation and exchange at all. The farmer who wants both food and shoes will not make more food than he wants and no shoes, unless he thinks that by doing so and exchanging part of his food with a shoemaker for shoes, he will be better off than if he tried to meet both his different wants directly. The fact that both farmer and shoemaker continue freely to specialise and exchange is itself proof that both feel themselves better off for doing so, that the needs of each and thus of both are satisfied in this way by a smaller total effort. In trade, one thing is given only for another thing; what is given, indeed, is necessarily of less value to the giver than what he counts on getting in exchange. Only on these terms will men trade at all.

These statements, which are obvious truisms for the imaginary case of the single farmer and single shoemaker in the same village, are no less true for trade between groups of producers in different districts. Regional specialisation has economic advantages as definite as individual specialisation. Sometimes these advantages are so obvious that no one questions them. Extractive industries like mining, and many agricultural industries—rubber, cotton, oil-seeds—are tied to certain portions of the earth; they could be carried on elsewhere only at prohibitive cost, if they could be carried on at all. In manufacturing generally the advantages of a particular locality are less overwhelming and less obvious, but they are none the less real. It is true that almost any kind of manufacturing can, at a price, be done almost anywhere. It is not true that every or any kind of manufacturing can be done as efficiently in one place as in another, *i.e.* that location is irrelevant to it. Nor is the economic advantage of particular locations for particular industries destroyed by the existence of international boundaries. Within any national area, prudent business men take pains to erect their factories at the point of greatest convenience, having regard to differences in sources of raw materials, location of markets, supply of labour or power, and so forth. Such differences do not disappear because the possible sites between which the choice has to be made have a political frontier between them. The development of international trade under conditions of freedom is in itself the proof of gain by national specialisation; if there were no gain, there would be no trade. "If goods, which can be produced at home, are yet imported freely from abroad, that shows that they can be got generally at less cost by making other things with which to buy them from abroad than by the direct method of making them at home."[1]

---

[1] Marshall, *op. cit.*, p. 391. The assertion made by Mr. Amery (*Empire and Prosperity*, p. 61) that " the greater part of modern

The fundamental argument for complete freedom of trade is that under it the different parts of the earth's surface will be put to those uses for which, taken as a whole and with regard to the labour available and to other factors of production, they have the maximum suitability. This does not mean that each product will be made in that place where, considered by itself, it can be made most easily—in the place that would be chosen if nothing else had to be made as well. All the different products have to be considered together; the same field in a farm may be the best both for growing wheat and for the farm buildings, but it cannot be used for both. To understand the nature of international trade, under conditions of freedom, it will be well to return for a moment to our imaginary farmer and shoemaker.

Concentration in work is the key to variety and abundance in consumption. Concentration pays even for Admirable Crichtons. As between the farmer and shoemaker, the advantages of specialisation and exchange do not depend on each being better at his own task than the other would be at that task. The farmer may be better than the shoemaker both at farming and at cobbling, but still find that it pays best for him to keep to farming. Suppose, for instance, that the production of a quarter of wheat and a pair of shoes represents in each case four hours' work of A, but that B would take five hours to make the shoes and seven to produce the quarter of wheat. Then, if each wants a pair of shoes and a quarter of wheat and sets out to produce them separately, A must work eight hours and B twelve hours, or twenty in all. But if A produces both quarters of wheat, taking eight hours, and B produces both pairs of shoes, taking ten hours, the same combined result will have been reached, not in twenty

economic production can take place in one country as well as another," is ambiguous. If it means, for instance, that motor cars can, at a price, be made almost anywhere, it is a true but idle statement. If it means that motor cars can be made and marketed as cheaply wherever they are made, and that it doesn't matter where the motor factory is put down, it is untrue.

[11]

hours, but in eighteen hours. Even though A is better than B both at farming and at shoemaking, it will be profitable for A to stick to farming because his advantage over B is there greatest; conversely, it will be profitable for B to stick to shoemaking because his inferiority to A is there least. The gains of specialisation and exchange depend not on absolute, but on relative advantages and disadvantages.

It may be asked whether this imaginary illustration of farmer and shoemaker has any practical bearing on the facts of life? The answer is that it certainly has. Consideration shows that parallel cases occur constantly in real life; their moral is of fundamental importance for an understanding of international trade. The general manager of a business may also be a first-rate accountant and a first-rate driver of cars, better at each of these things than most cashiers or most paid drivers. Yet it will almost certainly pay him to stick to his general managing and hire a cashier and a driver, rather than divert part of his time to keeping his own accounts or doing his own driving. It will pay him if, while excelling these others as cashier or driver, he excels them still more in managing business. In that case it will pay all parties best for him to concentrate on the work which they are least capable of doing, and leave to them that of which they are most capable. The moral of this, as applied not to individuals but to countries, is that even if one country be superior to another country at every kind of production, trade between them may still develop and be profitable to both. The maximum output of the two together will be obtained by the superior country concentrating on those branches of work for which it has greatest advantage, and leaving to others those where its advantage, though still existing, is relatively less. This principle, known to economists as the theory of comparative costs, has important practical bearings on the problem of trade between countries of widely different standards of living and wage rates. This is the principle which makes it advantageous often for one country to buy from another articles which it could itself make more cheaply. It will come up again and again in the discussions that follow.

In the simple illustrations given above, trade has been described as if it were barter, a direct exchange of shoes for wheat. In practice to-day trade, alike between citizens of the same country and between citizens of different countries, hardly ever takes the form of barter. It is conducted through a medium of exchange; it takes the form of selling goods or services for money. The use of money introduces complications of various kinds. One complication arises from the fact that money is not only a medium of exchange but is also a unit of account; things exchanged through the medium of money exchange at prices expressed in terms of money. Another complication is that money is not only a medium of exchange and a unit of account, but is also "a store of value"; it can be borrowed and lent, both domestically and internationally. Yet another complication is that different countries use different kinds of money; in contrast to domestic trade, international trade is generally complicated by considerations of currency and of rates of exchange between different currencies. These complications in the machinery of trade give rise to some of the most important arguments now current in favour of checking or controlling imports by tariffs. Because the exchange of goods and services in international trade does not take the simple form of barter, a reduction of imports is not automatically reflected in a reduction of exports. Because the prices at which goods exchange may change, and change differently for different classes of goods, the terms of trade between any one country and the rest of the world, that is to say, the quantity of imports that it can get for a given quantity of exports, may and do vary from one time to another. Because exchange of goods and services in international trade is bound up with movements of international credit and exchanges, it may appear possible for a country to gain advantages in the management of its currency or the guidance of investment by restricting the freedom of its citizens in trade. It will be desirable, accordingly, in the following chapter to describe in some detail the machinery of international trade. The arguments for tariffs arising from the nature of that machinery will be examined in Chapters VI and VII.[1]

Apart from these questions of machinery, what are the doubts that can be raised as to the general advantage of international trade, judged by its purpose of exchange based on specialisation? What reasons can be given for restricting the freedom of citizens to trade abroad as freely as at home? They are broadly two.

The first doubt arises from the possibility of conflict between the economic interests of the nation as a whole and of some of its individual members. The Free Trade case is that, if the individual citizens of a country are left to seek their own interest in deciding what to produce and how and where to buy and sell, the country will in general have those occupations and industries for which the people and resources are best suited, and which will therefore yield the largest measure of prosperity. Against this it is pointed out that individual self-seeking may not always lead to general good. Individuals naturally take narrower or shorter views than the State. Perhaps it would be safer to say that the State, if it knows its business, should take broader and longer views than individuals; should sometimes step in to prevent extreme individualism from sacrificing the greater good to the less, the permanent to the passing good. This

[1] There is one highly theoretical argument, as to the possible advantage to a country of shifting the terms of trade in its favour (*i.e.* lowering the prices of what it imports in relation to what it exports) by imposing a tariff, to which no further reference is made in this volume. Those who are interested in these matters may find the argument briefly stated and answered by Professor Jacob Viner in an article on " The Tariff Question and the Economist " in the *Nation and Athenæum* of 7th February 1931. " No economist, as far as I know " (Professor Viner concludes), " has ever maintained that the gain to any country from the favourable shift in the terms of trade due to Protection is ever likely, under conceivable circumstances, to equal her loss from the uneconomic re-allocation of her productive resources."

is the argument that has to be advanced, not for tariffs only, but for every kind of interference by the State in economic affairs; for factory laws and minimum wage Acts and all their like. Its application in the field of international trade is to serve as the philosophical basis underlying most arguments for protection of infant industries, for defence against dumping, and for customs unions or preferential trade within tariff walls.

A second consideration commonly influencing judgments on international trade is the conception of the State as existing for other than strictly economic purposes; for defence, or for a particular type of life or culture. This consideration, again, is not peculiar to problems of international trade, and boundaries between economic and other purposes are hard to define. But it is convenient to distinguish between arguments turning upon more or less of wealth measured in terms of money, and arguments directed to such ends as securing a fair proportion between urban and rural life in each country, or being prepared for war, or linking trade with particular political ideas and institutions such as those of the British Empire.

These are all serious arguments. They do not, any more than do arguments arising out of the mechanism of foreign payments and foreign lending, challenge the general case for freedom of international trade as a long-run economic policy. As such, indeed, the case is unchallengeable. "The fact of trade establishes an overwhelming presumption that the commodities obtained from abroad in exchange for exports are so obtained at lower cost than that which the domestic production of their equivalent would entail. If this were not the case, they would not be imported, even under Free Trade."[1] It is not immaterial whether an

[1] This is the "positive argument" for Free Trade, as expressed by Professor Jacob Viner ("The Tariff Question and the Economist" in the *Nation and Athenæum* of 7th February 1931). "The negative argument rests on the weakness of the objections which after several centuries of sustained effort Protectionists have been able to accumulate against this simple positive argument for Free Trade."

article is made abroad and imported or is made at home. It will not under Free Trade be made abroad and imported unless there is economic advantage in this. To justify causing it, by a tax or otherwise, to be made at home, it is necessary to prove some countervailing advantage, economic or other, in that special case. The burden of proof rests always with those who interfere.

For international trade is but one form and no peculiar form of the division of labour, and finds justification in the advantages which spring from division of labour and specialisation. Its purpose is to increase the wealth of all who take part in it, as definitely and as generally as is that of trade freely conducted between citizens of the same country.

CHAPTER III

THE MACHINERY OF INTERNATIONAL TRADE [1]

NOTHING for nothing is the rule of international trade as of all other forms of trade. Citizens of other countries will not freely send us imports unless they get or have got something in return; citizens of this country cannot afford to make and send out exports unless they get or have got something in return. There must be a balance of some kind between what goes into each country and what goes out of it.

What is it, however, that goes in and goes out? Suppose an observer gifted with miraculous vision, able to see through walls and roofs and the backs of books of account, yet lifted high enough above earth to watch international trade as a whole. What would it look like to him? He would see, in the first place, streams of goods in every stage of rawness or manufacture moving across seas and land frontiers into each country and out of it. The inward and the outward stream for each country would be on the whole different in kind and finish. Some countries would have an inward stream mainly of food and raw materials, and an outward stream mainly finished; for some the position would be reversed. But there would be very few countries which had not some nearly raw materials and some manufactures in each stream; nearly all the larger countries would send to each other and receive from each other copious streams of highly finished goods of different kinds. The flow inward and the flow outward for each country would seem to bear some relation to one another—a big or growing inward stream of goods would generally be associated with a big or growing outward stream, but

[1] This chapter, printed before the events of September 1931, should be supplemented by Chapter XVIII on the Balance of Trade.

the relation would be neither uniform for all countries nor constant for any, nor would it be one of equality. For some countries the inward stream and for others the outward stream would be more valuable than that which met it; these differences might be seen persisting for generations and even growing. The observer would see, in the second place, not only goods moving over the earth; there would also be ships to carry the goods, and messages and documents with them, and here and there a gleam of gold. The ships, wherever found, would bear the flags mainly of a few countries, and notably of one country, whose inward stream largely exceeded its outward stream of goods; the observer would be intelligent enough to guess that the services rendered by these ships and their crews in moving goods for other people were really an addition to the outward stream—invisible exports—from the country to which they belonged. He would observe also that, as goods left one country to go to another, there was recorded in one or both countries some kind of claim by persons in the first country upon persons in the second country, and that in all countries there were people who made a business of recording these claims and setting them off against one another, and sending documents and messages to one another about them. Some of these claims would at once cancel out against one another. Sometimes persons in one country would agree for a number of years not to enforce claims they might have against persons in another country, and for doing this—called foreign investment—would receive documents recording their right to satisfaction of the claim in due course, and to additional annual claims by way of interest; they would get long-dated securities. Sometimes they would leave their claims unsatisfied, without committing themselves for any long or definite period, and thus build up balances which could be called in from the other country at need, balances recorded in documents of various kinds, which might all be described as short-dated securities. Finally, as has been said, there would be seen gold, coming out as a continuous stream from one or two countries to spread over all the world, as between all other countries moving now this way and now that way, for all these other countries a gleam almost lost in the stream of goods.

All these things—goods, services, securities (long or short-dated), gold—our imaginary observer would see. One thing, somewhat oddly, he would not see: the movement of anything that men usually call money. Pounds sterling, dollars, francs, marks, lire, and the rest of them would all stay in their own countries; a few would be seen as occasional visitors elsewhere, but obviously not at home there, and having nothing to do or say to the streams of goods and services. The completion of a domestic sale or purchase is often said to be marked by the money passing. In international trade money does not seem to pass at all.

We shall come to the explanation of that apparent paradox in a moment. It will be best as a first step to complete our imaginary observer's view of international trade by bringing him down from the clouds, to see how his picture works out in the figures of inward and outward movement for a particular country, the country with which we are most concerned. The overleaf table sets out briefly the account of the United Kingdom in international trade in the last year before the War, and in three years since the War (1924, 1929, and 1930).

The table shows that in each year we received goods from abroad to a value much greater than the value of what we exported and that, while there were movements both inwards and outwards of bullion, these by no means made up the difference. Taking goods and bullion together the receipts of the United Kingdom exceeded what it sent out by £158,000,000 in 1913, £324,000,000 in 1924, £366,000,000 in 1929 and £392,000,000 in 1930.

This does not mean, of course, that in each of these years foreigners (including for this purpose inhabitants of the overseas empire) were making us presents of goods and gold to the amounts named. The excess of goods and gold

INTERNATIONAL TRADING ACCOUNT OF THE UNITED KING-
DOM IN 1913, 1924, 1929 AND 1930[1]

	(In millions of pounds.)			
	1913	1924	1929	1930
Due to United Kingdom:—				
For Exports of Goods produced in United Kingdom	525	801	730	571
For Exports of Bullion .	62	62	87	90
For Shipping Services .	94	140	130	105
As Net Income on Overseas Investments . . .	210	220	270	235
As Short Interest, Commissions and for other Services	35	75	80	70
As Excess of Government Receipts from other Governments . . .	—	—	24	21
Total . . .	926	1298	1321	1092
Due from United Kingdom:—				
For Goods Imported and Retained	671	1137	1112	958
For Bullion Imported . .	74	50	71	95
As Excess of Government Payments to other Governments	—	25	—	—
Total . . .	745	1212	1183	1053
Net Balance due to United Kingdom	181	86	138	39

[1] The values of goods and bullion imported and exported are taken from the ordinary trade statistics. The other figures are from a table on p. 68 of the *Statistical Tables relating to British and Foreign Trade and Industry* (1924-1930), recently issued by the Board of Trade (Cmd. 3737). The figure of retained imports in 1913 exceeds by £12,000,000 the figure usually given, because it includes the value of diamonds imported, which is now excluded. Diamonds must have been included by the Board of Trade in preparing the table on p. 68, as otherwise the excess of merchandise and bullion imports would be only £146,000,000 in place of the £158,000,000 shown by them.

sent to us was in each year materially less than they owed us—for shipping and other services and interest on loans, so that at the end of each of the three years taken they owed us materially more than at the beginning. Some of this additional debt represented fresh long-term borrowing by them, or, from our point of view, new investment abroad, *i.e.* export of capital by us. Some might represent increases in their temporary indebtedness to us. On the other hand, in any particular year there might be decrease of temporary indebtedness, and the long-term foreign investment might be greater than the additional debt shown in the table. Two lines of the table—relating to government payments overseas—represent a new feature brought into the account since the War. On the one hand the British Government now makes each year payments of interest and principal on its debt to the United States of America; on the other hand, it receives sums from the governments of debtor countries and from Germany as reparations; the payments exceeded the receipts in 1924, but in 1929 and 1930 receipts exceeded payments.

There are thus many items on both sides of the account—goods, services, long-dated securities, short-dated securities, gold. There may be payments of interest on former debts to be allowed for. It is all the items taken together on each side that must balance; not any one item. How is the balance of all those items taken together brought about? How do the wheels of international trade go round? They don't go by passing money to and fro. They don't go by barter. Is there any connection, and, if so, what is the connection, between the purchase (say) of a French motor car by a Britisher and the export of British produce overseas.

The answer to this question is found in asking how the motor car gets paid for. The British purchaser, no doubt, pays for it by a cheque on his bank in Britain; he transfers £500 sterling to the agent from whom he bought. But the car was made in France; the agent has to put someone in France in a position to pay wages and other costs of production in France. For this purpose sterling is of no use at all; nothing is of any use except francs, since they are the only legal tender in the country where the car was made. To complete the transaction, the £500 sterling (or so much of it as represents the French maker's share—less any commission and transport charges) must be converted into francs; the agent must, directly or indirectly, find someone in France who wants sterling and will give francs for it. For what purpose can anyone in France want sterling, and what can he do with it when he has it? The principal and most obvious use of the sterling—the money of England—is to buy things in England, but the owner of the sterling in this case is in France, and what he buys in England will give him very little satisfaction till he ships it to France. The most obvious use of British currency in the hands of a man in France is therefore in the purchase and export of British goods, or, what is the same thing in another form, payments to persons in England for services rendered by them. That, however, is not the only possible use of it. The Frenchman who gives francs and gets sterling can use the latter to pay interest on a debt in Britain or to pay off the debt if he owes one, or he can invest the sterling in Britain, or he can leave it lying about in his bank in Britain, or he can, since 1925, turn his sterling into gold and ship that to France, or he can even decide that with £500 in his control he will migrate to Britain or spend a long holiday there.

There is clearly no necessary connection between any single export of goods and an equivalent import. Each export and each import is a transaction involving, in the first place, simply a change of international credit. Export of a motor car from France to Britain creates a sterling credit in favour of someone in France, gives someone in France a right if he wills to buy things up to the value of that credit in England. There may be someone at the same time in France wanting to buy goods of that value in Britain and import them into France, and if so, he can pay for the British goods by getting command of the sterling credit created by the export of the French motor car. But he decides to buy the British goods, in the first instance, because he wants them, not because he has a sterling credit or thinks that he can get one. In fact, if he is a man of good repute in his country, and if the times are normal, he knows that he can always get a sterling credit. There are people who make a business of providing such credits, for a consideration. The French merchant who wants British woollens doesn't first have to see if there is any other Frenchman who has just made a sale to Britain. The French manufacturer who sells a motor car to Britain doesn't do so in order to help another Frenchman to get woollens from Britain. Each transaction in import trade and in export trade, as Ricardo pointed out long ago, stands by itself.[1]

There is, indeed, no automatic connection between any two items of any kind in the international trading account of a country. It is the account as a whole that must balance, not particular items. Sometimes, indeed, we can espy a direct connection between the two sides. If, for instance, a new and energetic country, like Canada in 1910-14, is deliberately borrowing heavily for future development, we shall expect to see its imports of goods going up without a rise in its exports of goods; it is in effect exporting securities in place of goods to pay for imports. There is a similar connection, the other way round, between the development of the export trade of the United States and its extensive investment abroad between 1924 and 1929; there is a connection also between the stopping of investment and the collapse of exports after the financial crisis of 1929.

[1] " Every transaction in commerce is an independent transaction. Whilst a merchant (in Portugal) can buy cloth in England and sell it with the usual profit in Portugal, he will continue to export it from England. His business is simply to purchase English cloth, and to pay for it by a bill of exchange with Portuguese money. It is to him of no importance what becomes of this money : he has discharged his debt by the remittance of the money." (*The Principles of Political Economy and Taxation:* Second Edition, 1819, p. 151.) The discovery which some modern Protectionists have made of the independence of export and import transactions seems to have been anticipated by Ricardo ; indeed it formed an integral part of his exposition of the arguments for Free Trade.

There is, again, every reason for connecting the fall in the value of British exports in 1929-1931 with the fact that in those years she was getting her food abnormally cheap; her customers were being impoverished. Nor can any one doubt that the tendency of gold to flow to America has something to do with the fact that gold is almost the only import into America that is not heavily taxed to keep it out.

But the fact that other demands than goods and services enter into the international trading account, that citizens of different countries not only wish to trade with one another, but at times wish to borrow and to lend—does not mean that any connection between imports and exports of goods and services can be ignored.

By importing goods, Britain gives to foreigners purchasing power in Britain; by importing more, she increases their purchasing power; by importing less, she decreases it. Because foreigners have more purchasing power, it does not follow automatically that they will then and there purchase more goods or services: they may exercise their power to take gold or they may forego its exercise and make loans, either at call or for a definite period. Because foreigners have less purchasing power, it does not follow automatically that they will then and there buy fewer goods and services; they may need the goods and services so badly that they will send gold or will borrow, and will find Britain able and willing to lend more than she has been lending in the past. But, in the long run, the connection between purchasing power and actual purchases must be expected to re-assert itself. The whole machinery of international trade is designed to set limits to the movement of gold. Lending does not go on indefinitely without return.

If the export of French goods to Britain is reduced, that may not make any difference to the desire of Frenchmen to buy British goods, but unless there is a simultaneous increase in the desire of British people to lend abroad, the Frenchman wanting British goods will find it increasingly hard to pay for them. There will be fewer sterling credits available for Frenchmen; their price will go up; the price of British goods to Frenchmen will be raised indirectly, and their purchase by Frenchmen discouraged accordingly.

It is not, of course, impossible that for a while the diminution of credits due to exports for a country wishing to continue its purchases overseas may be offset in other ways. It is not impossible for a country for a while to be living on the rest of the world to an extent which it cannot afford. France itself in the years between the War and stabilisation of the franc is a good example of this process. It is possible for a country for a time to outrun the constable, if it can persuade foreign merchants and financiers for that time to let short loans and balances pile up within its borders. By manipulating its interest-rates so as to make itself an attractive place for foreigners to lend in, a country can within limits prolong the period of thus living on credit.

But it is easy to exaggerate the extent to which, in normal times, foreigners will allow idle money thus to pile up in their hands in the offending country. Sometimes when tariff disputants first discover that international trade can be done on credit, the discovery seems to go to their heads, as the same discovery about private trade occasionally goes to the heads of young men at the universities. The young men find that they can get clothes and books and wines from obliging tradesmen without paying for them, and act as if this would go on for ever. The tariff disputants find that banks and other businesses in every country carry balances, often large and fluctuating balances, in other countries, and that a change in those balances could offset a change in exports or imports of goods. Or they find that for decades together people in one country are willing to increase their lendings to another country. They propose to act as if these balances could be used again and again, without replacement, to go on paying for imports by a country which had not been allowed to export; as if a loan did not contemplate a return by way of interest; as if the stopping of a country's exports, whether by a revolution at home or by tariffs abroad, did not affect both its power to buy goods from other countries on a cash basis and its prospects of being able to buy on credit. The young spendthrifts at the universities are just as sensible as the people who, because credit as well as goods and services enters into international trade, think that they can ignore the relation between imports and exports.

Those who hold that a reduction, say, of imports of goods is likely to be offset, not by a reduction of exports of goods or services, but in some other way, *e.g.* by import of gold or by increased lending abroad, must give reasons for their expectation; the burden of proof from the special circumstances of the time rests on them. Clearly it would be impossible for all countries simultaneously to reduce their imports and maintain their exports. Those who argue that one country can do so, even for a short run, must show what gives her the special power to do so, and how long that special condition is likely to last.

For the long run, the only rational general assumption is that the larger on the whole the import trade of a country the larger will be its export trade. It may well be that the citizens of that country may have a settled practice of lending largely abroad, and these loans will enter into its international trading account, as will the interest on past loans or repayments of principal. Allowing for whatever movement of goods inward or outward is needed to adjust this, the greater beyond that point the value of the exports (or imports) the greater will be the value of the imports (or exports).

In the sentence last written, the word "value" has twice been inserted. Goods and services exchange of course by value and not by quantity. If the prices of what a country exports rise relatively to the prices of what she imports, the quantity of her exports may fall materially in relation to the quantity of her imports without affecting the balance of trade. She will be able to pay for her imports by a smaller volume of exports; if she goes on exporting as much as before she will be able to lend more abroad; the terms of trade will have moved in her favour. Conversely, the prices of a country's exports may fall relatively to the prices of its imports; it will then have to send more exports or to borrow (if it can) to get the same imports; the terms of trade will have moved against it.

As compared with the time just before the War, the terms of trade have in fact moved sharply in favour of Britain. Taken on the whole, the prices of what her people sell abroad have risen relatively to the prices of what they buy from abroad. This in itself is an advantage; she is able to get from abroad the food and raw materials that she needs, without having to give so many of her own goods in exchange; this, more than anything else, has made possible the maintenance of her population in spite of so much unemployment. But an improvement in the terms of trade, particularly if it is as violent as that now affecting Britain, may have a bad side also, for it may cause unemployment in the export trades. And there is another way in which the relative rise of prices of British products has damaged her, without redeeming features; that is their rise, relative not to the prices of what she buys, but to the prices at which competing industrial countries can sell. The price of British exports has gone up relatively to most other prices, and this has restricted the demand for them in two ways: those who buy them cannot afford to pay for so much of them, and some customers have gone elsewhere.

This, however, is a special problem foreign to the main theme of this chapter, which is the working of international trade in general, as exchange of desirable things for one another. The positive account of how trade does work may, in conclusion, be illustrated negatively by showing how it does not work—by examining, that is to say, one of the most popular fallacies about it, the fallacy of "keeping money at home."

"I do not know much about the tariff, but I know this much, when we buy manufactured goods abroad we get the goods and the foreigner gets the money. When we buy the manufactured goods at home we get both the goods and the money."

This remark, once attributed to Abraham Lincoln, puts

in its simplest form what economists call the mercantilist view of international trade. As Professor Taussig has shown, there is no ground for believing that these words were ever used by Abraham Lincoln, who was dead thirty years before they first appeared in print, in an oration by Mr. Robert Ingersoll. The remark, with Abraham Lincoln's authority attached to it, has naturally had more vogue in America than in Britain. It has, however, from time to time made its appearance here, and embodies a view that must be examined on its merits.

Briefly, it has no merits; the only sensible words in it are the first eight words. It represents a complete misunderstanding of the nature of international trade. If we buy goods abroad we have to pay for them, but we do not pay for them with money. Ultimately, they have to be paid for in the currency of the country where they were made; apart from temporary adjustments through movements of gold we cannot get command of that currency except by shipping abroad goods that we ourselves have made; we get the foreigner's goods and he gets ours. As the case has been put in this country by Lord Beaverbrook, by buying goods abroad we are employing foreigners to work for us, paying them wages week by week. As this case has been answered, the foreigners do not work for us for nothing; they work for us only because and so long as we make and send to them things that they want; if we employ them, they employ us just as truly.

But what about the exception made above for possible movements of gold? We can by shipping gold abroad get hold of foreign currency to pay the foreigners for the goods we buy. Isn't gold money? Isn't gold what Mr. Ingersoll meant in his oration?

Of course, in a sense gold is money; it can be turned almost at will into the money of almost any country in the world. If we buy goods from the foreigner without sending him goods of our own in exchange, we can send him gold instead; if we sell goods to him without buying goods from him, he may have to send us gold.

The last phrase sums up the mercantilist theory which dominated the economic policy of most nations in the eighteenth century and before. It was conceived that the object of trade was to amass bullion; each country set out to sell as many goods as possible to every other country, and by tariffs and otherwise to keep down as much as possible its buying of goods from abroad so that it would have to be paid in gold or silver bullion. The impasse that would result if every country played this game equally well is obvious. But suppose one country played the game much better than the rest, and had an ever-mounting stream of gold pouring into it. What good would that do to the country? A certain amount of gold is needed by each country which has a gold standard currency, as a basis for its currency, but that amount is limited. Gold beyond that amount is sometimes held to be desirable by some countries as a preparation for war; this was the idea underlying mercantilism in the Dark Ages; but even this quantity would, by most countries in their senses, be thought to be limited. A permanent policy of acquiring gold or "money" indefinitely by refraining from purchases abroad is nonsensical.

Gold, after all, is only a special kind of goods. For a country like South Africa, gold is the goods which she makes for a living. For other countries, the gold they have has mainly been acquired by making goods and shipping them abroad; gold represents past goods made by them. Gold is in many ways best thought of as a lubricant to the machine of trade. Like other lubricants it has to be produced and one or two countries live largely by producing it. Most countries have to buy it—by making other goods— and use it as a lubricant. Some may think it worth while to keep for an emergency more than they need for daily use. What is in use moves about constantly with the movement of the machine; but if the machine is working well it gets distributed according to the work it has to do. Tariffs, in so far as they interfere with this distribution, and they undoubtedly can interfere with it, cause either friction or waste of the lubricant.

[29]

Tariffs, and yet more direct restrictions on imports have, nevertheless, since the War, been imposed or justified in certain countries mainly on monetary grounds—in order to prevent an outflow of gold or to secure its inflow as the basis of a new currency. The desirability of using a tariff in Britain specifically for monetary purposes, as an instrument of international equilibrium, has recently been urged by an economist of very high standing, and will be considered in Chapter VII. Proposals of this nature rest on possibilities remote from the simple conceptions of Mr. Ingersoll. For him and his views there is nothing to be said. The idea that as a piece of permanent policy it is good for a nation to cut down imports in order to keep its money in its country is just a simple fallacy and no more. If money in this connection means the particular currency of the country—sterling or dollars or francs—that stays naturally in the country, because it is practically of no use outside the country; it isn't legal tender anywhere else. If money means gold, no country except one that lives by producing gold, like South Africa, pays in gold for any considerable proportion of its foreign imports.

CHAPTER IV

THE NATURE OF TARIFFS

THE last two chapters explained the nature of international
trade as one form of the division of labour—of international
trade as it arises under conditions of freedom through
individuals seeking to satisfy their varied wants with the
smallest expenditure of effort. In the present chapter a
brief account must be given of the ways in which States
seek to limit this freedom and influence the course of
international trade by tariffs or other devices.

The essence of a customs tariff is the imposition of taxes
on commodities as they cross a national boundary. As a
condition of their admission to the territory of the State
admitting them, the State requires payments from the
persons seeking to bring them in. With this definition, the
term tariff is restricted to payments demanded for entry
across a national boundary. It is possible for a similar tax
to be imposed by an authority less than the State at the
boundary of a municipal area; such municipal customs,
generally known as *octroi* duties, were at one time common
and still exist in many of the towns in France and elsewhere.
With this definition a tariff is restricted also to the case of
taxing imports. It is possible for a State to tax goods not as
they enter, but as they leave its territory. Such export duties
were a common device of mediæval state-craft and are not
unknown to-day, though they are now far less common than
import duties. The last example in Britain was the tax of
1s. a ton on coal, imposed from 1901 to 1906. It is interesting to recall this export duty on coal to-day, when policy
has swung to the opposite extreme, and a levy can be made
in each mining district on all the coal raised there in order

to give a bounty on each ton exported. In those days, it was thought that British coal was going abroad too freely and cheaply, enabling foreign industries that used it to compete too strongly with our own manufactures. The Chancellor of 1901 defended the duty as neither a direct nor an indirect tax, because it could be passed on to the foreign consumer. To-day it is thought right to tax all our other industries and weaken their competing power, in order to subsidise and encourage the export of coal to their rivals.

The term "tariff," used originally for any arithmetical table, implies as a rule the imposition of taxes, not on one article only, but on a number of articles entering a country. It is a table of the charges to which they will be subjected. In countries with a general tariff, that is countries taxing many or most imports, this table of charges is a very complicated affair and tends to grow in complexity. The articles to be taxed at varying rates call for elaborate definition. The form of tax varies, being sometimes based on weight or quantity, sometimes on the value of the article, sometimes on a combination of both. It is here necessary to refer only to one main complication—the need of allowing a loophole in the tariff for articles which, having been admitted, are to be exported again, either without change or after some finishing process. If the article is to be exported again just as it came in, and is simply passing through the country on the way to its final destination, it is usually admitted and kept in bond, without payment of duty. Allowance for articles which are worked up further before exportation is a much more complicated process, usually involving payment of the duty on import and a subsequent return of the duty by way of "drawback" to the exporter. For Britain, with its entrepôt trade and with its exports so largely based on imported materials in different stages of rawness or finish, both these matters would, under a general tariff, be of great importance.

A tariff, or series of taxes on imports, like other taxes, may have two main objects—the raising of revenue or the discouraging of the activity which is subject to tax. The raising of revenue is to-day perhaps the less important of these two objects. Yet receipts from import duties are an important feature in the budget of every modern State. Even Britain has never allowed imports of all kinds to enter untaxed. The Free Trade doctrine bars not all taxes on imports, but only taxes intended to influence directly the course of international trade. Taxes on articles which cannot be produced in Britain—tea or wines or tobacco—may, by raising their price, discourage their consumption in favour of substitutes, but will not cause them to be produced in one place rather than in another. Except in so far as they may be differentiated to favour importation from one country in preference to another, they are in essence taxes for revenue alone. An import duty on some article which can be produced at home, such as beer or spirits, can be given the same character of being a revenue tax only, by imposition of an equal excise duty on the domestic product; in respect of duties, the domestic product and the imported one continue to compete on equal terms.

Tariffs for revenue, though calling for discussion in this volume, lie apart from its main theme. The desirability or the reverse of the State's raising by duties on imports part of the money required for its expenditure is a question of the principles of taxation, and of the rival merits of direct taxation and indirect taxation of various types. In so far as a tariff yields revenue, it fails as a rule to carry out any other purposes for which it may have been imposed. Revenue is obtained from import duties only in so far as the imports on which they fall are not checked but continue to come in. The checking of the taxed imports, which is the second object of a tariff, may, in turn, have a variety of remoter objects. First, the State may desire that the articles taxed shall, so far as possible, be made in its own territory in place of being imported. This policy, generally described as Protection, may be either general or special, either permanent in intention or temporary. It may be advocated for or applied to the industries of the country generally or all those in which

C
[33]

imports are possible, as a means of increasing or maintaining the general prosperity of the country. It may be advocated for or applied to particular industries, on the ground that there is some particular reason why they, even more than other industries and, if necessary, at the expense of other industries, should be carried on in the country. It may be advocated as part of the abiding economic policy of the country or as a measure of defence against some special passing danger, such as dumping. Second, the State may desire that the articles taxed shall be imported from one country rather than another. This involves the charging of a lower tax or no tax at all on imports from the country to be favoured, and is described as preference. The preference is usually accorded in return for reciprocal privileges from the favoured country; the extreme form of preferential arrangements is a customs union in which each of a group of countries allows importation without tax from other countries of the group, but taxes imports from all countries outside the group. In such an arrangement, freedom of trade within the group may be a more important object than Protection against the rest of the world. Third, a State may impose a tax on imports, not with a view to maintaining it, but with a view to taking it off, if and when it obtains some other concession from the country or countries from which the imports come. In particular, a tariff may be advocated as a means of bargaining to secure the lowering or removal of tariffs by other countries.

Whatever the remoter objects, all tariffs other than tariffs solely for revenue have one common feature. The taxation imposed by them is discriminatory, falling on some articles and not on others, falling on articles produced in one place and not at all or more lightly on the same articles if produced elsewhere. It is intended on the one hand to discourage or prevent consumers from buying as they would like to buy, as they would buy if there were no tariff. It is intended, on the other hand, to encourage producers to produce as they would not produce if there were no tariff. It is both a restriction of the liberty of consumers and a changing of the environment for producers. This effect on production is the most distinctive feature of tariff taxation as compared with direct taxation. A tariff is nearly always intended to influence directly men's lives and livelihoods, to mould the economic structure in which each man must find his niche. That is the intention nearly always. It is always and inevitably the result. The fact that they thus mould economic structure is in itself an argument against frequent changes of tariffs; they cannot be changed constantly without destroying the stability on which business rests. Direct taxation—such as income-tax—is also a restriction of the consumer's liberty; it has not the same effect as indirect taxation upon production and on livelihoods; it can go up or down without causing instability and unemployment.

There is, finally, one more feature common to nearly all tariffs, that of making the prices of articles subject to the tariff higher in the country imposing the tariff than they would be if there were no tariff. This is not an invariable feature, but nearly so, and the exceptions are not for practical purposes important. Two only need be named here, and each is little more than formal.

In the first place, it is possible to imagine circumstances in which the burden of duties imposed by a country on articles imported into it could be thrown upon the foreign producers of those articles rather than on the consumers. It is all but impossible, indeed, to imagine any circumstances in which the foreign producer would have to pay the whole of the duties, so that the price was not affected at all by the tariff; this would involve so complete an economic domination of one country by another, one both having a practical monopoly of certain goods indispensable to the other and being practically its only market for exports, that it has probably never occurred between two independent states. Nothing even remotely resembling it exists to-day. The question is not whether any country can throw on foreigners the whole burden of its import duties, but whether it can throw on them any appreciable part of them.

[35]

In regard to this country, the conclusion reached by Alfred Marshall in 1903 was that there was "no considerable exception to the rule that England has now to pay the burden of her own import duties." Whatever inconsiderable exceptions there were a generation ago must have been diminished by the great development since then of industry and trade throughout the world. The kind of monopoly power which England possessed in the Middle Ages through her exports of wool, or in the early nineteenth century through her manufactures, has gone beyond recall.

The second exception is even more formal than the first; a tariff duty does not raise prices if it is, or becomes, wholly inoperative, so that nothing comes in under it and nothing is kept out that would come in if it were not there. Inoperative duties, of course, do exist. There are duties on motor cars entering America; British cars, however, are kept out of America not by the duty but by the lower costs of production of American cars; the price of the latter is not affected by the tariff. But a tariff which has any protective effect at all has that effect only because and so long as it makes prices higher than they would be without it.

This is a truism on which it would be unnecessary to insist, except for the frequency with which it is denied, directly or by implication. Thus the fact that the price of a protected article has fallen during the period of Protection is sometimes adduced to prove that "tariffs do not raise prices." It does not, of course, prove anything of the sort in any fair sense of the words. The price of an article is the result of many factors—general monetary conditions, cost of materials, efficiency of production and so on—all of which may vary; their changes over a period of years may easily lower the price of the article even below the point which it reached before any duty was imposed.[1] Yet so long as the

[1] A typical argument of the kind here referred to is used by Sir Henry Page Croft in a letter to the *New Statesman and Nation* of 28th March 1931. He regards it apparently as some answer to the fear of raising prices by a tariff that " in every single safeguarded industry prices showed a substantial drop except in the case of gas mantles, in which case there is a definite rise in the cost of raw materials." This

duty is having any effect in keeping out imports of that article, it will be having that effect only because it is making the price higher than without the duty. The phrase that a proposed tariff will not raise prices is used in a more straightforward way, when it is being argued that after a period of Protection the costs of production can be so lowered that the protection will not be needed, that is to say the proposed tariff will become inoperative (as some parts of the American tariff are inoperative). Whether in any particular case that expectation will be realised is a matter of argument. It does not affect the statement that so long as a tariff is having any effect at all it is keeping up prices within the tariff area. It is either doing that or doing nothing.

is either a very bad argument or a very disingenuous one, according to how Sir Henry means it to be taken. He does not mention the dates which he is comparing to show the drop of prices, but the general period covered by the Safeguarding Act is from 1922 onwards, that is to say a period in which wholesale prices generally have shown a marked fall. Any industry which did not show a fall or exceptional circumstance would rightly be accused of profiteering. The rise in the price of raw materials is used by Sir Henry Page Croft to justify the rise in the price of gas mantles, but no mention is made of the fall of raw material in other cases. The real point, however, is that no safeguarded industry has got to the point of being prepared to do without safeguarding.

CHAPTER V

PROTECTION AND THE STANDARD OF LIFE

OF all the varied arguments for Protection, two transcend all others in popular appeal to-day. One is the argument for keeping work at home and so reducing unemployment; this will be examined in the following chapter. The other is the argument that Protection is needed to defend the standard of life of a high-wage country against the competition of goods made under worse conditions. This argument, with an allied argument for equalising costs of production generally and not wages only, forms the subject of this chapter.

The standard of life argument has been stressed more than once in recent speeches by Mr. Stanley Baldwin. "The dry bones in the trade union world are stirring. Men are beginning to see that you cannot maintain your standard of life in this country so long as you leave that standard of life open to be attacked by goods coming free into this country and produced under conditions where the standard of life is lower."[1]

As applied to the existing wage situation in Britain Mr. Baldwin's proposal is open to the charge of irrelevance. The workmen whose standard of living is most in peril in Britain to-day, having gained least or not at all since the War, are to be found for the most part either in trades dependent on export or in agriculture. The coal-miner, the cotton operative, the boilermaker, and the fitter will find small help to their standard of life through the taxation of imports; they are being threatened not by imports into

[1] Address at Kingsway Hall, London, reported in *The Times*, 26th November 1930.

Britain, but by competing exports into neutral markets. The British farm labourer on the other hand, is suffering mainly from imports, but the imports are mainly the product not of worse-paid but of better-paid workers in other lands.

As an argument which, if good for this country is presumably good also for all countries, it leads also to perplexing conclusions. It would mean that a high-wage country could never compete successfully with a low-wage country. Yet the contrary was demonstrated throughout the nineteenth century by Britain and is being driven home by the United States of America in the twentieth century.

There must be something wrong somewhere with the argument. What is wrong? What is the effect on international trade of the wages in different countries being at different levels? What is the effect on differing wages of allowing trade between two countries where they differ?

The main thing wrong about Mr. Baldwin's argument is, of course, the assumption that a high standard of life in a country necessarily, or even normally, causes the cost of production there to be high. When we speak of a country as having a low standard of life, we mean that all the efforts of people unremittingly applied only just suffice to produce the bare necessities of life, the irreducible minima of simple food, clothing and shelter. By contrast, a country with a high standard of life is one whose people get or could get these minima with a fraction only of the toil of which they are capable, and either use their surplus power to produce the means of faring better or prefer the luxury of leisure. One country is able to have a higher standard of life than another country, only if and because human labour in that country is more productive. So far from a high standard of life being a cause of high costs of production, it is truer to look at the matter the other way round and say that a high standard of life is the result of low costs of production, low costs, that is, reckoned in terms of human toil.

That, however, is reckoning costs in terms of human toil. In the world to-day things are not reckoned in terms of

[39]

human toil, but in terms of money. What difference does that make?

It still does not mean that a high general level of money wages in a country necessarily or normally means high costs of production reckoned even in money. The price of every article entering into international trade, and most articles now do enter, must tend to be the same, however and wherever it is produced. If the people who make particular articles, say shoes, in one country get at the end of each week a much higher wage than those who make the same quality of shoes in another country, this must mean that, in general, each workman in the high-wage country makes more shoes in a week than each workman in a low-wage country; otherwise his produce could not sell at the same price per pair. The differences of wages in different countries represent, at bottom, differences in the productivity of their labour. A country can and does have a relatively high standard of life, because and so long as its labour is relatively more productive than those of other countries.

If we go on to ask what it is that makes labour in some countries so much more productive than in others, we see that this may be due to one or all of at least three main causes. The workmen themselves may be more efficient— stronger, cleverer, more educated; their labour may be better applied—either because the employers are more efficient, or for another reason that will appear in a moment; the natural resources of the country—in soil, minerals, climate, situation—may be richer. Different people are apt to stress one or other of these elements as the chief cause of difference, according as they are most concerned with it. For the present purpose the cause of the difference in productivity is less important than the fact of difference. The productivity of labour does vary greatly from one country to another and these differences of productivity are reflected in, and for purposes of international trade are offset by, differences in the standards of life.

Up to this point we have been talking in general terms, have related the standard of life and wages in each country generally to the productivity of its labour. Now a distinction has to be made. There is such a thing as the general standard of life in a country. There is no such thing as the general productivity of its labour, that is productivity irrespective of occupation.

Within any one country employers in different industries cannot for the same quality of labour pay in the long run very different wages. A country cannot have an American standard of life in some of its industries and a Chinese standard in others. If it ever got into that position, fresh capital would flow into the American standard industries and would try there to use Chinese standard labour; labour would flow out of the Chinese standard industries into the American standard ones. If capital and labour have free choice of industries in an area, something like a general level of wages for equivalent types of labour is bound to establish itself for that area.

On the other hand the productivity of labour in a country is by no means the same in all directions. Labour must always be applied to particular purposes—to digging coal or growing wheat or making shoes or building ships. In any given country it may be highly productive in some of these occupations, and very unproductive in others. If all the coal in a country is more than 5000 feet below the surface, there will be small result for much labour in digging coal there, but the miners will have to be paid at least as much as the shoemakers and agricultural labourers on the surface; in effect the coal will not be mined but will be got by exchange from another country. Each country has its special aptitudes and special disabilities; can do some things better than others, and some things not so well; can afford high wages in some occupations but not in other occupations. Even if a country is so favoured by nature that it is better than others in practically all forms of production, it will not be equally better in all. In accordance with the theory of comparative costs, explained in the second chapter, it will then still be profitable for that country to trade with others instead of making everything it can at home. The average productivity of all its labour will be higher, that is to say its standard of life will be higher, the more its efforts can be concentrated on those things which it can do best. This is the purpose and justification of international trade and the fundamental reason for leaving trade as free as possible.

If a country has a number of important industries of high productivity, able to pay good wages yet hold their own in the markets of the world, these industries set a standard of wages which other industries in the country must follow. If there are other industries which cannot produce as cheaply as their rivals abroad, if they have to pay those wages, then under conditions of Free Trade those industries will not be maintained in that country. This does not mean that the country will do without the commodities which those industries would have made; it will simply make more of the things that it can make best, and use part of them to buy from abroad what it cannot make quite so well. By Protection the less efficient industries can be maintained in the country; but Protection will operate, not by raising their efficiency and decreasing their costs of production, but by increasing to the people of the country the cost of buying things abroad.

The relation of Protection to the standard of life of a country is now becoming plain. The relation is the direct opposite of what Mr. Baldwin suggests. The general effect of Protection on the standard of life in a country is to lower the standard, not to raise it. A high standard of life in a country depends on its labour being highly productive; that depends, in turn (among other things) on the labour being well applied. Good application of labour, as was said above, is partly a question of organisation by employers. It is at least as much—probably more—a question of applying the labour in the right direction, to the industries best suited to the country, rather than to industries in which the country is at a disadvantage or has no special advantage over other countries. The high standard of life which Britain was able to establish in the nineteenth century, was manifestly achieved by concentrating on those industrial occupations in which, through the earlier development of her coal and other circumstances, she was then ahead of other countries, and by getting cheaply from other countries of lower standards the food and raw materials in which she had less advantage or which she could not produce at all. Protection of agriculture at that time would have checked this concentration and kept the standard of life from rising as fast or as far. Protection to-day cannot operate in any other way on the general standard of life. There is no sense at all in a country which has a high standard of life refusing to trade with some other country because its standard of life is low. This does not mean that a high-wage country has never anything to fear from the competition of a low-wage country. It may have much to fear. The practical questions are: where can danger threaten it, and what can be done to keep the danger off? In answering those questions, the vital distinction is between the home market and export markets.

Wages, hours, and conditions of work enter, of course, into the cost of production of any article and so affect its price and the demand for it. To raise the wages or reduce the hours of the workmen engaged in making that article, without any simultaneous change in the efficiency of production, will increase the price of the product. The rise of price may lead to people in a country buying that product, if they can, from abroad; foreign manufacturers may undersell domestic manufacturers of that particular article in their home market; this, be it noted, may happen alike in a Free Trade country and under a tariff, if the tariff wall, before the rise of wages, was just high enough to keep out the foreign article and no more. The same thing may happen also, not through raising of wages in the country which we are considering, but through maintenance of its wages while rivals abroad lower their wages or increase their efficiency or enter new lines of production. But, though the wages which the manufacturers of any one article have to pay may cause these particular manufacturers to be undersold in their own market, no raising of wages or costs of production generally in a country, and no increased competition from abroad, can cause all its manufacturers in all lines to be undersold in the home market. The goods that come in to undersell any one product come by way of trade, not of gift. In considering long-run results like the effect on standards of life, the possibility of paying for imports otherwise than by exports can be left out of account. In the long run the foreign goods underselling any one product in its home market must necessarily be paid for by some other product or service of labour. Raising wages and the cost of its productions generally may diminish the whole trade of the country—both imports and exports; it cannot lead to the country having as many imports as ever and no exports. What actually comes in and what goes out is determined by comparative costs.

The theory of comparative costs has one aspect of special importance for the present topic. Foreigners sending exports to a country try to get in return the largest possible value; they take the goods which, being produced most cheaply in that country, can be sold by it most cheaply. The various export industries of the country compete with one another for the privilege of paying for its imports. In so far as success in this competition turns upon the efficiency of the winning industry or its suitability to the natural conditions and resources of the country, its results are wholly beneficial; it tends to concentrate the activities of the nation upon those things which it can do best. In so far as success in this competition turns on anything else— subsidies or sweating or dumping from behind a tariff wall —it is harmful; the activities of the nation are concentrated on things that hurt it or that it cannot do well.

A nation cannot be undersold in its home market in all its industries at once, either as a result of lesser efficiency or as a result of excessive wages. The position in the export markets is different. The raising of the standard of living in a country generally, if it is unaccompanied by greater efficiency of production, may, and almost certainly will,

[44]

restrict the world's demand for its products and so, if it is engaged in export, may tend to put it out of business. This will happen in two ways.

First, the higher price of its products abroad will, even if there is no alternative source of supply, restrict the market for them; the foreign customers will pay as much or more for each unit that they buy, but will take less in quantity, and the volume of exports will fall even if their total value keeps up. In one sense the country may gain, getting as many imports as before for a smaller volume of exports; in another sense it will lose, as some of the men in the export trades will be unemployed.

Second, if there are alternative sources of supply which are now cheaper, the foreign customers may turn to them. The country which has raised its wages may find itself undersold in neutral markets, and this, unlike the under-selling in the home market, can be generalised, can extend through all its industries at once. Moreover, it may happen not because the country under consideration has raised its wages, but through some other country with lower wages going into new branches of manufacture in competition with it. In such a case the first or high-wage country will find its trade in neutral markets cut down by the competition of a low-wage country. But it cannot defend itself against this by protecting the home market. It can, in fact, do nothing at all except by some means or other lower its cost of production so as to compete on economic terms with the new country. Or, rather, the only alternatives to this are either to give up its exports or to maintain them un-economically by subsidies or systematic dumping, keeping prices high in its home market by a tariff or other legal device and selling permanently cheaper outside. Something like this would have been possible for coal under the pro-posed levy on home consumption for cheapening exports. The demerits of that proposal were sufficiently shown in debate; the policy is one which obviously cannot be generalised.

In neutral markets a high-wage country can hold its own

against a low-wage country only so long as its products are as cheap as those of the other country, that is to say, only if its labour is more productive fully in proportion to its higher wage. This may of course be the case. The country of highest wages in the world—the United States of America —is in a number of important industries able to compete successfully in neutral markets with goods made in other countries by less productive labour at lower wages. It may, however, also happen that, after a country with high standards has established an export trade, some new country with lower standards comes into the same business, and trades to make the same articles more cheaply. Japan's undertaking of textiles is part at least of the explanation of the difficulties of the British cotton industry to-day. The high standard country may find its export trade in one direction destroyed, without any kind of compensation in other directions. That is a real danger. It is a danger threatening Britain to-day, not in one industry but in many. Protection, however, is no defence against the danger to our exports; by raising costs at home it would weaken our only possible defences.

Let us look for a moment at another aspect of international competition and another argument that is often put forward for a tariff. The argument that a tariff should be imposed to defend the standard of living of a high-wage country is only a special case of a more general plea for equalising all costs of production. This plea has had a great vogue in the United States. "Offset the higher expenses of the American producer, put him in a position to meet the foreign competitor without being at a disadvantage, and then let the best man win. Conditions being thus equalised, the competition will become a fair one. Protected producers will only get the profit to which they are reasonably entitled, and the domestic consumers are secured against prices which are unreasonable." So the argument is summarised by Professor Taussig, before he criticises it; so set forth it has, as he notes, "an engaging appearance of fairness," and has been urged as the principle on which a scientific tariff should be based.[1] Though it has not yet come to play so prominent a part in tariff controversy here as it does in America, it may easily do so. The idea underlying it enters into Mr. Amery's argument for a 33 per cent. tariff on foreign manufactures—to compensate for the higher level of British taxation.[2] It is worth examination for its own sake as an illustration of tariff problems.

As a principle for the construction of a scientific tariff "equalisation of costs of production" is, in fact, worthless. It means that if an article costs a quarter as much again to produce at home as it does to import, the import duty is to be 25 per cent.; if it costs half as much again, the import duty is to be 50 per cent.; if it costs twice as much to produce as to import, the duty is to be 100 per cent., and so on.

The greater the disadvantage of the home producer as against the foreign producer, the greater is the protection he needs and, on this principle, will receive. The less suitable an industry is for domestication or the less efficient its conduct in a particular country, the higher will be the tariff imposed in its favour. The logical conclusions of the principle, as Professor Taussig points out, are "universal and unlimited protection" and "the complete annihilation of foreign trade."[3]

Of course, none of its advocates would admit pushing the principle to such logical conclusions. But in that case

[1] *Free Trade, the Tariff and Reciprocity*, p. 134. The principle has actually received the support of an American economist of high standing—Professor J. B. Clark of Columbia—in a work on *The Control of Trusts*, published in 1901. Professor Clark, however, used it to argue for a reduction of the indefensibly high tariffs which were leading to exploitation of the consumer by monopolies. It is most unlikely that a man of his capacity would have given the principle any wider application.

[2] *Empire and Prosperity*, p. 34 *seq.*

[3] Another logical conclusion is that, since goods may be imported from more than one country, and since the costs of production in different countries vary, the principle would involve different duties against each country. Smart (*The Return to Protection*, p. 73).

they have to say where they will stop and why. They have to find some ground, other than the principle of equalising costs, for deciding which industries, unable to meet foreign competition without a tariff, shall be enabled by a tariff to do so, and which shall not be so assisted. "Equalisation of cost of production," unless carried to its absurd logical extreme, will not save them from the risk of deciding this according to the vigour with which each industry makes its case or by counting the votes that it can command.

Even when the decision has been reached on some other grounds, as to which industries should receive protection, equalisation of costs of production will not serve as a principle even to answer the secondary question, as to the rate of duty to be levied. The higher cost of production in the importing country may be due to any of several distinct causes or a combination of them—to the higher wages of the workman, to the greater cost of materials, to heavier taxation, to the lesser suitability of climate, geographical position or other physical conditions, or to lower efficiency of management in relation to technical appliances, organisation, and half a dozen other matters. To take into account the last of these is to put a premium on inefficiency. Yet how can it in practice be excluded? Efficiency of management enters into every element of cost—except perhaps taxation—into wages, materials, choice of location and transport. To allow the home manufacturer to throw the additional costs of his production over that of foreign rivals upon the consumers is to take away one main incentive to progress.

What is to be said, however, of equalising, not all costs of production, but, as Mr. Amery suggests, only those which are imposed by the State itself by way of taxation? Taxation has nothing to do with the efficiency of the manufacturer. It seems manifestly unfair that British manufacturers, crushed by taxation, should have to compete with manufacturers in countries where taxation is less. Should not the State which taxes British products see that, by import duties, at least an equal burden is placed on competing products seeking to enter Britain?

The extent to which direct taxes on profits, such as income-tax and super-tax, enter into costs of production is a debatable point. Most economists would deny that they do enter directly into costs, and very few business men would believe them. Most economists would point out that, on the other hand, import duties on articles used in manufacture do enter into the costs of that manufacture, and that the tariffs of other countries must be taken into account in comparing British and foreign tax burdens. Here the point can be dealt with more simply.

Even if it is assumed, in opposition to the best authorities, that the greater burden of British taxation is a net addition to British costs of production, the position of British manufacturers as a whole cannot be bettered either in neutral markets or in the home market by equalising duties on imports. This is obvious for the neutral markets; if British manufacturers have to carry, as part of their costs of production, an undue share of war debts or of charges for interest which rivals have destroyed by inflation, they are to that extent handicapped as exporters in neutral markets, but they cannot be helped there by duties on imports into Britain. As regards the home market, the general argument applies—that in the long run goods will not come in to Britain except to pay for goods or services going out.

The additional burden of British taxation, like any other disadvantage—bad climate or inefficient labour or lack of mineral resources—will not prevent international trade; as has been shown in Chapter II, trade may and does take place to mutual advantage even between countries, one of which is in all industries inferior to the other. The burden of taxation, if entering equally into all costs of production, will not even change the character of trade. Import duties, if imposed evenly, will equally leave the position of the different trades unchanged; those industries which are relatively best suited to Britain will continue here, and will export; those which are relatively better suited to some

D   [49]

other country will settle in them. The only effect of the equal tariff all round will be somewhat to diminish international trade and the division of labour; it will be an addition to all transport charges.

This does not mean that heavy taxation does not matter. All taxation, even when necessary, is an evil, in so far as it diminishes freedom, compelling people to spend their money or have their money spent for them not in the way that they themselves would choose. Taxation needed to pay interest on foreign debt or tribute to foreign countries is a direct impoverishment of the country which pays it. But, in relation to trade, taxation is an evil to which tariffs are irrelevant. They cannot equalise the costs of production of the British manufacturer and his rivals in competing for neutral markets. For British manufacturers competing with one another as to whose products shall, as exports, pay for imports into the British market, tax burdens are already equal.

The broad result of this discussion is that, alike for equalisation of costs of production generally and for defence of general standards of living against the competition of low-wage countries, Protection is either unavailing or not needed. It is unavailing to secure neutral markets. It is not needed for the home market, because there is no possibility of a low-wage country underselling a high-wage country in all branches in the home market of the latter.

This does not mean that protection of a particular industry may not keep the standard of life of workpeople in that industry higher than it could be without Protection. Obviously Protection may make it possible to maintain in a country an industry for which it or its people have no special aptitude; the less suitable industry may thus be enabled to pay wages as high as more suitable industries, at the expense of the domestic consumer. It will not be able to export, save by dumping. The growth of the more suitable industries which could export at a profit will be checked by the cutting down of international trade.

Protection, as it will often appear again, is a means of favouring some industries only at the expense of others. If the State insists that all agricultural labourers shall have a given standard of living—represented, say, by £2 a week at present prices, and desires also that the number of agricultural labourers shall not fall materially, it must not merely fix a minimum wage; it must secure to the farmers a sufficient market at a price justifying that wage. If the home market is large enough, it can secure both its aims *for agriculture* by a protective tariff; if the home market is not large enough, the State may still break a way into sufficient foreign markets *for agriculture* by bounties on export. Broadly speaking, a country can have any given industry at any given standard of life by paying for it, because this is a problem of distributing the national dividend.

But it cannot generalise this for all industries. It cannot raise the standard of living of the population as a whole by Act of Parliament, whether a Minimum Wage Act or a Tariff Act, because the standard of living of the population as a whole is a simple quotient, is the total of all good things produced by the population divided by the number of the population. Nothing can be added to that except by robbery from other peoples or be taken from it except by being given away.

CHAPTER VI

PROTECTION AND UNEMPLOYMENT

"THE one thing that Protection cannot do," wrote Mr.
J. M. Keynes in 1923, "is to cure unemployment. . . . There
are some arguments for Protection based upon its securing
possible but improbable advantages to which there is no
simple answer.   But the claim to cure unemployment
involves the Protectionist fallacy in its grossest and crudest
form."[1]

In writing thus eight years ago, Mr. Keynes was dealing
with the claim that Protection can cure unemployment as
a whole.   That selective Protection afforded to particular
industries can increase employment in them, and so, if there
is a surplus of labour attached to them, bring that labour
into work and cure its unemployment is unquestionable.
The issue to be examined in this chapter is a different one—
whether and under what circumstances the increase of
employment which Protection may give in one industry can
be obtained without corresponding loss elsewhere, can be
a net increase of employment over all industries and not
simply a diversion from one industry to another.

On this issue Mr. Keynes eight years ago, in the passage
cited above, took for practical purposes a strongly negative
attitude.   Within the past year, as will be seen below, he has
expressed with almost equal emphasis, an opposite view.
Comparison of these two views is as good a way as any to
an understanding of those aspects of the tariff problem which
have been prominent recently.

In writing as he did in November 1923, Mr. Keynes was
attacking protectionist proposals made just before that time

[1] The *Nation and Athenæum*, 24th Nov. 1923.

by Mr. Baldwin and arguments used then by Mr. L. S. Amery, as they are still used by him.

In proposing "a duty of 33⅓ per cent. on finished manufactures with a lower scale on semi-manufactured goods (say an average 25 per cent. all round)" Mr. Amery estimates, "that within three years some £200,000,000 out of the £334,000,000 of retained foreign manufactured imports would be transferred to British production"; he infers that directly and indirectly this would "increase our normal demand for labour in this country by at least 1,500,000 a year, and that we should soon be confronted not by a surplus, but by a real shortage of labour."[1] This prospective result of so simple a device as putting a tax on manufactured imports is so dazzling as to lead to the immediate question why it is not adopted forthwith by every country which has serious unemployment; that is to say, at this moment nearly every country in the world. The answer must presumably be that most of those countries can hardly now adopt Protection because they adopted it long ago—yet unemployment continues.

The plain fact is that Mr. Amery's device is of the same nature and efficacy as the philosopher's stone for transmuting all metals into gold, or the innumerable machines for perpetual motion. It ignores all the elements of the problem. The imports which it is proposed to "transfer to British production" are goods which people in foreign countries send us because they want something from us in return—either goods or services. If we refuse their goods they cannot pay us for our goods or services; that is, they cannot employ us, unless we will take either useless gold or promises to pay later. If we keep on refusing their goods, they won't be able to pay later; they won't be able even to send us interest on our loan. We cannot, by cutting off imports, avoid in the long run cutting off a comparable value of exports that we should otherwise have made.

Thirty pages later, indeed, Mr. Amery sets out to deal with the criticism that exports must balance imports.

[1] *Empire and Prosperity*, p. 35 (Faber & Faber, 1930).

Recognising that "imports and exports as a whole are to this extent connected that an excess of one or the other sets up a situation in the international exchange tending to redress the balance," he argues, first, that the restriction of one import may just as much tend to increase other imports as to diminish exports; second, that even if exports were reduced it does not follow that they would be exports of manufactures giving employment. As to the first point, the substituted imports will either be manufactures—displacing labour in some other field—or food and raw materials. We certainly cannot increase our consumption of imported food by £200,000,000 a year (what about the farmer if we do?), and if we take raw materials we can take them only to work up into manufactures—to be thrown on the world market, where there are already £200,000,000 of foreign manufactures excluded from us and seeking an outlet. As to the second point, what exports from this country would not give employment in making them? To this Mr. Amery suggests no answer, except in saying that, after his scheme had been adopted, Americans might not be quite so favourably placed for buying English country houses or their treasures. As support for a proposal to stop imports to the value of £200,000,000 a year, this is misplaced frivolity.

The foregoing criticism would apply if Mr. Amery had said not £200,000,000, but £100,000,000 or £50,000,000. The actual figures given by him are nonsensical. The total of £334,000,000 from which he starts is not that of retained foreign manufactured imports in any year ever recorded; it is the figure of total imports of manufactured goods in 1929 from all countries overseas, whether British or foreign, including goods re-exported. Re-exports of manufactures in 1929 amounted to £29,000,000; of the £305,000,000 retained, £28,000,000 came from British countries, while about £60,000,000 had already paid tax at something like the rate proposed by Mr. Amery, and would not be affected by it. The £217,000,000 remaining includes about £17,000,000 worth of non-ferrous metals—copper, tin, lead, zinc—coming from foreign countries as crude materials for our industries in bars, slabs, ingots, and other forms. The remaining £200,000,000 of foreign manufactured imports include not only all kinds of finished articles—machinery, electrical goods, paper, apparel, glass—but many goods partly manufactured and forming crude material for our industries, such as hides, plywood, wool tops, dressed furs, pulp for newsprint; many articles both finished and half-manufactured have never been made to any extent in this country. Mr. Amery proposes to make them all here now. The idea that within three years the factories necessary for making them here could be built, the labour trained, and the businesses financed, is fantastic. If all the manufacturing processes could be transferred, a large part of the value of the present imports would still have to be imported as raw material. Transference to British production of even the £200,000,000 means including in what British workmen could do, not only the turning of wood pulp into newsprint, but growing the trees and pulping them; not only dressing furs brought in, but finding the fur-bearing animals to shoot in Britain.

Finally, Mr. Amery has to assume that three years of a 25 to 33 per cent. tariff would in future exclude foreign manufactures, many of which we have never made, though ten to fifteen years of similar duties still let in motor cars, electrical and optical goods, watches and many more things which we can and do make.

Mr. Amery's argument for curing unemployment by a tariff is just plain, straightforward nonsense. Despite the lip service paid by him here and there to economic science, it is "the protectionist fallacy in its grossest and crudest form."

Mr. Amery, however, is a singularly bad advocate of Protection, defeating himself by his own extravagance. It is certain that no protective tariff could have any effect comparable to that which he predicts, or could cure unemployment as we know it to-day. It does not follow that a protective tariff can never under any circumstances reduce unemployment. There are at least two sets of circumstances in which it could have this effect. That is to say, there are two theoretical arguments sufficiently plausible to deserve examination, for holding that stoppage of imports by a tariff may lead to a net increase of employment in a country and not simply to a diversion, not simply to favouring one industry at the cost of hurting another.

The first argument rests on the undoubted fact that, since movements of capital as well as goods and services enter into the international trading account, imports and exports of goods and services alone need not balance. As it was put by a correspondent in *The Times* some months ago: "Imports do not necessarily pay for exports. They give rise to bills, which are used to pay for some exports, but the balancing factor in this country's account with the rest of the world is always an export of capital."[1] That is to say, we can restrict imports of goods by a tariff and so increase employment in trades making for the home market, yet keep up our exports of goods, if at the same time we increase our foreign investments. There is nothing new or surprising in this. It is exactly the point put by Mr. Keynes when he said, in 1923, that "an artificial interference with imports must *either* interfere with exports *or* involve an artificial stimulation to capital to leave the country," or again that "in so far as the keeping out of an import does not involve a corresponding restriction of export, it must drive some capital out of the country."[2] This statement of alternatives is as true to-day as it was then. Though by a tariff excluding imports we reduce the power of foreigners to pay us for our goods, we may still sell them as many goods as before, if and so long as we go on lending them the money with which to pay us. This, on the face of it, does not appear a prosperous proceeding or a possible permanent policy. Before we embark on it, even as a short-range policy for dealing with a particular crisis of unemployment, we need answers to two questions.

[1] " Mercator " in *The Times*, 31st March 1931.
[2] *loc. cit.*

We must ask, first, what reasons there are for being certain that restriction of imports will in the circumstances of the day be accompanied by increase of our foreign lending and not by the alternative of reduced exports, and for how long we can trust to these reasons. The burden of proof in such an issue rests heavily on those who urge this particular result. We must ask, second, how much of our total problem of unemployment could in any case be affected by a measure of the kind now suggested.

The kind of answer which can to-day be given to the first question is illustrated by arguments recently advanced by Mr. Keynes in certain passages of his *Treatise on Money*, and in an Addendum to the Report of the Committee on Finance and Industry. These arguments are set out in the following chapter and examined there. Though Mr. Keynes claims some direct increase of employment through the protective operation of the tariff that he proposes this is for him only a subsidiary gain. His object is primarily the use of a tariff as an instrument of international equilibrium; he knows, it may be suggested, too much about the actual facts of British unemployment to make for his or any tariff proposals the extravagant claims of most protectionists.

Here the results of the next chapter must be anticipated briefly. It is not certain, and on balance improbable, if we reduced imports, that even for a few weeks or months our foreign customers would go on buying substantially as many of our goods as before, with the prospect of paying for them by borrowing; they would probably not want to buy as much at any price (for they would be and feel poorer) and, unless bribed by export bounties they would certainly not want to buy as much at our increased prices. If, nevertheless, the circumstances were at the time of imposing a tariff such as to lead to a substantial increase of exports on credit, it is a pure gamble as to how long these circumstances would continue. In so far as these circumstances did continue and exports were maintained by increased lending, it would mean the diversion of British capital abroad and the probable further cramping of home investment. Finally, while all the possible purposes to be served by a tariff in this field are temporary, the tariff itself would almost certainly prove to be irremovable.

Restricting imports on the chance that exports will be maintained by increased lending is a pure gamble, in which permanent advantages are risked in hope of temporary gains. Nevertheless, if the possible temporary gains were very great indeed, the gamble might seem worth while. This is the point of the second question—as to how much of our actual unemployment could be affected by restriction of imports. The answer here is decisive: for the reduction of actual unemployment in Britain to-day there is hardly anything that could be done directly by restriction of imports. The dangerous game of tariffs is emphatically not worth the candle. As this answer, however, and the facts on which it rests, have a direct bearing also on the second theoretical argument for Protection as a cure for unemployment, they should wait till that argument has been expounded.

This second theoretical argument goes yet further than the first in admitting a connection between imports and exports. Even if a restriction of imports by a tariff leads to a corresponding loss of exports, it urges that employment as a whole may be increased.

Granted, it is said, that the employment given to men in our export industries now depends on imports, *e.g.* that the foreign purchaser of a ton of coal exported from Britain pays for it by the proceeds of a suit of clothes imported into Britain, why not by a tariff shut out the foreign suit, get a suit made at home by a tailor now unemployed and let that exchange for the ton of coal as before? It has to be admitted at once that if there is a tailor now unemployed and likely to remain so, and if by shutting out the foreign suit he can be brought into employment, and the coal-miner be kept in employment as before, a definite improvement will have been brought about. The tailor and the miner will both be in work. The customer who under the tariff buys the home-made suit, whereas under Free Trade he would have bought a foreign suit, will as consumer pay a little more for his clothes, but as against that he will as tax-payer save his contribution towards the maintenance of the unemployed tailor.

But can a tariff bring all this about? The only thing that a tariff on clothes from abroad can do for certain is to drive the home consumer to pay more for foreign clothes, or, if the tariff is high enough, to do without foreign clothes and to buy what clothes he wants at home. If there are not more tailors altogether than could make all the clothes needed at home, they can all be brought into employment by shutting out imports. Beyond that, all the consequences of the suggested tariff are uncertain. The tailor now employed on making the suit of clothes formerly made abroad doesn't want and won't take a ton of coal for it. His product does represent a demand for labour, but not necessarily or probably for that of the miner. It isn't certain that anyone else in the country wants more coal as a consequence of the foreign clothes being shut out; the miner may have been working for a highly specialised demand. The tariff may simply bring the tailor into employment at the cost of throwing out the miner; the buyer of the suit in that case will be paying more for his clothes, without saving on his contribution for unemployment.

The assumption that exclusion of the foreign clothes will both bring the tailor into employment and leave the miner in employment simply begs the whole question at issue. The retort may be made that to assume that the miner will not be employed is also a begging of the issue. The real position appears to be this. At present the tailor is unemployed and the miner is employed in working for a foreign demand. On the assumption made as to the balancing of exports and imports, exclusion by a tariff of the foreign clothes will mean that the tailor finds a market at home, and the miner loses his market abroad. At present the tailor is looking for a market; after the tariff the miner, having lost his former market abroad, will be looking for a new one either abroad or at home. Is the miner more likely to find that new market after the change, than the tailor is likely to find it for himself, if things are left as they are? If that question can be answered definitely in the affirmative, a case for a tariff is made out. But if it cannot be so answered, if the chances of the two appear equal, then the balance of advantage rules against having the tariff; for the one thing certain is that it is going to cost more labour to make the clothes at home than to mine and export a quantity of coal sufficient to pay for importing them from abroad.

On equal chances for the miner and the tailor of finding new markets for themselves, the advantage remains with Free Trade as against a tariff. On worse chances for the miner, the case against the tariff is decisive, and the general presumption is against the chances being as great for the miner as for the tailor; the tailor was presumably in a job before, under Free Trade, and may by a return of former conditions find himself in work again; the miner has lost for good his former market and has to find a new place in a changed world.

There is, however, one case in which the presumption is the other way, that is to say, in which the miner's chance of fresh employment appears better than the tailor's. Suppose that the tailor has lost his job, not through temporary depression, but through the development of a rival industry in some other country which, by using new methods or new machines, is able to make clothes more cheaply than he can ever learn to make them. Then the tailor, unless he can take to a new trade, will be out of work for the rest of his life. If, on the other hand, the foreign demand for the miner's coal is a growing one, the disturbance that might be caused to international trade by a tariff protecting the tailor might be only temporary. On these suppositions, protecting the tailor, even assuming the balance of exports and imports, might cause a net increase of employment. This is a theoretically valid argument for Protection as a means of reducing unemployment. But two simple considerations show that this theoretical possibility is no ground for endeavouring to reduce unemployment in Britain to-day by a tariff.

The first consideration is one of policy. In so far as the tailor in our theoretical case is being put out of work through development of a rival industry which can under-sell him, he is the victim of industrial progress. Because labour can never be perfectly fluid, because all men as they grow older get set in their ways and places and less able to follow changes of industrial structure, such changes may cause unemployment and will cause it if they come rapidly. Stopping those changes or slowing them down may reduce unemployment. But that means stopping or slowing down progress.

This illustrates a general point often lost sight of in dis-cussions of the tariff issue. The goal of economic effort is not employment but wealth.

It is undeniable that by tariffs, if they are high enough, a country can cut off international trade altogether, so that none but its own citizens are employed in meeting their own needs. It does not follow that even so all the citizens would be always or more regularly employed than before. It does follow, for certain, that they would as a whole be poorer rather than richer than before. As Mr. Amery says, "It is obvious to ordinary common sense that there is more employment in making an article ourselves than in buying it from abroad."[1] So there is more employment—much more employment, absolutely no end of employment—for a person who tries to build his own house and make his own shoes and cook his own food and do every single thing for himself, whether he can do it well or badly. If any Free Trader is so foolish as to doubt this, let him try making his own bicycle! That, however, is the kind of employment which means starvation and drudgery. Employment by itself is not prosperity. Employment means prosperity only if it brings a good return for the effort it involves.

Mr. Keynes has put this point, like most others against tariffs, as well as it can be put.

[1] *Empire and Prosperity* (1930).

[61]

"If Protectionists merely mean that under their system men will have to sweat and labour more, I grant their case. By cutting off imports we might increase the aggregate of work; but we should be diminishing the aggregate of wages. The Protectionist has to prove, not merely that he has made work, but that he has increased the national income. Imports are receipts and exports are payments. How, as a nation, can we expect to better ourselves by diminishing our receipts? Is there anything that a tariff could do, which an earthquake could not do better?"[1]

The second consideration destroying the theoretical argument now in question, is a consideration of fact. The suppositions underlying the theoretical case in which a tariff can reduce unemployment are the direct opposite of the facts of British industry and unemployment to-day. The suppositions are of unemployment being caused by imports into the home market and of a vigorous demand for our exports, or, in other words, of international trade tending to grow at the expense of domestic trade. What are the facts of British industry and unemployment?

To begin with, unemployment presents not a simple problem but a complex problem. Unemployment is not itself a disease amenable to a single specific, but a symptom which may show the presence of one or more of many distinct diseases, for each of which the appropriate remedy is different.[2]

In the complex causes of unemployment at least four main strands must be distinguished, each itself composed of several threads. There are, first, the causes of unemployment as they were diagnosed just before the War by the

---

[1] The *Nation and Athenæum*, 1st Dec. 1923.
[2] See *Causes and Cures of Unemployment*, by Sir William Beveridge (published by Messrs. Longmans in August 1931, 2s. 6d.). The analysis of present-day unemployment is partly summarised from there and has in fact appeared as an article in the *Fortnightly Review* for February 1931.

Royal Commission on Poor Laws, and still operating to-day: disorganisation of the labour market, both generally and in its special forms of casual employment and mis-direction of juvenile labour; seasonal fluctuations; cyclical fluctuation; changes of industrial structure. There is, second, the dead weight addition to pre-War unemployment experienced in Britain from 1922 to 1929, between the two slumps of 1921 and 1930. There is, third, the world slump of 1930, perhaps no more than an acute case of cyclical fluctuation, but so overwhelming in its incidence as to call for special study. There is, fourth, the administrative factor, the effect in increasing unemployment of the provision made for unlimited relief of unemployment in the guise of insurance.

To three of these four main types of unemployment, Protection is clearly irrelevant. It can have no bearing on the administrative factor—the working of unemployment insurance. It has as little bearing on cyclical fluctuation, as illustrated by the world slump of 1930. This is not, indeed, universally recognised; the delusion is persistent that by Protection it is possible to diminish the violence of trade fluctuations.

This is the thought underlying the manifesto issued by Sir Oswald Mosley and his associates, in so far as that manifesto proposes Protection of the home market. Sir Oswald Mosley himself makes Protection only the first step to general control of economic activities by the State. As to Protection alone—Protection as it might be advocated by Conservatives rather than by Socialists—the answer to be given is clear. There is no reason whatever for supposing that Protection can diminish the violence of trade fluctuations.

Cyclical fluctuation before the War was common to all advanced industrial countries, irrespective of their fiscal policy. An American authority, writing in 1902, expressed an opinion shared by most observers in stating that "crises are more severe and frequent in the United States that in any other country"; he added that they were felt "with diminishing force in England, Germany, France, Holland and Switzerland."[1] The crisis of 1908, occurring after this was written, was certainly worse felt in America than elsewhere. This pre-War experience has been repeated since the War. The depressions of 1921 and of 1929 have been common to Protectionist and Free Trade countries alike; all the available evidence suggests that in each year the recession of economic activity has been more violent in the United States than in the United Kingdom, and at least as violent in some other Protectionist countries. This appears alike in the figures of stock prices, of physical volume of production, and of foreign trade. Between September 1929 and September 1930 the prices of industrial shares in Britain have fallen as from 100 to 83; from 100 they have fallen in the United States to 63, in Germany to 77, in France to 75, in Belgium to 60, in Holland to 63, in Italy to 68, in Sweden to 78. From the third quarter of 1929 to the third quarter of 1930 the physical volume of industrial production is estimated to have fallen in the United States by 25 per cent., in Germany by 21 per cent., in Canada by 16 per cent., and in Britain by 10 per cent. France alone stands out as showing substantially no change.[2] The United States has lost in the depression more of its foreign trade than Britain has, both relatively and absolutely.

In the first ten months of 1930, as compared with the same period of 1929, imports into Britain fell by £131,000,000 or 13 per cent., while imports into the United States fell by £218,000,000 or 25 per cent.; exports from Britain fell by £139,000,000 or 20 per cent., while exports from the United States fell by £220,000,000 or 29 per cent. For unemployment itself no statistics are available in the United States, and none of the various guesses made deserve quotation; the seriousness of the problem there is beyond

[1] T. E. Burton, *Financial Crises and Periods of Industrial and Commercial Depression*, p. 66.

[2] See table of " National Indices of Industrial Production, 1924-30 " at p. 375 of Cmd. 3737.

question. In Germany the numbers officially recorded as unemployed have risen from 2,036,000 at the end of November 1929 to 3,683,000 at the end of November 1930; the percentage of trade unionists wholly unemployed has risen in the same period from 13·7 to 26·0, and of those on part time from 7·6 to 16·1. In another country, not only highly protected but highly organised in some of the directions desired by Sir Oswald Mosley, namely, Australia, the percentage of unemployed trade unionists from 1922 to 1929 averaged about 10 per cent.—very near the British figure. By September 1930 the percentage had doubled to over 20, and since then it has risen further; half-way through 1930 it had risen to 18·5 and by the end of 1930 to 25.[1]

For Britain the effects of the world depression have been accentuated by special misfortunes, such as the political disturbances in two of her principal markets—India and South America; her unemployment figures have been swollen by administrative changes transferring men from the Poor Law to the Insurance Fund. The depression itself seems to have been less violent here than in most other countries.

All the obvious facts tell against the view that fluctuations of industrial activity are made less violent by Protection. So does consideration of the probable causes of fluctuation. While there is much that is obscure as to the precise causation of the slump of 1930, while the means alike of prevention and of cure for similar disasters in the future are uncertain, there can be no risk of error in regarding it as being in essence and origin a monetary phenomenon. It represents a failure in the world as a whole to manage the mechanism of cash and credit with even tolerable success, and so to keep industry on an even keel. This failure relates both to gold, which for most countries is now the basis of their currency, and to the superstructure of credit, which in nearly

[1] See "The Australian Problem," by Professor D. B. Copland in *Economic Journal* for December 1930, p. 645, and *The Times*, 6th January 1931.

all countries is erected thereon. The second type of failure is probably the more important; the experience of America shows that abundance of gold is no preventive of depression, and makes the cruder forms of mercantilism more patently foolish than ever before. But whether the root of the trouble lies mainly in gold or mainly in credit, Protection is no cure. No advanced country, least of all Britain, can cut itself off from the financial system of the world. The idea that by taxing foreign goods it can keep away depressions is like supposing that by a smoke screen it can keep away bad weather.

The world slump of 1930 is probably only an acute form of the price and credit fluctuations which ran their course and made recurrent crises of abnormal unemployment in the nineteenth century. The other pre-War causes of unemployment are as clearly beyond the influence of tariffs, and independent of the growth and prosperity of industry. Their remedy must be sought in carrying out after twenty years the main recommendations of the Poor Law Commission, in abolishing at last the hawking of labour and casual under-employment and the anarchic recruiting of trades and the blind choice of careers.

What, however, of the fourth remaining type of unemployment—the dead-weight burden borne by Britain from 1922 to 1929? Here the argument that a remedy might be found through abandonment of Free Trade appears, and is, stronger than with any other type of unemployment. It appears strongest on the face of things because, while the slump of 1930 is common to all the world, the troubles experienced by Britain before the slump—from 1922 to 1929 —are to some extent peculiar to her. During these years the United States and some other countries prospered exceedingly; though some, like Germany, had good and bad fortune, few if any showed such a record of long-drawn heavy unemployment as Britain. May not her exceptional policy of Free Trade and her exceptional distress be connected, as cause and effect?

It is easy to follow up this general argument by a specific

one. The case for Free Trade is that it causes the various factors of production of each country—natural resources, capital and labour—to be put to those uses for which experience shows that they are best suited. If a country which could make boots gets the boots it needs, not by making them, but by making gramophones and importing the boots in exchange for exported gramophones, that shows that making gramophones is a more advantageous use of its energy than making boots, and leads to its getting its boots by importation at less cost than by making them. All this, however, amounts only to saying that, where the question is between employing its factors of production in one way rather than in another, Free Trade will lead to a more profitable use of them than State interference can. What if over a long period some of the factors of production never get employed at all? The Free Trade case is all very well, when it could be shown, as it was shown before the War, that there was no real surplus of labour in Britain, and that unemployment represented simply fluctuations incidental to the growth of industry. Does it ring as true when the question is not one of using labour and other factors of production more or less advantageously, but of finding any use for them at all? Many who formerly supported Free Trade are inclined to say that the existence of a permanent mass of unemployment alters the case.

This is one of the points urged by Mr. Keynes:

"In ordinary circumstances, when abnormal unemployment is expected to be quite temporary, it is impossible to justify a tariff by reference to its effect on employment. For when the productive resources of the country are likely to be almost fully employed in most directions, a tariff means a diversion of output, not a net increase. I have often argued the Free Trade case on these lines, and would do so again in the appropriate circumstances. But at present the necessary conditions are not fulfilled."[1]

[1] *The Times*, 21st March 1931.

Those who are familiar with Mr. Keynes' arguments against tariffs in the past will feel that this hardly does justice to their variety and vigour. Nor does it in any way represent the real argument that Protectionists have to meet. If the Free Trade case amounted only to saying that when all the productive resources of a country are likely to be almost fully employed in most directions, they cannot by Protection be given much fuller employment in some industries except at the cost of diverting them from other industries, the Free Trade case would be the most barren of tautologies. It is of course true that the existence of permanent unemployment—of productive resources not simply standing by for a fluctuating demand but surplus to the needs of industry—is a pre-condition of being able to increase employment by a tariff. This, however, is not only true, but a truism. It applies not only to increasing employment by a tariff, but to increasing it by any other means, for if there is no permanent unemployment, it cannot be cured and does not need to be cured by anything. But it does not follow in the least, that if there is permanent unemployment, then Protection will cure it. The question has still to be asked: to what is the permanent unemployment due? What is preventing the full use of the productive resources of the country? Or rather, what was preventing this in Britain from 1922 to 1929, for that, rather than the present slump, must be the basis of Protectionist argument?

If the circumstances of that time be looked at more closely three principal facts as to unemployment emerge.

First, at the beginning of the period there was still substantial unemployment due to the cutting down of War industries to peace-time proportions. In the War some industries were bloated, others starved. The return to peace-time proportions involved a change of industrial structure of unprecedented scale and speed, and so caused unemployment of labour too fixed in its ways to follow the change.

Second, as this change passed, another change from pre-War conditions became apparent—the decline of the export trades. To quote the results of an analysis made by myself elsewhere: "The cramping of Britain's trade overseas appears to be one of the more enduring dislocations involved in the War. Whether this is to be explained simply by growth of economic nationalism and tariff barriers or has some deeper cause will be considered later. Whatever the cause, the result is a shifting of industrial structure and of quality of labour demanded, too swift for the labour supply to follow. From 1923 to 1929 all the staple industries on which the former prosperity of the country was founded— coal, iron and steel, cotton, wool and other textiles, ship-building, even engineering, have lost in numbers and suffered more than the normal unemployment. In contrast, new and minor industries have expanded, with, as a rule, little unemployment."[1]

The third special feature of the period, though bearing on unemployment, is a fact about wages rather than about unemployment. As compared with the last years before the War real wages in Britain have risen very substantially. That this, through its bearing on the costs of production of what we sell, has been one of the factors in the decline of exports as well as in unemployment generally, is hardly open to question. I can only refer those who wish to go more fully into the point to what I have written more fully elsewhere.

The position from 1922 to 1929 may thus be summed up as one of decline in the staple trades mainly concerned with export, inadequately compensated by growth of minor trades mainly making for the home market. In such a situation, Protection of the home market is not a cure for unemployment, but an aggravation of it; it is a means of hastening a transition—from export to home industries— already violent enough to cause unemployment. There is a theoretical case in which Protection of the home market might directly reduce unemployment; that is to say, if at any given time unemployment was occurring in a country predominantly through underselling in its home market of its former principal industries. This would presumably

[1] *Unemployment : A Problem of Industry* (1930), pp. 357-8.

be stimulating the growth of some of its other industries making for export, but, since labour could not move readily from the declining to the rising industries, unemployment would result. Unemployment of this kind might be diminished by temporary protection of the old industries slowing down the violence of the transition.

It is, no doubt, possible to find industries in Britain which have suffered from 1923 to 1929 from invasion of their home market. But this is emphatically not the main feature or an important cause of unemployment in that period. "The mass of unemployment has been, and is, mainly concentrated in the heavy industries, and latterly in certain of the textile trades, all of which figure largely in our export business."[1] The actual incidence of heavy unemployment[2] from 1923 to 1929 is the reverse of that in which Protection of the home market might lead to less unemployment.

In so far as unemployment from 1922 to 1929 was due to a change of industrial structure—from making for export to making for the home market—it could only have been aggravated not reduced, by Protection. For the effect of Protection would be to make the change more violent.

It is probably felt, indeed, by some supporters of a tariff that though hastening the change over from export to home industries may aggravate unemployment at the moment, yet the change over is inevitable, and that it had better be

[1] *Report of Committee on Finance and Industry*, § 108.

[2] The theoretical case in which unemployment can be diminished by Protection is most likely to occur in practice, when the question is one not of imposing Protection but of removing it. Suppose that under high Protection an industry has been built up to an extent to which it could not maintain itself without Protection. Then a sudden removal of Protection, however much it may stimulate international trade and some other industry of the country making for export, will cause unemployment, through delay in the transfer of labour from the first industry to the second. The nearest important parallel to the theoretical case in Britain is the agricultural depression from 1870 onwards, resulting from the underselling of her agriculture by grain from overseas, combined with a rise of export industries. Employment in agriculture was thereby cut down severely. Unemployment did not occur to any large extent because the displaced agricultural labour was in fact able to migrate to the rising industries.

made quickly in place of being long drawn out. "If it were done when 'tis done then 'twere well 'twere done quickly." To that the only answer is: why? To adjust oneself as rapidly as possible to unpleasant changes that have occurred in one's economic position is wise. To hasten such changes is meeting trouble half-way; it may even mean making trouble that would not come of itself. Once the idea that a protected country is less liable to depressions than a Free Trade country has been dispelled, as it is dispelled by the facts, any advantage of the protected over the Free Trade condition vanishes; desire to hasten to the former becomes absurd. If the economic conditions of the world are going to drive Britain back more and more upon her own limited natural resources and territory for maintenance of her population, the more slowly she can so retire the less pain there will be in the process. At the end of it she must be less prosperous than if international trade and division of labour had grown.

This deals, however, only with one case of Britain's exceptional unemployment from 1922 to 1929. What about the other, more general cause, the abnormal rise of real wages?

One of the common arguments against Protection is that it would raise prices. If that is so, ought it not to be regarded, in the circumstances of to-day, rather as an argument for Protection than against it? If Protection raises prices it will, other things remaining unchanged, lower real wages and so correct the previous rise. Will not that reduce unemployment? This is not the kind of argument for Protection that is much used in political speeches. But it weighs undoubtedly with many minds, and has been expressed with his usual candour by Sir Josiah Stamp.[1] If wage rates are to be regarded as sacred and prices, left to themselves, keep tumbling down, may we not be driven to Protection as an indirect way of lowering wages with them? The suggestion is plausible, but for three good reasons is beside the mark.

[1] *The Observer*, 15th March 1931.

First, the manufacturer for export (and the main though not the only trouble is with him) is affected by money wages rather than by real wages. If he has to go on paying the same money wages as before for the same output, it is of no advantage to him that his workmen find their wages not going as far as before in buying food and fuel and clothing. He must either get the price of what he produces raised in terms of gold or get a bigger output for the same money wages or give lower money wages for the same output.

Second, the lowering of real wages by Protection raising prices, even if in any indirect way it can be shown to be good for employment, depends entirely upon the workmen being prepared to sit quietly on their money wages while prices rise against them. What is the chance of this?

Third, though wages *on an average* may have risen out of relation to productivity the rise has been by no means uniform. The wages of different occupations are badly out of gear with one another, and are unequally out of gear with prices. The remedy is certainly not a uniform depreciation of wages by raising the cost of living. Greater flexibility and detailed readjustment of wages are needed rather than a general concealed attack on wages through the cost of living.

Every consideration of common sense and common honesty points to bringing about directly and not secretly the necessary readjustment between the costs of our production and the prices we can command for the product—between wages and output.

Failure to make fast enough the adjustments needed to fit a world changing perhaps more swiftly than ever before is the explanation of Britain's dead-weight of unemployment from 1922 to 1929. In one word it is rigidity—on the one hand of occupations and on the other hand of money wages and other money costs of production in face of a falling price level. One form of the Free Trade argument is that, given fluidity of labour and wages, all of the productive resources of a country, alike under Free Trade and under

[72]

Protection, will eventually find employment, but that the kind of employment which prevails under Free Trade will be more profitable than that which prevails under Protection.[1] If we assume rigidity in place of fluidity this form of argument becomes inapplicable, but the normal advantage of Free Trade is not destroyed. Some of the implications of assuming rigidity will be examined in the following chapter. In regard to unemployment the position seems clear. In so far as British unemployment, as experienced from 1922 to 1929, is due to rigidity of occupations, it would on balance be increased, not diminished, by Protection. In so far as it is due to rigidity of money wages, Protection designed to raise prices is an indirect, unjust, and ineffective way of correction.

If men are chronically unemployed because they are not employable at the wage demanded, there are all sorts of devices which can be suggested for getting them back into employment. Some of these devices involve a subsidy to the working classes at the expense of the general tax-payer; such are the organisations of unremunerative public works, the remission of insurance contributions, or direct subsidies to private industry. Others involve a concealed lowering of the real wages of the workman; devaluation of the pound sterling in terms of gold is one of these and Protection is another. Protection is for two reasons among the least reputable of such devices. It is among the least open. It chooses for stimulation just those lines of production in which our comparative efficiency is lowest.

Unless it can be shown that Protection adds to the productivity of the factors of production already employed in a country, it does not provide any source out of which additional factors of production can be drawn into employment without sacrifice of real income on the part of somebody. If we are prepared for such sacrifices in the cause of employment, it is more sensible to concentrate on the production of things such as better houses or better roads

[1] See *The Tariff Question and the Economist*, by Jacob Viner (the *Nation and Athenæum*, 14th Feb. 1931).

which have a high social value and cannot be imported more cheaply from abroad. Opinions may differ among Free Traders, as amongst others, as to how far it is wise to press such schemes of public expenditure and how far they will merely delay natural and necessary re-adjustments. But the fundamental case for Free Trade remains unshaken by the demonstration that there is a standing pool of unemployed factors of production: for Free Trade ensures that such amount of the factors of production as the wage-policy of trade unions and the conditions of investment and enterprise between them allow to be employed, are at least not utilised in producing things which can more easily be obtained by exchange, in accord with the principles of international division of labour.

It is impossible to say that under no circumstances will exclusion of certain imports by a tariff cause a net increase of employment. There are certain cases in which it may for a shorter or longer time have that effect. The theoretical cases of this kind examined above are among the "arguments for Protection, based upon its securing possible but improbable advantages, to which there is no simple answer." That is to say there is no simple answer theoretically. Practically to-day there is. Anything that Protection could do to lighten unemployment of any type can be done more directly and better in some other way. In relation to the main types of British unemployment to-day, Protection in all its forms is grotesquely irrelevant.

It cannot touch directly—if it can touch at all—the pre-War unemployment due mainly to seasonal fluctuations and disorganisation of the labour market, the post-War pre-slump unemployment of 1922-29 due mainly to decline of international trade and a rise of real wages out of relation to productivity, the slump unemployment of 1930 due to world-wide dislocation of prices, or such unemployment as may result from weaknesses in the law or administration of insurance and poor relief. Those who urge that it can are blind raisers of false hopes that darken still more the difficult and clouded way to real remedies.

[74]

CHAPTER VII

TARIFFS AS INSTRUMENTS OF INTERNATIONAL EQUILIBRIUM[1]

In the days of the gold standard before the War, the international equilibrium of imports, exports, prices and exchanges was secured, it now seems to us, almost automatically. If, in any country, those who were importing goods tried to bring in more than the country's balance of outward trade, after taking account of services, interest payments and changes of foreign investment, would pay for, the foreign exchanges would move against that country; that is to say, its currency would become depreciated in terms of other currencies. At a certain point of depreciation, this would cause gold to flow out from that country. The flow of gold would cause the central bank to raise the rate of interest, contract credit, and so bring about a lowering of prices and later of wages. The country, compared with its former state, would, through its lowered price-level, become a worse country to sell in and, through its lowered costs of production, a better country to sell from; that is to say exports would tend to rise and imports to fall. The original disequilibrium of excess of imports over exports would be corrected.

This is the classical theory of international equilibrium in its simplest form. On the whole, it worked before the War with reasonable smoothness. It may be, as the Committee on Finance and Industry suggest, that the automatic operation of the gold standard, even before the War, was more or less limited to the sphere of the Bank of England.

[1] This Chapter written before the events of September 1931, deals with international equilibrium on the assumption of a gold standard or other convertible currency. It is supplemented by Chapter XVIII on the Balance of Trade, for an inconvertible currency.

[75]

"London was then by far the most powerful financial centre in the world, had 'sight' claims on the rest of the world much greater than those of the world on her, and could thus by the operation of her bank rate almost immediately adjust her reserve position. Other countries had, therefore, in the main to adjust their condition to hers."[1] At any rate for this country the gold standard worked. Actual movements of gold were small; each successive contraction of credit and depression of trade was liquidated; there was no chronic unemployment. Moreover, on a rising tide of prosperity even the liquidating of depressions by contraction of credit was in practice less painful than it sounds in theory, and encountered few obstacles. The general course of money wages and money incomes was upward; contraction meant often little more than ceasing for a while to rise.

The post-War position appears radically different. Whatever the causes, on various occasions since the War, the operations of the Bank of England, in defence of its gold reserves, have not met with so ready a response or led smoothly to equilibrium. Depressions do not work themselves out; unemployment and disequilibrium have become chronic.

The former weapon of the Bank of England for securing equilibrium, that is, the raising and lowering of the rate of interest, seems insufficient for its purpose. The most distinguished English authority on problems of international trade and finance has been led to propose, accordingly, that this weapon should be supplemented, among other ways, by direct interference with trade through tariffs. Mr. Keynes' recent advocacy of a tariff for Britain is based essentially on its possible service as an instrument of international equilibrium. He has supported his argument by claiming other advantages for a tariff, in raising revenue or in indirectly increasing employment for the home market. These aspects are discussed in other chapters of this volume. But for Mr. Keynes, these advantages appear incidental. Primarily he advocates a tariff as an instrument of inter-

[1] *Report of Committee on Finance and Industry*, § 295.

[76]

national equilibrium, as an alternative or supplement to measures of monetary control. Even within this restricted scope his advocacy covers a bewildering variety of aims and arguments. In the *Treatise on Money* (October 1930) the taxing of imports is an alternative to differential rates of interest for investment at home and abroad. In the Addendum to the Report of the Committee on Finance and Industry (June 1931) it is an alternative, among other things, to devaluation. In a recent newspaper article (September 1931) the short-period argument of "improving our current balance of trade on income account" comes to the fore; incidentally Mr. Keynes in this article puts first as the right remedy devaluation. Failing devaluation "we must restrict our imports." [1]

The various arguments used by Mr. Keynes are naturally not all independent, even when his practical conclusions are different, and many of the same considerations apply to all of them. The short-period argument, however, for using a tariff to adjust a balance of trade that has gone wrong is so intimately related to the exchange crisis of August 1931 and to the attempt to keep on the gold standard at the old parity, that it becomes out of date so soon as the attempt has failed. [2] The present chapter, substantially written before the crisis arose, deals with arguments of more permanent application advanced by Mr. Keynes in the *Treatise on Money* and in an Addendum to the Report of the Committee on Finance and Industry. Whether Mr. Keynes' arguments or the criticism of them here will have any immediate bearing on Britain's problems depends on the future policy of Britain in relation to the gold standard.

The case put by Mr. Keynes in his *Treatise on Money* [3]

[1] *Evening Standard*, 10th September 1931.
[2] This is, of course, recognised by Mr. Keynes, and has led to his withdrawing (or suspending) the argument in a letter to *The Times*, 29th Sept. 1931.
[3] The passages quoted are from vol. i, p. 162, and pp. 346-7, and vol. ii, p. 189. Chapters 21 and 30, from which these passages come, and from which the rest of the argument is summarised, should be read in full by those who wish to go further into the point at issue.

relates, in his own terms, to the securing of equilibrium between the foreign balance and foreign lending. The foreign balance in each year of Britain or any country with a favourable balance of trade is the amount by which the sums due to it from abroad, as payments for exported goods or services or for loan interest and the like, exceed the sums due from it as payments for imported goods and services or loan interest and the like. The foreign lending in each year is the amount by which the country increases in that year the debts due to it from abroad, the excess of new loans, long or short-dated, over repayment of loans to it or borrowing by it. "The amount of the Foreign Balance in any given situation depends on the relative *price-levels* at home and abroad of the goods and services which enter into international trade. The amount of Foreign Lending, on the other hand, depends on relative *interest rates* (corrected, of course, for variations of risk, etc., so as to represent the net advantage of lending) at home and abroad. Now there is no direct or automatic connection between these two things." Foreign lending and the foreign balance may tend to differ.

Foreign lending, however, and the foreign balance cannot, in fact, differ in any period except to the extent that gold moves out of or into the lending country. A country cannot in any year lend abroad more than its foreign balance except by sending gold; if it lends less, it will receive gold. The function of a Central Bank in each country is to keep these gold movements as small as possible—to reserve them for the detailed final adjustment of each year—by keeping foreign lending and foreign balance as near as possible to one another in other ways. "The weapon of a Central Bank," for this purpose, "consists in the power to alter interest rates and the terms of lending generally." It has no direct means of altering relative price-levels (upon which the foreign balance depends). But it can change directly or nearly directly the interest rates (on which foreign lending depends) and, assuming plasticity of money wages and money earnings of the factors of production other than labour, this in due course changes indirectly relative price-levels also. Up to the Great War the Central Bank in Britain found no difficulty is securing by these means equilibrium of foreign balance and foreign lending with a comparative absence of friction. But since the War another picture presents itself.

"In an old country, especially in one in which the population has ceased to expand rapidly, the rate of interest at which borrowers for home investment are able to absorb home savings must necessarily decline. Meanwhile, in the new countries the rate will be maintained, and as these countries get over their early pioneer difficulties, the estimated risks of lending to them—provided they are careful about their reputation as borrowers—will decline. Consequently the old country will tend to lend abroad an ever-growing proportion of its total savings. This will be partly cared for by the interest on its previous foreign lending. But for the rest its costs of production must fall so as to stimulate its exports and increase its favourable balance on trading account. If there is a resistance to this fall, gold will flow, bank rate will rise, and unemployment become chronic. This is particularly likely to happen if the prevalence of tariffs against manufactured goods (and a readiness to raise them when imports of such goods are increasing) renders the foreign demand for the old country's exports inelastic, whilst at the same time Trade Unions in the old country present great obstacles to a reduction of money wages.

"I leave it to the reader to work out in detail what a pickle a country might get into if a higher rate of interest abroad than can be earned at home leads to most of its savings being lent abroad, whilst at the same time there are tariffs abroad against most of its exports and a tendency to raise these tariffs from time to time to balance the gradually rising level of costs in the protected countries due to the outflow of gold from the lending country."[1]

[1] J. M. Keynes, " *A Treatise on Money*," vol. i, pp. 346-7.

The reader, as Mr. Keynes notes, will have perceived for himself that in this passage from his first volume—on the Pure Theory of Money—Mr. Keynes has partly in mind the position of Britain in 1929-30. In his second volume—on the Applied Theory of Money—the case of Britain is considered directly. Assuming that money wages cannot be lowered and that the greater attractiveness of foreign over home investment continues, excess of foreign lending over foreign balance for Britain leads to an impasse of chronic depression and unemployment. From this there are four possible ways of escape:

(1) To increase the foreign balance by decreasing money costs of production as a result, not of reduced money wages, but of increased efficiency.

(2) To increase the foreign balance by diminishing the volume of imports through the agency of tariffs or analogous measures.

(3) To decrease foreign lending by establishing, by means of a subsidy or other equivalent arrangement, a differential rate of interest for home investment as compared with foreign investment.

(4) To stimulate investment throughout the world, both at home and abroad, by an international cheap money policy.

The first of these ways is attractive but slow. The fourth is also attractive, but not within the power of Britain by herself. Both are unexceptionable, but Mr. Keynes, looking not only at the present but some years ahead, is not sure that they will serve; they may need support by one or other or both of the other methods named, the second or the third.

"It may be that the attainment of equilibrium in accordance with our traditional principles would be the best solution—if we could get it. But if social and political forces stand in the way of our getting it, then it will be better to reach equilibrium by such a device as differential terms for home investment relatively to foreign investment, and even, perhaps, such a falling off from grace as differential terms for home-produced goods relatively to foreign-produced goods, than to suffer indefinitely the business losses and unemployment which disequilibrium means. Of the two types of devices indicated above, I much prefer that of differential rates for home and foreign lending to that of differential prices for home and foreign goods; for I believe that there is a much greater scope for this device without risking injurious reactions in other directions, and, in some cases indeed, with positive social advantage. But I am coming round to the view that there is also room for applying usefully some method of establishing differential prices for home and foreign goods."[1]

The method thus cryptically suggested by Mr. Keynes is left in the *Treatise* without further explanation. The two passages here quoted might easily be read by most Protectionists without its being thought that they gave any support to Protection. To anyone, indeed, who believed almost any of the common arguments for Protection, the whole of Mr. Keynes' treatise, with its subtle analysis of economic reactions, would be incomprehensible. Mr. Robert Ingersoll, if he had survived to read Mr. Keynes, would have felt that he knew even less about tariffs than he thought he did.[2] So far from tariffs being a means of keeping both the goods and the money from the foreigner, their object, in Mr. Keynes' new doctrine, is to let the foreigner have both the goods and the money, to supply him with exports and lend him the money to pay with, and to put ourselves in a position to lend the money by doing without imports which we should like to have. Though, however, in the *Treatise on Money* Mr. Keynes does not explain himself further, his later writings[3] make

---

[1] J. M. Keynes, " *A Treatise on Money,*" vol. ii, p. 189.
[2] See Chapter III, p. 27, above.
[3] These writings, besides *Addendum I to the Report of the Committee on Finance and Industry* (Cmd. 3897 published in June 1931), include in the *New Statesmen and Nation* an article entitled *Proposals for a Revenue Tariff*, on 7th March, a letter on 21st March, and three articles on 28th March, 4th April, 11th April, and in *The Times* letters on 21st March, 27th March, and 2nd April.

explicit what careful readers would infer from the context, that he is thinking here of protective duties on imports. Such duties would serve, at least, to establish differential prices for home and foreign goods. In so far as they checked imports without diminishing exports they would increase the foreign balance.

To this proposal Mr. Keynes comes, in the *Treatise*, very dubiously; he comes to it as a subsidiary to better plans or because better plans seem politically not available. His support for a tariff here is the embodiment of caution. For this caution there is ample ground in the speculative nature of Mr. Keynes' own argument, and in the criticisms to which that argument lies exposed.

Mr. Keynes' diagnosis of the disorders to be remedied rests on two main premises. One is a particular assumption as to the relations between saving and investment in Britain in the immediate future; the other is a general theoretical conclusion as to the lack of connection between the foreign balance and foreign lending. Each of these premises is unsafe.

The assumption that for equal security [1] lending abroad yields and will continue to yield better interest than lending at home is not, as Mr. Keynes seems to think it, an almost self-evident axiom. If Britain is an old country, there still is limitless room for capital improvement there; if Britain is getting older, so are other countries—both as borrowers and as competing lenders. The low rates of interest in the United States of America and the financial strength of France point to possibilities of competition in lending abroad which Mr. Keynes seems to overlook. Nor, again, is it self-evident, as Mr Keynes suggests in another passage, that the rate at which borrowers for home investment will be able to absorb home savings must necessarily decline, while the savings themselves continue without change. On

---

[1] Equal security is of course fundamental. Mr. Keynes' unhappy illustration of a socialised Australia by the offer of 6 per cent. outbidding Britain at 5 per cent. in borrowing was clearly written some time ago.

the contrary, it is practically certain that some of the causes which since the War have diminished the attractiveness of home investment—high taxation and redistribution of the product of industry in favour of labour against capital—are diminishing also the proportion of saving to total income.

When we turn from Mr. Keynes' particular assumption as to British savings and investment to his general view as to the possible discordance between foreign lending and the foreign balance, further doubts arise. It has been urged with much force that Mr. Keynes under-estimates the degree to which, without special devices, the foreign balance of a country tends to adjust itself to the transfers abroad which that country needs to make, whether for foreign lending or by way of reparations or similar tribute. As a matter of history, this adjustment came about with great regularity and ease in Britain before the War, though even before the War wages in Britain were not wholly plastic. Since the War it seems to have happened in rather a remarkable way in Germany; after American lending to Germany stopped, an export surplus commenced to develop there to pay reparations, just as Mr. Keynes' critics would have predicted. In the slump of 1930 the proportionate declines of exports and imports of the three largest trading countries have been curiously in accord with their respective positions as international creditors or debtors. Britain is still the chief creditor nation. A substantial proportion of her imports are required to meet the interest on her overseas investments and would tend to come though she exported nothing. Germany is the chief debtor nation; to provide reparations and interest on post-War debts calls for a steady stream of exports. The United States of America occupies a position between these two. In the slump of 1930 British imports have fallen notably less than those of either the United States or Germany and less than her exports; German exports have fallen notably less than those of the United States or Britain and less than her imports. In the United States exports and imports have fallen in much the same proportion.

[83]

As a matter of theory, accounting for these historical results, there are connections between foreign lending and foreign balance which Mr. Keynes neglects or undervalues. The connections are not rigid, but they exist. One is on the side of imports. If a loan is raised for abroad or taxes imposed to pay reparations, the spending power of consumers is diminished. Some of what they would have spent otherwise would presumably have been spent on imports; there will be a tendency to reduce imports. Another link is on the side of exports. The conditions of demand for exports are not unaffected by the fact that a transfer is to be made. If I lend a man £100 out of a fixed income, that involves, in the language of economists, that my demand curves are moved to the left and his to the right, or, in the language of plain men, that at any price I demand less and at any price he demands more. This does not follow as simply when the lending is abroad, but it follows none the less.

The foregoing criticisms relate to Mr. Keynes' diagnosis, considered without regard to any of the remedies that he suggests. Even if these criticisms could be answered, and the diagnosis so far made were accepted, remedy by a tariff would be inappropriate and harmful.

In the first place, both the need for any such remedy and its utility depend upon the assumption that money-wages are and will continue to be rigid, that they cannot be made to fall and will not rise. Mr. Keynes himself points out that the need for any method, other than the traditional one of raising the rate of interest, to keep foreign balance and foreign lending in equilibrium is bound up with the failure to lower money-wages with world prices.[1] It is equally

[1] See particularly Mr. Keynes' footnote in vol. i, p. 348 : "Whilst I regard the relative attractiveness of Foreign Lending as a serious aggravation of the difficulties (of Britain in 1929-30), I do not regard this factor as so important a cause of the disequilibrium between Foreign Lending and the Foreign Balance as the factors decreasing the volume of the latter, due to the failure to deflate earnings and costs of production in as great a degree as the international value of sterling had been raised in the period ending in 1925."

true, though he seems not to notice this, that the efficacy of any tariff device to bring about equilibrium depends largely on money wages remaining fixed though domestic prices rise. Anything like a general tariff is bound to raise prices to the workman and lower his real wages unless money wages rise also. But if they rise, money costs of production will rise, the market for exports will contract, and the foreign balance will be cut down.

In the second place, the efficacy of a tariff for adjusting foreign lending and the foreign balance depends absolutely on the view that the cutting down of imports will not be offset by a decline of exports. What are the certain and what are the probable or possible effects of a restriction of imports into Britain by a general tariff?

The only thing certain to result from there being fewer imports of goods into Britain is that there will be fewer people in other countries holding bills of exchange on London payable in sterling; foreigners will be in a worse position for paying for goods or services from Britain. It is almost equally certain that, imports being restricted, their prices will rise and the costs of production of our exports will be higher; foreigners will get less value for the money that they spend in Britain. How can we be sure that, nevertheless, they will be so determined to go on buying British goods and services that they will send us gold or stop taking gold from us, or will buy on credit and be able to find some in Britain ready to lend to them? The answer is that there is no means of being sure beforehand that this will happen. Mr. Keynes himself does not go beyond a guess at probabilities. He hazards the opinion that diminishing the volume of imports through the agency of tariffs or analogous measures "in present circumstances would probably not result either in a diminution of our exports to an extent equal to the diminution of imports, or in a diminution of home investment, but in some increase of foreign investment, which increase would be mainly a net gain to the wealth of the community." He does not, in the immediate context, give any grounds for this opinion. If he

[85]

did give his grounds he would say, presumably, that our anxiety to lend abroad more than our export surplus will allow, will cause us to go on exporting as much as ever even though imports are reduced substantially by a tariff; that we would sell more exports on credit, as against the fewer exports for which we get immediate payments. The assumptions underlying this argument, as to the course of saving and investment, are, as has been shown, unsafe for the present and still less safe for the future. But even if these assumptions were safe, instead of unsafe, they would not bear the weight of the practical conclusions drawn by Mr. Keynes. International lending and international trade are not generalised activities in the air, but transactions between particular countries; they are not carried on in water-tight compartments, but affect one another in many ways. If increased lending is to keep British export trade unchanged, in spite of a restriction of imports, the additional loans must be made just to those countries whose exports to Britain are being stopped; it is of no use their being made to anyone else. Is it possible to conceive of a tariff having this effect—of severely curtailing the trade of a foreign country and simultaneously increasing both its desire to borrow and our desire to lend to it? Frankly, the suggestion seems little short of fantastic. It is by selling their goods that the people of the Argentine and Germany and other foreign countries earn their living; it is in order to finance business (including the export trade to us) that they chiefly want loans; it is on their prosperity that their credit depends. To expect that a severe blow to their trade by British tariff would leave them not merely as anxious and as able as before to borrow, but even more anxious and able to borrow is to ignore elementary considerations. In private trade, few firms stop buying goods from another firm and simultaneously buy shares in it, however eagerly they may be looking for a good investment. Few employers dismiss a workman and at the same time lend him a year's wages. But it is to the Argentine and Germany and the countries whose imports we cut off that the loans must be made by us or by someone, if they are to keep on taking our exports. The fact that at any given moment Argentine or German banks may hold large balances in Britain, which could be used to pay for imports from Britain if exports to Britain were reduced, is beside the point. Once they had been used they could not be used again; they would not provide for a permanent stream of imports not paid for by exports or by borrowing.

Mr. Keynes has carried his diagnosis of possible discordance between foreign lending at once not far enough and too far. He has not carried his diagnosis to the point of realising that there may be discordance of locality or direction as well as of quantity. This discordance may exist, even before the adverse effects of a tariff on loans to a country hit by it are taken into account: as a matter of recent history the most eager borrowers in London have been the Dominions. But it is hard to regard as practicable a tariff aimed particularly at the Dominions. He has carried his diagnosis too far, in so far as he seems to think it possible for lending and trade to continue without any kind of relation to one another at all. A blow to trade is a blow to credit and so to borrowing and lending at all times and in all places.

In the Addendum to the Report of the Committee on Finance and Industry, appearing some time after the *Treatise on Money*, Mr. Keynes clearly has in mind the objections just made to a tariff—that it cannot be relied on to decrease imports without decreasing exports, and therefore may leave the foreign balance just as it was. He adds to his proposed tax on imports accordingly an equal bounty on exports; the figure he suggests—whether practically or by way of illustration—is 10 per cent. in each case. This it is pointed out, "would have precisely the same effects as those produced by a devaluation of sterling" by the same percentage except that it *"would leave sterling international obligations unchanged in terms of gold."*

The presentation of this scheme of tariffs plus bounties as an alternative to devaluation makes clear its monetary character. It is an attempt to put right the alleged damage done to our export trades by the return to the gold standard in 1925 at par. This is said to have given an upward jolt to all prices, wages and other money incomes in England, in terms of gold; failure to reduce money incomes and money costs of production sufficiently has acted as a clog on exports ever since. Had the return to the gold standard been made not at par but after devaluation of sterling, the jolt would have been avoided. Devaluation now would jolt things back again, but devaluation must be ruled out on grounds of general policy. The tariffs, plus bounties, proposal, "would avoid the injury to our national credit and to our receipts from foreign loans fixed in terms of sterling which would ensue on devaluation. . . . A plan of this kind would be so immeasurably preferable to devaluation that it is foolish even to discuss the latter while the former remains untried."[1]

The form of the Addendum makes it difficult to be quite certain how far the plan of tariffs plus bounties as a means of adjusting price-levels is put forward as a serious practical proposition. It can hardly be taken seriously, as soon as its implications are understood. Whether or not it would be desirable now, if possible without injury to national credit, to get the precise effects of devaluation, that is to say to reverse the jolt given to our economic system in 1925, is a matter on which there may be two opinions. That it would be impracticable to get it and foolish to attempt it by a plan of tariffs plus bounties is beyond question.

It would be possible, of course, for a State determined to increase its foreign balance at all costs to combine taxing imports with subsidising exports. Stranger things have been done in the Middle Ages. On purely theoretical grounds there is no greater (and no less) objection to the State's subsidising export industries directly by a bounty, than there is to the State's subsidising home industries indirectly by a protective tariff. The practical and political aspects of the two plans, however, are by now profoundly different. An announcement that Britain was about to adopt a general

[1] *Report of Committee on Finance and Industry*, pp. 199, 200.

plan of State-aided dumping would be greeted by humanity with incredulous derision. The carrying out of such a plan would be negatived at once by every kind of discriminating countervailing duty.

That a national policy of export bounties should at this date be put forward by men of high authority in economics and business, as a contribution to solving an international problem, would be incredible if it were not true. Have those experts never read the history of the sugar bounties, or heard of anti-dumping legislation and tariff wars?

That Mr. Keynes and his associates of the Addendum should, in their suggestion of export bounties, omit all reference to its inevitable repercussions in other countries would be remarkable in any case. It is the more remarkable, because in arguing just before against reduction of salaries and wages as a means of adjustment, Mr. Keynes has laid great stress on the re-action of other countries, that is to say, the possibility that cutting costs in one country may be countered by competitive cutting elsewhere. His argument approaches at times the impasse that every existing wage-rate in every country at all times is to be regarded as unalterable for fear of repercussions elsewhere. It ignores throughout the fact that wage-rates in different countries are notoriously at widely different levels without anyone troubling about them; it ignores the very solid forces which in each country, irrespective of what is happening elsewhere, custom and trade union organisation oppose to any down-ward move of nominal wages. But whether or not competitive wage cutting is possible, countervailing tariffs would be inevitable, if Mr. Keynes' proposal were carried out.

Like everything that Mr. Keynes writes, the passages cited here are full of suggestion and of food for thought. They are no justification for his proposal of a protective tariff. Apart from all theoretical niceties, Mr. Keynes' favourite remedy is a bad one, for three practical reasons. It does not go to the root of the trouble, but accepts and thus perpetuates the rigidities from which trouble comes. It is discriminatory and national in character, while the disequilibrium is one of international relations. It is permanent in character, while the disequilibrium is the creature of particular time and circumstance.

First, remedy by a tariff does not go to the root of the trouble. Even if Mr. Keynes' diagnosis be correct so far as it goes, the diagnosis does not go far enough and must be carried a stage further. If depression in Britain is due to savings made in Britain seeking investment abroad rather than in Britain, that means that the return to capital in Britain is not high enough, as compared with the return in other countries. That means in turn either that the productivity of capital and labour together in industry must be increased or that labour must accept a lesser share of the joint product and leave more to capital. We are back once more at higher productivity or lower wages. These and these alone go to the root of the trouble.

This is a point that Mr. Keynes himself has urged forcibly in the past. With freedom of international lending, the return to capital in any one country cannot without danger be reduced, in favour of wages, without regard to what capital can earn in other countries. This does not mean that the rate of interest in any one country must be as high as the maximum that can at that moment be earned for equal security elsewhere, and that wages must be kept down accordingly. The actual earnings of different undertakings and their attraction for capital vary; a certain amount of foreign lending is desirable. All that it does mean is that a large sustained difference in the return to capital as a whole between domestic and foreign investment, may tend to starve the former and drive capital abroad. Conversely, if capital is tending to go abroad too generally, as Mr. Keynes' diagnosis suggests, this points to undue inequality in the rates of return to it.

This deals with Mr. Keynes' diagnosis as set out in the *Treatise on Money*. On the diagnosis of the Report of the Committee on Finance and Industry and Mr. Keynes' Addendum, the charge of palliating instead of curing rigidities applies yet more plainly. Prices have always been recognised as the adjusting factor in economic relations, ever since economics became a science; they lose their *raison d'être* if they lose their flexibility. The fundamental cause of disequilibrium to-day is that money prices for some things since the War have shown even more than normal flexibility, those of other things—notably labour and invested capital—have become abnormally rigid. Yet Mr. Keynes devotes all his ingenuity not to breaking down this rigidity but to getting over its results.

Second, Mr. Keynes' proposal is discriminatory and national. It is so even as a tariff proposal alone, without the bounty needed to secure its desired results. It cannot, that is to say, avoid injuring directly and openly particular foreign countries and particular interests in them. The counter-measures that this must inevitably provoke would at once frustrate its objects. The spirit that it must provoke would provide the worst possible atmosphere for planning the international co-operation in finance upon which international equilibrium must ultimately rest. Mr. Keynes cannot really suppose that the crude devices of nationalist self-seeking proposed in his Addendum will run well in harness with the international re-planning of finance postulated by the main Report.

The third and final objection to a tariff, as the means to the end that Mr. Keynes desires, is that the end is transient and the means proposed are not transient. The trouble that Mr. Keynes seeks to cure arises out of the circumstances of a particular time. Even if his diagnosis in the *Treatise* be right for the moment, the circumstances may change; apart from half a dozen other possibilities, a cure may be provided by the increase of income from previous foreign investments financing the new investment. He himself says only that "it looks as if there may be an interim period," during which difficulties will arise and continue. In the *Treatise* he himself, even during this interim period, would prefer measures other than taxing imports.[1] The view taken

[1] In the Addendum Mr. Keynes got to the point of preferring a tariff *plus* bounties to all other measures. Yet if the diagnosis of the

here is that, whether or not these other measures or any other measures are needed and admissible, a tariff is not admissible. Just as certainly as tariffs damage one set of people, so do they benefit another set, and establish an environment favouring, and making possible, activities of particular kinds, rather than activities of other kinds. The suggestion that we should use a tariff for short-period financial adjustments ignores the essence of tariffs—that they become the basis of men's livelihoods and breed vested interests. Tariffs once put on do not easily come off. Tariffs once imposed must be taken as permanent; and permanent tariffs, in the long run, are as certainly an impoverishment of the countries which they hold apart as are frozen seas or rock-bound coasts.

Addendum is right, it furnishes in itself one of the strongest arguments against this preference. It is argued there (on p. 197) that the present standards of living are not higher than our productivity would justify if we could secure equilibrium and bring all our resources into play. The difficulty is essentially one of the short run. Yet the tariff once put on would remain.

CHAPTER VIII

THE ECONOMIES OF MASS PRODUCTION

In certain branches of industry, the economies of mass production are undoubted. One of the characteristics of many British industries, as compared with similar industries in America, Germany, and elsewhere, is the smaller size of their producing units, whether coal-mines or blast furnaces or motor factories or farms. This love of smallness seems deeply ingrained in the British character. In the organisation of industry it is more and more coming to be regarded as a weakness. Here is the case as put by Lord Melchett:

"It is a commonplace of business that economy of production frequently depends on the size of the market which is available. . . . In the United States of America there is a very large Free Trade Area inside a high tariff wall; the producers inside that area have at their disposal the market of 120,000,000 people belonging to the most prosperous community in the world, and accordingly the market is sufficiently large to enable the mass production of the most diversified types of nearly every commodity . . . Except in those trades which have been safeguarded, the British home market is in no sense secure to the British manufacturers, and, accordingly, in spite of many products, the scale of manufacture is insufficiently large to ensure a maximum of efficiency of production." [1]

The case has been set forth more recently by Sir Eric Geddes, with special emphasis on the growing proportion of fixed charges under mass production and the consequent importance of making many units in order to lower the cost of each unit. [2]

[1] *Imperial Economic Unity*, p. 72.
[2] *Mass Production : The Revolution which Changes Everything*, by the Rt. Hon. Sir Eric Geddes, G.C.B., etc. (June 1931).

The same point has been urged by Sir William Morris, with a special emphasis on prices:

"As manufacturers we know that the spreading of our overheads over a much larger volume of production will enable us to lower prices."[1]

Protection accordingly need not mean higher prices. Security in the home market, it is suggested, by increasing the scale of production, may actually lower prices.

To this general argument, that a secure home market will lead through larger output to lower prices there is often added a financial argument. Industries now in difficulties can be rationalised and put into a sound condition if they can raise capital for the necessary re-construction. Security of the home market for the products of those industries is urged as the best way of giving the needed confidence to investors.

What is to be said of this argument? Theoretically a case can be put in which it would be plausible. That is to say, it is possible to imagine circumstances in which imposition of a tariff might lead, through increased scale of production at home, to lower rather than to higher prices for the article subject to tariff. Suppose that the market for a given article in a country is being supplied partly by a number of home manufacturers, partly by foreign manufacturers, all competing with one another at a price determined by their costs of production. Though the circumstances may be such that one or two of the home manufacturers, by increasing their scale of operations, could lower their costs, undersell their rivals at home and abroad, and capture the market, they may not realise the position or they may shrink from the risks involved. They may hesitate to lay down more plant or launch a selling campaign, in ignorance of what reply their rivals abroad or at home would be able to make. Their hesitation may be overcome, if the State by a tariff

[1] Letter to *The Times*, 2nd October 1930.

shuts out the foreign supplies and suddenly increases the demand on the home manufacturers. One or more of the home manufacturers more vigorous than the rest may lay themselves out to meet the new demand and find themselves able by their larger scale of production to reduce costs and so reduce prices, even below the point at which imports had come in before.

This is the theoretical case in which a tariff might lower prices rather than raise them. How far it is from justifying anything like a general system of permanent Protection appears from a few simple considerations.

First, the argument is not one for a general tariff at all. Not all industries are in need of or susceptible of reorganisation for purposes of large-scale production. The argument, at highest, is one for safeguarding particular industries after investigation.

Second, the industries which could show themselves to be in the delicately balanced position required by the argument must always be few and far between. They must be ripe for large-scale production, but with none of the manufacturers in them prepared to undertake it. The argument assumes something that looks perilously like lack of initiative on the part of the home manufacturer. If the circumstances are such that, after the tariff, one of the home manufacturers by enlarging his scale of production could bring prices below those of his foreign rivals, it must have been open to him to do the same thing before the tariff. Lord Melchett, writing as a Free Trader some years ago, himself put this difficulty in the way of his later argument:

"If it is true that by working full time such a reduction of cost can be made as to enable the British manufacturer to produce at a sufficiently low price as to compete with the foreigner, the remedy is in his own hands. All he has to do is to set his works going at the full rate, and then make the articles the foreigner is making to-day."

There remains a third difficulty, more serious still.

[95]

Assuming that the circumstances are such as the argument assumes and that a tariff by suddenly enlarging the market *might* stimulate some of the home manufacturers to enlarge the scale of their production, and lower costs, what chance is there that it *will* have just this effect, and not an opposite effect?

As manufacturers, Lord Melchett and Sir William Morris know the advantages of large-scale production. As writers on economics they seem to confuse scale of production with total volume of production. A large total volume of production may be achieved by many small-scale producers as much as by a few large-scale producers. To diminish by a tariff the imports of any article in strong demand will, of course, lead to more of it being made at home. But the larger volume of production may be spread over innumerable small factories as before; there is nothing in Protection itself to favour large-scale rather than small-scale production. Sometimes it seems to work in one way and sometimes the other way. A prohibitive tariff may stimulate a movement towards monopoly with a view to exploiting a helpless home market; the American tariff has probably at times had this effect, and the South African sugar monopoly is perhaps another case in point. On the other hand, Protection may lead to multiplication of small firms rather than to amalgamation. That tendency has shown itself in Australia. It is certainly not absent in the industry which Sir William Morris himself has done so much to develop. The motor industry of Britain has now for fifteen years enjoyed a high measure of Protection, under duties imposed avowedly as an experiment with no guarantee of permanence. Manufacturers in the industry had every ground for treating their Protection as a temporary breathing space, for rationalisation, for standardisation, and for framing plans of large-scale operation. Little of the sort has resulted from the tariff. Protection has served instead to keep alive and separate multitudes of small makers of innumerable types of car, competing with one another, not by standardisation and cheapness, but by unimportant small variations. Sir Eric Geddes is particularly insistent that without Protection of their home market, manufacturers cannot take the risks of mass production. "*Because* the unprotected manufacturer . . . cannot be sure of his minimum market, he dare not spend the capital which would enable him to manufacture at competitive cost." But Protection, except to a monopoly, is no guarantee even of a minimum market. So the British motor makers seem to have thought, for they have not tried mass production.[1]

Another British industry affords another illustration of the same British characteristic. The coal-owners of Britain have for generations had a monopoly of the home market and a large export market. Have they ever, as a body, realised or aimed at the economies of large-scale production? Was it, on the other hand, his security of the protected American market, or was it the need of underselling his free competitors in that market, that led Mr. Ford up the path of mass production? Is the mass production of 200,000 pairs of boots and shoes a day now being achieved at incredibly low costs by a famous Czechoslovakian manufacturer really dependent on his security in a home market of 14,000,000 persons?

Fourth, even if in any industry a tariff could have been and was shown to be likely to have the effect desired—of stimulating large-scale production—the case would be made out at most for a temporary tariff, not for a permanent one.

To show this, it is necessary to ask exactly how much lowering of prices is meant by those who speak of Protection enabling them by economies of large-scale production to lower prices? If the motor-car industry, or any other industry, is going to be able, by reorganisation and large-scale working, so to reduce its costs of production as to compete on level terms with its rivals, Protection will

---

[1] Sir William Morris himself makes seven distinct types of engine in six different chassis, each with two to six different bodies. As compared with his British rivals Sir William gives admirable value for money, but it is not by multiplying models that the Americans with higher wages contrive to make cheaper cars than he can.

become needless, as soon as reorganisation has been completed; the industry will hold the home market and share export markets by its own strength. If reorganisation, though it may cheapen British costs of production somewhat, is still going to leave them above those of rivals, then the industry can hold its home market only under Protection and can export only by dumping from behind the tariff wall, at the cost of the home consumers.

This clearly is what Sir Eric Geddes wants. He praises what some call "dumping" as "perfectly fair competition." Free Traders should face up to the fact that "it pays a modern manufacturer to sell far below the full cost of production if thereby he can get volume." Almost in the same breath he complains of the "inadequate and temporary Protection" afforded to the motor industry by the $33\frac{1}{3}$ per cent. McKenna duties. His vision of international trade is that of a series of mass production industries, each inviolably entrenched in its home market, each competing furiously with its rivals to sell its products below cost of production outside, in order to "get volume." The outside price in each case will clearly be below the home price, else what is the need of say 50 per cent. or more of permanent Protection? For Britain, whose home market is notably smaller than some at least of her rivals, and which above all countries must have exports (that is the foundation of Sir Eric Geddes' paper), the export price will have to be a particularly low one. For Britain Sir Eric Geddes' vision can have few attractions.

Whether Sir William Morris and his associates contemplate temporary Protection or permanent Protection is not so clear from their published declarations. It is probably fair to say that they use arguments applicable only to temporary Protection but contemplate permanent Protection; the McKenna duties have already had their fifteen years. It may be suspected also that the effect of a tariff in improving the credit of an industry for borrowing depends as a rule on expectation that the tariff will stay, not that it will become needless. If, however, this is the case contemplated, if in any industry rationalisation under Protection is still going to leave the industry unable to compete with its rivals abroad, there can be no pretence of advantage either to the consumer or to other industries. The consumer will have to pay more than he would under Free Trade; the protected industry will hold its own market only by keeping out imports which in the long run would have meant a demand for some other product, and will get export markets only by dumping. If, on the other hand, the argument is treated as one for temporary Protection, it becomes a special form of the well-known argument for nurture of infant industries. Industries in need of rationalisation are to be helped by a tariff till by rationalisation they can stand alone.

It will be appropriate accordingly to consider here the argument for Protection of infant industries, first in its original form, then in its special bearing on projects of rationalisation. The general argument runs thus:

A particular industry may be well suited to a particular country, but under Free Trade may be hard to introduce there, in competition with other countries where it is already established on a large scale. Beginnings in the new country must almost certainly be on a small scale, with untrained labour. Exposed in its early days to the full strength of competition with established industry elsewhere, the infant industry may never grow up, though, if it could grow up, it would be able in time to do as well as its rivals or even to beat them. This is a case in which individuals, left to themselves to buy what is cheapest now, may sacrifice the future to the present. Protection, on the other hand, while it may for the moment raise prices, may in the long run lower them.

This is the reasoning which was made by List the basis of his scientific protectionism for Germany. "As List phrased it, the question of the *productive powers* of a country and their possible development is far more important than present *values*; it might be well worth while to incur a loss for a time in order to secure a more than proportionate future gain."[1] The theoretical validity of this argument was admitted by John Stuart Mill in a passage which has been quoted often, though not always correctly quoted and seldom fully quoted. It is given in full below for almost the first time since Mill wrote. It has been one of the commonest arguments used to support the beginnings of Protection. What is to be said of it?

The first thing to be said of the infant industries argument is that it is not really an argument for Protection in general. It is an argument for nurturing particular industries, as to which there is reason to believe that, after nurture, they will be able to hold their own without Protection. In the countries in which during the nineteenth century it carried most weight—Germany and the United States, and later, Australia and Canada—the argument could without too much strain be applied to most industries, seeking to compete with the established power of Britain. For Britain itself in the twentieth century its appropriate place is in the Safeguarding of Industries Act, or in such measures as the Dyestuffs Act, for domesticating here some new industry, in which by inadvertence or accident we have allowed others to get ahead of us.

Second, while it is impossible to say that Protection of infant industries has never been helpful, there is, as Professor Taussig of Harvard points out, "at least one striking phenomenon which proves it to be not indispensable." Professor Taussig may be left to speak of his own country:

"Here we have seen, under a regime of the most absolute Free Trade, the gradual and steady growth of manufacture in communities that a few decades ago were exclusively agricultural. In our Southern States the cotton manufacture has grown and prospered in face of the competition of the established industry of New England. It found in the South advantages of situation, and a labour supply which proved amenable to profitable

[1] So List's argument was paraphrased by Professor W. J. Ashley in 1903 (*The Tariff Problem*, pp. 25-6).

exploitation. But these advantages could not be utilised without an initial period of experiment and uncertainty, and during this the older industry had all the advantages against which Protection is supposed to be necessary. Even more instructive is the transformation of the great Central region—the States north of the Ohio and east of the Mississippi. Here we have seen, under a regime of complete Free Trade within the country, the steady growth of manufactures. When the field was favourable for a new industry, whether from rich natural resources, from advantage in location, or from ingenuity and enterprise among the leaders of industry and the rank and file, there the industry has expanded and flourished, unchecked by the competing establishments of the older States. Some of the industries that so sprang up in the central region have been of the kind that felt the stimulus of Protection against international competition. Some have been quite independent of this stimulus, the question being not whether they would spring up within the country, but where within the country—whether along the sea-board or in the interior. In either case, the full competition of the older regions of our own country has been felt by the newer regions. The diversification of the newer regions has, nevertheless, proceeded smoothly and steadily. That diversification continues and will continue, notwithstanding the most absolute Free Trade throughout our own borders. No artificial fostering as against the manufactures of the East has been possible; though, if possible, it would doubtless have been asked. Yet the growth of manufactures in the central region has been perhaps the most striking change in the industrial structure of the country during the last generation."[1]

Third, the argument is one for temporary Protection, not permanent Protection, yet the Protection secured by it has seldom if ever been willingly renounced by the in-

[1] Taussig, *Free Trade, The Tariff and Reciprocity*, pp. 21-2.

dustries concerned, and has in nearly all cases become permanent. Here is the place to give Mill's concession in full:

"The only case in which, on mere principles of political economy, protecting duties can be defensible is when they are imposed temporarily (especially in a young and rising generation) in hopes of naturalising a foreign industry, in itself perfectly suitable to the circumstances of the country. The superiority of one country over another in a branch of production often arises only from having begun it sooner. There may be no inherent advantage on one part, or disadvantage on the other, but only a present superiority of acquired skill and experience. A country which has this skill and experience yet to acquire, may in other respects be better adapted to the production than those which were earlier in the field; and besides, it is a just remark of Mr. Rae that nothing has a greater tendency to promote improvements in any branch of production than its trial under a new set of conditions. But it cannot be expected that individuals should, at their own risk, or rather to their certain loss, introduce a new manufacture, and bear the burthen of carrying it on until the producers have been educated up to the level of those with whom the processes are traditional. A protecting duty, continued for a reasonable time, might sometimes be the least inconvenient mode in which the nation can tax itself for the support of such an experiment. But it is essential that the protection should be confined to cases in which there is good ground of assurance that the industry which it fosters will after a time be able to dispense with it; nor should the domestic producers ever be allowed to expect that it will be continued to them beyond the time necessary for a fair trial of what they are capable of accomplishing.[1]

[1] *Principles of Political Economy*, book v, ch. x, par. 1 (p. 922 of the edition edited by Professor W. J. Ashley). As the editor notes, in the

Many economists would accept this as a theoretical possibility. It is hard to see how to-day any economist not living wholly in his lecture room could think it an argument of any practical importance.

The plain fact is that, however economists may theorise about temporary Protection of infant industries, Protection once given is in practice not temporary; it proves as hard to get rid of as an amendment of the American Constitution. The infant industries never feel themselves grown up; if they grow up at all they devote their manly strength to fighting for bigger and longer Protection. This is the lesson of all tariff history in every country with a tariff for the past sixty years. It is the moral of every temporary duty imposed in Britain since the War. " One of the fathers of Canadian Protection—Sir Charles Tupper—declared long ago that 'given fifteen years of Protection the infant industries of Canada would be able to stand alone.' The fifteen years are gone; twenty-five years are gone. The infants are still in arms ! " Thus Professor Smart wrote in 1903. To-day fifty years are gone; in the fifty-third year the infants have to be rescued by an emergency tariff.

For this tendency of Protection, once it has been granted, to become irremovable there is a specific cause other than conservatism. The suitability of an industry to a country is partly a question of the size to which it is extended. There

last sentence but one, " will " of the original (1848) edition was changed by Mill to " might " in 1871 and the words, " it is essential that," were then added in the sentence following. In Professor Ashley's book on *The Tariff Problem*, the opening of this passage, referred to as " a remarkable concession," by John Stuart Mill, is printed as follows :

" Protective duties can be defensible, on mere grounds of political economy, when they are imposed temporarily (especially in a young and rising nation) in hopes of naturalising a foreign industry in itself perfectly suitable to the circumstances of the country."

The omission of the first words, with the transposition of order following thereon, entirely change the emphasis. In a writer of Professor Ashley's standing and familiarity with Mill's writings, the mis-quotation is obviously accidental. But it calls for correction.

[103]

may be natural scope for that industry, that is to say possibility of establishing it on a basis competitive with other countries, up to a limited extent, for special types of work or markets, in a few specially favoured localities, or under exceptionally able management. But high Protection over a period of years will not cause or allow it to be limited in that way. During the protective period the industry will be profitable beyond its natural scope, and will come to be established on an excessive scale; that is to say, on a scale and in places where it cannot be maintained without Protection. Each industry within a country is not homogeneous, but of varying degrees of efficiency and rates of profit. At the end of the period, those who cannot carry on without Protection will fight for its continuance. They will argue, correctly, that a removal of Protection will cause unemployment; they will be joined in their plea by those who could get on without Protection, but can make larger profits or do larger business with Protection and at least cannot lose by it. Protection is not an instrument of precision, which can be used to do just one desired good thing and no more. It is a blunt instrument which if it touches the spot aimed at at all, at the same time makes a blur all round it.

The "infant industries argument" is a leading example of academic theorising remote from realities. List, who made most use of the argument, described Protection as a period of apprenticeship which should lead on to Free Trade; for England he held Free Trade the best policy throughout. Mill himself had too much common sense[1] to regard the concession which he had made for it from Free Trade doctrine as of any importance; he devoted great energy to repudiating the use made of his concession by protectionists in America and Australia; he altered the text of what he had first written, and he finally came to the view that if any subsidy to a new industry were needed "this had better be done by a direct annual grant, which

[1] Described by Professor Ashley as " inconsecutiveness of thought " (*The Tariff Problem*, p. 25).

is far less likely to be continued after the conditions which alone justified it have ceased to exist."[1]

Alfred Marshall, as he stated in his memorandum in 1903, was so much impressed by the arguments of Carey and his followers that he visited the United States in 1875 to study the problems of national industry and international trade from the American point of view. He came back convinced "that a protective policy, in fact, was a very different thing from a protective policy, as painted by sanguine economists, like Carey and his followers, who assumed that all other people would be as upright as they knew themselves to be, and as clear-sighted as they believed themselves to be."

The infant industries argument, in its general form, may be theoretically valid, but practically has been exploded by experience. As applied to rationalisation, it is not worth anything at all. If the people of a country are determined that some industry till then unknown to them shall settle in their country, they can make nearly sure of this by giving suitable Protection. Whether they will ever get the Protection off again and prices down to world level is another matter; but they will at least have done something of what they set out to do. But when the aim is not to domesticate a new industry, but to make an old one change its ways and reorganise itself, Protection may bring nothing at all of what is desired. The giving of Protection cannot in practice be made conditional upon steps for rationalisation having been taken; it cannot in practice be withdrawn if sufficient steps are not taken. No one but an interested person now argues that a tariff once put on comes off again easily. No one but a child believes him.

The diagnosis leading up to rationalisation—that one of Britain's weak spots to-day is lack of industrial planning and co-ordination, is having too small and too separate units of production — is possibly correct. The further

---

[1] *Letters of John Stuart Mill*, vol. ii, p. 155 (To a Minister of New Zealand in 1868). Other repudiations are at pp. 27, 57, 116-17, 149 and 200.

diagnosis may also be correct—that industries needing capital for profitable reorganisation cannot now get it in the ordinary way of business—though there is no presumption in favour of this view. If it were so, and the State had to come in, then even more obviously than with the infant industry, it would be better for the State to come in, as Mill suggested, by direct subsidy than by the indirect subsidy of Protection. A direct subsidy—whether by provision of cheap capital or in some other form—can be made conditional upon specific steps for rationalisation being taken. A direct subsidy can be withdrawn or ended when it becomes either needless or unavailing. Finally, a direct subsidy can be used to strengthen trades suited to the country; to choose for help trades that need Protection is to choose those which on the face of things have the weakest claim. Protection, here as elsewhere, shows itself as a remedy which does not touch the spot. As a means to rationalisation it is like giving to an invalid a dose from a bottle labelled "sleeping mixture," and hoping that it is really a tonic or will turn into a tonic when it gets inside him.

CHAPTER IX

A TARIFF FOR A TARIFF

Sixty years ago Britain seemed the victorious leader of a march of all nations to Free Trade. To-day she stands by Cobden waveringly and almost alone. The camp of the Protectionists becomes yearly larger and more deeply entrenched. No country goes back upon Protection. Old areas of Free Trade—Austria-Hungary and the British Empire—break up into strictly protected units. Nearly every revision of an old tariff is upwards. New tariffs multiply.

There arises in Britain not unnaturally an argument which is really a double argument for a tariff to meet these tariffs. On the one hand, it is urged that the economic advantages of Free Trade depend upon its being mutual; that nothing is gained by a policy of free imports if other countries tax all our exports. On the other hand, it is urged that, Free Trade or a lowering of tariffs all round being the best policy, the only practical way of getting towards that to-day is ourselves to have a tariff which we can offer to lower for concessions from other countries.

Those who use the first of these arguments usually admit the theoretical advantages of Free Trade. Their view is well expressed in the first resolution moved by Sir William Morris, in establishing the "National Council of Industry and Commerce."

"That while the universal adoption of the policy of Free Trade may be as desirable to-day as when first promulgated by Cobden, it is unattainable and our adherence to it as against the tariff system of other nations of the world is injuring our trade and destroying our employment."[1]

[1] Reported in *The Times*, 26th September 1930.

Those who use the second of these arguments necessarily admit the theoretical advantages of Free Trade, or at least the damage done by tariffs. Their view has been well expressed by Mr. Stanley Baldwin in a recent speech at Glasgow:

"I am all in favour of lower tariffs in the world; we want the barriers lowered. I admit at once that high tariffs are a check to trade, but as long as there is one market left of the importance of our market which exists for every tariff country to fling its surplus into, no move will ever be made. The only hope we have to secure lower tariffs is to put a barrier round that free market and say, 'Anyone who wants to come in here has to give us reciprocal advantages.' You will find that there will be a new spirit in the world, that many a country which has never listened to any of the academic or book arguments will begin to realise quickly that business is business, and that they may be able to do better for themselves if they enter into tariff agreements with us as Cobden made with France seventy years ago."[1]

These two arguments for a tariff to meet tariffs will be examined in turn. After them, one last question arising out of the same fact, of the apparent growth of Protectionism throughout the world, will be asked and answer attempted. Why if the case for Protection is so bad and the case for Free Trade so strong as nearly all economists make out, do most countries flout the opinion of nearly all economists and go in for Protection?

ONE-SIDED FREE TRADE

As a matter of history, the assertion that the advantages of Free Trade depend upon its being mutual, has always been made by people who were attacking Free Trade. It has never been made or admitted by any of the principal

[1] Reported in *The Times*, 13th December 1930.

advocates of Free Trade. For this there is a simple reason. It represents complete misunderstanding of the nature of international trade and the working of tariffs.

International trade, like every other kind of trade, arises from the advantages of the division of labour and specialisation of function. This division and specialisation cannot as a rule be carried so far in international trade as within the boundaries of one country, from mere consideration of distance and the cost of transport. Of two countries, each capable of producing both potatoes and wheat, one may be able to grow potatoes more cheaply and the other wheat more cheaply, so that if the countries lay next door to one another and the cost of transport could be neglected, each would get both potatoes and wheat more cheaply by specialising on one crop and getting the second crop by exchange from the other country. But if the countries are at opposite ends of the world, costs of transportation may more than offset the advantages of specialised production; it may be cheaper for each country to grow both wheat and potatoes. Distance of the alternative sources of supply is a natural protection to the home producer to the extent of his costs of transport. So is a dangerous coastline or bad harbours or a bad railway system from the coast. So is the perishability of the product; the fresh milk consumed in each country is almost invariably produced at home, though actual production may be cheaper in some other country; the cheapening of Britain's meat supply has depended on refrigeration.

International trade is never free of all obstacles. The argument of the Free Traders has been directed to making the obstacles as few as possible. The gain through removing one obstacle depends in no way at all upon the removal of all the other obstacles or any of them. As Professor Pigou puts it: "The advantage which a policy of freedom possesses over one of Protection does not, and never has been believed to depend upon its being reciprocated. The high customs duties of foreign countries do, indeed, inflict an injury upon us. They have this result, however, simply because they put a check on exchange. They impose a burden upon the outward branch of our foreign trade, which, of course, diminishes both our exports and our imports. If that country were to add a further burden upon the inward branch of it she would diminish them both still further.''[1]

Gain through freeing imports from taxation does not depend on other countries doing the same. For other countries to tax our exports to them is an injury to us and an obstacle to trade. For us to tax their exports to us is not a correction of that injury; it is just a separate additional obstacle to trade. By allowing free imports we allow competition to determine what goods we can get most cheaply by making them ourselves and what goods we can get most cheaply by something else to sell abroad in exchange for them. If other countries are taxing what we sell to them, the resulting distribution of our capital and labour among various industries will not be quite the same and not quite so profitable as if other countries also allowed free imports. But it will be more profitable than if, by taxing imports ourselves, we forced ourselves to do and make things for which we were less fitted rather than things for which we were most fitted. If one country has good harbours while all the rest have bad ones, it will not realise the advantages of its good harbours so fully as if all the rest had good ones also. But it will realise some advantage; it will be better off than if it, too, sank rocks all round its coasts.

This general argument disposes of the general assertion that the advantages of Free Trade depend on its being reciprocal. It does not meet the whole of Sir William Morris's case or the point that he probably has most in mind. The tariffs of other countries are not only a barrier to our exports. They are a wall behind which foreign manufacturers may raise prices and make profits, sending their surplus to our market at lower prices, at prices with which our home manufacturers cannot compete, at prices just

[1] *The Riddle of the Tariff* (1903), p. 29.

covering or not covering the specific costs of production without overheads or profits.

This point, raising the general problem of differential prices and "dumping," is of such importance as to call for a special chapter. It must be dealt with specially for another reason also—that it is not really an argument for Protection as a general policy. Dumping comes, as a rule, not from all countries at once, but from a particular country. Moreover, only particular articles are dumped. When dumping takes place it often comes at prices defeating any ordinary tariff; even the most highly protected countries are liable to dumping. In so far as it needs to be dealt with and can be dealt with, it calls for other measures than the protection of a permanent tariff.

A Tariff for Bargaining

The argument cited above from Mr. Baldwin is not in spirit an argument for Protection. It is the argument of a Free Trader, an argument for using a tariff to lower tariffs, for doing evil that good may come. It recalls with curious exactness the conclusion of Mr. Balfour's famous tract of 1903 on *Insular Free Trade*. After summarising the evils then threatening Britain, evils all "due to Protection," he proceeded:

"The source of all the difficulty being protective tariffs imposed by fiscally independent communities, it is plain that we can secure no concession in the direction of a freer exchange, except by negotiation, and that our negotiators can but appeal to self-interest, or, in the case of our colonies, to self-interest and sentiment combined.

Now, on the Free Trade theory self-interest should have prevented these tariffs being originally imposed. But it did not; and if argument failed before powerful vested interests were created, it is hardly likely to be effective now.

The only alternative is to do to foreign nations what

they always do to each other, and instead of appealing
to economic theories in which they wholly disbelieve, to
use fiscal inducements which they thoroughly understand. We, and we alone, among the nations are unable
to employ this means of persuasion, not because in our
hands it need be ineffectual, but because in obedience to
'principle' we have deliberately thrown it away. . . .

. . . I hold myself to be in harmony with the true
spirit of Free Trade when I plead for freedom to negotiate
that freedom of exchange may be increased."[1]

The echo of Mr. Balfour's words by Mr. Baldwin is
unmistakable. Mr. Baldwin, indeed, does not, as Mr.
Balfour did, call himself a "Free Trader," though sometimes
he comes near to this; his grasp of economic theory is not
so sure as Mr. Balfour's, and he can and does believe in
Protection and Free Trade together. A more significant
difference is that, while Mr. Balfour asked just for liberty
to negotiate, Mr. Baldwin wishes to begin by putting on a
tariff—just to show them.

If negotiation came before the tariff and if the negotiation could in substance be complete at once; if as part of a
great reciprocal treaty—with the British Dominions or
with the United States of Europe—the tariff barriers of
half the world against Britain could be made to fall
for ever, as British tariffs were raised against the rest
of the world, that would be a negotiation well worth
attempting.

But that is not the prospect to which Mr. Baldwin
beckons. The proposition that we should begin by putting
on a tariff and then use that for bargaining is something
different, and is unpractical, because it ignores the tendency
of tariffs to make vested interests.

Those who argue that it is the policy of Free Trade
which makes it impossible for Britain to secure the lowering
of tariffs, seldom try to show that protectionist countries
have any better success in such bargaining; they could not

[1] *Economic Notes on Insular Free Trade* (1903), pp. 29-31.

show it if they did try. For this there is the simple reason that tariffs are of hardly any practical use for bargaining. It is easy to put them on, but bargaining with them means taking them off, or offering to do so. That is another story. When a tariff is put on, the benefit to the home trade protected thereby is clear and definite, the damage to the rest of the community is dispersed. Suppose that we now put on a tariff against leather goods from Germany and elsewhere. The immediate effect will be to stimulate the production of such goods in this country; more capital and labour will be drawn into the leather industry, more factories opened. Is it conceivable that three or five years hence we should be able to offer to lower the tariff on leather goods from Germany in order to secure freer entry into Germany of some other article made by ourselves— woollens or motor cars? The gain to the woollen or motor industry would be as obvious as in the case of putting on a duty, but so would the loss to the leather industry. Why, it would be asked, should we directly cause unemployment in one industry in order directly to benefit another?

If we had any doubt before what tariff bargaining means in practice, we should have none after the Imperial Conference of 1930. The Dominion Premiers, anxious as they were, alike on grounds of sentiment and of business, to make a bargain with us that would find a market for their wheat and wool, could not offer for this purpose to lower a single duty of their own. The vested interests of their protected industries blocked the way.

The idea that tariffs can by bargaining be made a way to freer trade is not an economic fallacy like most of the common arguments for Protection. It is just a disastrous misunderstanding of human nature. Bargaining with tariffs is bargaining with livelihoods. Those who wish to put on a tariff at once that Free Trade may follow, go one stage further than those who seek peace by preparing war. They seek peace by making war, not by preparing it.

The Argument from Example

By now all the principal arguments for a policy of
Protection have been reviewed, in this or earlier chapters.
They have all, if the reasoning of these chapters is sound,
been proved to be unsound. The lay reader, even if he
accepts this reasoning, may still be puzzled by a doubt.
Why do other nations not accept it? Are they and their
governments all incapable of economic reasoning?

A full answer to this question would involve making an
examination of the fiscal issue for each country, and writing
a history of how its tariff came to be. No answer on such a
scale can be attempted here. The short answer is that the
growth of Protection has depended very little on reasoning;
its beginning—in most countries—can be explained by
circumstances which have passed away, while its persistence
and development once it has come are all but inevitable.

These last words give the dominant facts of the situation.
Protection directs production into particular channels,
breeds vested interests, shapes men's livelihoods. Any
protective tariff which is not just nugatory is keeping prices
higher than they would be without it; its abolition would
lower the prices that makers of the protected articles could
command in their home market. Sudden removal of a long-
established high Protection, such as that of the United
States, would cause dislocation, business losses and unemployment on a vast scale. Even those who disagree, as
practically all economists of any standing in the States
disagree with its protective policy, realise that a reversal
of policy would have to be slow and for a long time partial.

Two quotations from Professor Taussig of Harvard put
the view of most American economists admirably. "As to
most of the familiar arguments for Protection, either all the
economists are hopelessly in the wrong, or else the Protectionist reasoning is hopelessly bad." Yet, "no rational
person, even though he were the most radical Free Trader,
would propose to abolish at one fell swoop protective duties
to which a great industrial system had accommodated

itself. We may not like the result, but it is there, and not to be suddenly modified without widespread loss. Moreover those engaged in the industries may plead with weight that they have entered on their operations with the sanction of government, nay, with its direct encouragement, and that the government cannot in justice leave them in the lurch."[1]

The persistence of Protection, once it has been established, is only half the story. Once introduced, on however small a scale, it tends to grow and get established on a large scale. The benefit of Protection to the capital and labour engaged in an industry seeking Protection is immediate, direct and obvious. If Protection is granted to one industry, it is always difficult and often impossible to find reasons for refusing Protection to any other industry. If granted in any one industry, indeed, it tends to make Protection seem not merely equitable but necessary for others. There is hardly any product of one industry which does not enter, directly or indirectly, into the productive process of some other industry as raw material, or instrument of manufacture or transport, or basis of wages; if by Protection its price is raised above the world price, some other industry has its costs of production raised and gets a convincing special plea for its own Protection; this in turn affects other producers. The tariff grows like a snowball. For as against these clear sectional gains, the advantage of Free Trade is usually less obvious and more thinly spread. Once admitted in principle or for one case, Protection spreads through a succession of victories won by concentrated organised sectional interests over dispersed unorganised general interest.

The spreading and entrenching of Protection once it has begun are easy to explain. What, however, makes it begin? The answer to that question must be sought in economic histories; it is not the same for all lands. Sometimes the need of revenue has played a leading part.[2] The most

---

[1] *Free Trade, the Tariff and Reciprocity*, pp. 4 and 143-144.
[2] As with the British North American colonies at their foundation and the United States after the Civil War. See *The Return to Protection* (pp. 60-6 and 67-8), by Professor W. Smart.

common reason has been the desire of other countries to follow Britain down the industrial path to wealth, and the belief that as against her established industries their new industries could not be begun without Protection for their infancy. This belief was probably well-founded for some countries and badly founded for others. Good or bad, the infant industries argument has played a great part in the justifying of Protection everywhere.

This much it has seemed necessary and worth while to say about the argument from the example of other countries. It is enough to show that their example is no argument for us in Britain. They may in their special circumstances be right or wrong. Most of their own economists would tell them now that in the degree of their Protection, if not in the fact of it, they are emphatically wrong. But whether they are partly right or wholly wrong, their action is not based on reasoning which applies to us. Britain, having decided nearly ninety years ago to merge herself in world economy, has a vested interest in international trade, as large, as free, as various as possible, surpassing all her other interests.

CHAPTER X

THE GENERAL INTEREST

NATIONAL policy in the economic sphere, as in all other spheres, should be directed to ensure permanent advantages for the population as a whole. The presumption in favour of a policy of Free Trade is that it is so directed—it secures in the long run the use of the national resources of a country in the way shown by experience to be most economical, that is to say, to yield the greatest results for the least effort: the certain advantage of Free Trade is both permanent and general. The advantages, on the other hand, to be obtained by tariffs are either sectional if they are certain, or uncertain if they are general; in each case a strictly temporary gain, if any gain, is far more probable than a permanent one.

There is no doubt at all that Protection by a tariff can, in its immediate effects, benefit the employers and work-people in particular trades. Free Traders who argue as if Protection did not protect are on wrong lines. An import duty imposed on a particular article, so long as it is having any effect at all, means that buyers of that article are paying more for it than they would be if the duty were not there; it means that manufacturers of the article whose products are not subject to the duty, that is those within the tariff wall, can get a higher price for what they sell. A manufacturer who, without other change in his costs or other conditions, secures a higher price for his product is, of course, benefited. He can make larger profits; he can, and almost certainly will, be driven to share some of his advantage with his employees by raising wages; he can increase his production and take more men into employment and still retain enough profit to make this worth while. But the conditions and limitations of this benefit to employers and workpeople in particular trades must be carefully noted. In the first place, they depend on the Protection being selective. The benefit comes out of the higher price paid by consumers, and every one is both a consumer and a producer. If one industry alone is protected, or is protected more highly than the rest, employers and workpeople in it will gain more as producers by the higher prices that they obtain than they will lose as consumers by the higher prices that they pay to other producers. But if the tariff becomes general and equal all round there is no such net gain to anybody. In the second place, unless the employers in the protected industry can establish a monopoly, the advantage to them will not be lasting. In so far as selective Protection raises their profits and wages above the level of other industries, it will tend to draw additional capital and labour into the protected industry, till prices and profits sink again to the general level; the industry will be larger, but ultimately the employers and workpeople engaged in it will not be better off than they would be without Protection. Selective Protection can benefit a trade in the sense of bringing into existence in a country, or keeping in existence there, a trade which would not be there without it. But, unless they can establish a monopoly to exploit consumers, the employers and workpeople engaged in that trade will not be better off, indeed they will be worse off, than if their capital and labour had gone into a trade which could exist without Protection, that is to say, a trade representing a better use of the resources of the country.

This, however, is a long run view which naturally does not appeal to any existing body of employers and workpeople in any existing industry. Their capital and labour are committed to a particular line and cannot easily be transferred to anything else. They will gain if, by placing an import duty on things they make, making such things free of duty within the tariff becomes more profitable. They will lose if by removal of a duty it is made less profitable. If they are being threatened by the competition of foreign rivals who for any reason can make the same things more cheaply, the imposition of a duty will appear the simplest and may be almost the only way of saving them from loss and unemployment. But all these advantages, in so far and so long as they depend upon the import duty, are simply advantages at the expense of the rest of the community.

It may, of course, be held that the giving of selective Protection to a particular industry, even at the expense of the rest of the community, is justified for some special reason —of national security in war or of maintaining a balance between town and country—or the like. The case of agriculture is considered from this angle, among others, in a special chapter. The case of dyestuffs is similar. Selective Protection and its various implications may be illustrated by reference to iron and steel.

The iron and steel industry represents probably the strongest case for selective Protection on purely economic grounds in this country. It is an old-established industry and an important industry threatened, not only in export markets, but in the home market by competition of foreign rivals with lower costs of production. The competition does not extend over the whole industry; there is no question of the whole industry disappearing. In many kinds of manufacture, particularly the more advanced stages, it retains its competitive power and has a large export trade. But in many other kinds of manufacture, hitherto undertaken in this country, and for which plant and labour in this country have been adapted, it cannot now, with present methods and wages, compete on equal terms with the rival industries of several other countries. In so far as this competition cuts down exports, a tariff for the British industry would not help, except on the basis of the industry dumping from behind the tariff, charging more to home consumers and less to foreign consumers. But in so far as this competition causes loss of contracts for iron and steel in the home market, it throws out of employment plant and labour which it may be difficult to employ otherwise. To some extent this undeniably is happening to-day. Iron and steel is the leading, perhaps the only case, of an important industry in which unemployment is now resulting from imports. It is a case, therefore, in which on the grounds indicated in the sixth chapter, Protection might lead to a net reduction of unemployment.

But what are the implications of a tariff protecting the iron and steel industry of Britain? Two in particular must be noted. First, iron and steel, while they are manufactures, are the raw materials of many other industries—engineering, shipbuilding, motors, cutlery, window-frames and so on. Most of these are also in competition with foreign industries at home and abroad. If, by a tariff on steel, these other British industries are going to be made to buy British steel at one price, when equivalent foreign steel is on the market at a lower price apart from the tariff, they are to the exact extent of the difference going to be taxed in favour of their rivals. The cheaper foreign steel or the power to produce it will not go out of existence because it is kept out of Britain. The British industries using steel, will, of course, seek and may get protection in their home market also. But this will not help them in exports and will involve a general rise of prices, which in due course will injure their exports still further; the foreign industries using steel will get the cheaper supplies which have been kept out of Britain. It is not practical for any country that wishes to be a great exporter to neglect the cheapest sources of such fundamental raw materials as iron and steel. What would be the position of our iron and steel trade now, if, at the time when its own raw material of iron ore first began to be imported, a heavy duty had been imposed thereon in the interests of the ironstone miners?

Second, while it would be absurd to make accusations of inefficiency against all parts and members of any industry, it is beyond question that one of the difficulties of the British industry is that it is old established. Later rivals have benefited by our experience. A larger proportion of our plant is old and out of date. Certainly there is a striking difference between the average size of each of our blast-furnaces and those of all other countries. Certainly conservatism is of the essence of British character. Protection by a tariff of an old industry threatened by modern rivals involves serious risk of condoning excessive conservatism and delaying acceptance of new ideas and methods.

Consideration of the iron and steel industry brings out with peculiar force the clumsiness of a tariff as an instrument, and the difficulty of getting by it any desired result, without harmful re-actions. If, with a view to preparedness for war or for any other reason of State policy, it is desirable that parts of the iron and steel industry which might otherwise disappear from this country should be kept alive, this can be done better by almost any other means than a tariff. Public authorities not working for profit can be required, subject to safeguards against exploitation, to use British rather than foreign steel; in effect this is the rule with such customers as the Admiralty and the railway companies. Better still, the process of re-construction and rationalisation of the industry can be assisted by cheap capital. In such ways help can be given so as both to secure the desired end and to avoid undesirable re-actions.

The help that can undoubtedly be given to any particular trade by selective Protection is thus given as a subsidy from the consumers of its products. It is hard to see how a permanent subsidy for a particular trade can be justified except on "non-economic" grounds, e.g. preparedness for war. If a temporary subsidy seems justified, e.g. to bring about re-construction or meet an exceptional difficulty, it is far better given directly than through a tariff. To give help directly and openly offers the only hope either of making help temporary or of ensuring that the purpose for which it is given gets carried out.

The gain to the employers and workpeople in any particular trade of getting Protection for their trade is obvious and direct and dependent nearly always on continuance of the Protection. When we pass from consideration of particular trades to the possibilities of economic advantage through a tariff to the community as a whole, the position is almost exactly reversed. The advantages are never obvious and seldom direct and they usually depend upon removing the tariff as soon as a particular object has been obtained. Nearly all the common arguments for Protection are simple fallacies. The few arguments which are theoretically valid involve nearly always highly complicated calculations of gain and loss with the net gain depending on assumptions which are usually improbable, and can practically never be taken as certain. One of these theoretical arguments—involving the relations of the export surplus and foreign lending—has been examined at some length in Chapter VII. Similar examination of all the other arguments of its class leads to the same kind of conclusion. As arguments for action they are nearly all open to the same practical objection, of doing permanent certain harm for the sake of a temporary speculative good. As Professor Jacob Viner puts it of one of these protectionist proposals, it "seems very much like the current medical procedure of inoculating patients with malaria in order to cure them of paresis. Malaria, however, is unquestionably a less serious disease than paresis, whereas it is extremely doubtful whether Protection would be for England a less serious evil than is the amount of unemployment which Protection could abolish. The doctors, moreover, have a specific for malaria, but none has yet been discovered for Protectionism once it has gotten a firm hold." The fact that Protection does confer such definite and obvious advantages upon particular sections of the community, while it lasts, is the fact that makes the scientific use of tariffs to bring about subtle economic re-adjustments impracticable.

If the matter be looked at broadly it is easy to see why the advantage of a tariff to a particular section is so obvious and direct, whereas the advantage to the community as a whole is so indirect and speculative. A tariff after all is simply a form of taxation—of taking money away from people; taxation can be and often is to-day a means, not simply of taking away money from one set of people, but of using it for the advantage of others. It is a direct redistribution of wealth. There is nothing surprising in a tariff being able often to act in this way. But taxation is not a form of production; it does nothing directly to increase wealth. The suggestion that a nation can turn adversity into prosperity by so simple a device as taxing the things that its citizens want to buy from abroad is a paradox that should need no refutation.

The only way in which taxation can affect the production as well as the distribution of wealth is indirectly, by leading people to do things that they would not do otherwise. Here in the long run the influence of taxation by a protective tariff is almost inevitably harmful. The central Free Trade position lies not in the balance of exports and imports—though of that too in the long run and in the sense described above there is no doubt—but in the doctrine, accepted without question by nearly every economist since Adam Smith, that the greater the freedom of international trade, the more nearly will the productive powers of each country —in natural resources and labour—be used to their maximum of efficiency. Free Trade will not make possible a high standard of living in a country where the natural resources are poor or the labour ill-trained or feeble or the managers of industry behind the times; but it will make the standard higher than under Protection. Free Trade will not make an end of unemployment; that occurs through many causes, under Free Trade and Protection alike. Apart from all other causes, any change of economic conditions, by displacing capital or labour from its chosen occupations, may cause unemployment. The imposition of a new import duty, the taking off of an old one, the introduction of a new machine, may all alike cause unemployment. But the first kind of change is undesirable because it changes the industrial structure of the country ultimately for the worse; the other two change it ultimately for the better. Free Trade, finally, will not bring prosperity to a people which seeks to consume more than it produces, and will not change old habits to suit the changing world outside it. But Protection will not help that people either. Protection to such a people will be just a chance to each section to fight for more than its share of a steadily failing total.

The circumstances of Britain to-day are widely different from what they were when the fiscal issue was raised and settled twenty-five years ago. The new circumstances compel a different outlook and call for action of many kinds not tried before. Whether this action should include tariffs for such special purposes as revenue or the promotion of imperial preference or the prevention of dumping or should include measures alternative to tariffs, but having the same purpose, such as import boards or quotas, will be considered in the chapters that follow. At the end of the first part of this volume the negative conclusion stands clear. The new circumstances give no warrant for returning after ninety years to the policy of Protection.

CHAPTER XI

"Dumping" is both a term of art and a term of abuse. As used by economists, dumping implies "price discrimination between national markets"; it is "the disposal of commodities in a foreign country at one price, and to domestic purchasers at another and higher price."[1] As used by politicians, business men, legislators and the public generally, dumping has a variety of meanings, with little in common between them, except the denoting of a price which the speaker objects to as too low. Thus, under Part II of the Safeguarding of Industries Act, for the prevention of dumping, the term covers selling not only below cost of production (which almost inevitably must be dumping in the sense of the economists), but also selling abroad cheaply as the result of depreciated currency, and selling abroad cheaply as the result of having lower wages or standards of living; neither of these last need involve any price discrimination between home and foreign markets. South African legislation provides also against "freight dumping," that is to say sales which one particular importer can make at low prices because he has secured carriage at charges below those ruling for his competitors. These and other occasions of exceptionally low prices for imported goods will be considered later. For clearness it will be well to begin with dumping as defined by economists.

On this two preliminary points must be noted. First,

[1] The latter form of words is taken from Professor Taussig (*Prin. of Econ.*, 3rd Revised Ed., 1907). The former, from Professor Viner (*Dumping : A Problem of International Trade*, p. 4), is slightly wider, since it would cover discrimination with the price in the domestic market below that in the foreign market. This practice, sometimes called " reverse dumping " does not call for consideration here.

there are circumstances in which systematic dumping, that is to say, selling more cheaply abroad than at home, may be a prudent business practice to which no objection can reasonably be taken. Second, price discrimination, under the economists' definition, only becomes dumping when it is international discrimination—between markets in distinct countries, but price discrimination is in no sense peculiar to international trade.

As to the first point, a manufacturer may find that by selling at a certain price at home and a lower price abroad, he can secure a market and total output and costs of production making his price in each market lower than if it had to be the same in each market. This implies that the demand for his product is inelastic at home and elastic abroad; that is to say, that lowering his home price would not greatly increase his sales and that raising his foreign price would greatly decrease them. Such a difference between market conditions is perfectly possible. The demand for some kinds of cotton cloth is often said to be of this nature, the number of shirts that an Englishman will buy being little affected by changes in the price of the cotton entering into it, while the Indian demand is greatly affected. Acting on this difference means that the manufacturer throws his overhead costs disproportionately more upon the home market than upon the foreign market, because if he tried to spread them evenly he would lose the foreign market. He goes in for systematic permanent dumping. If he does this from a Free Trade country, neither his home consumers nor his rival manufacturers abroad have any legitimate grievance. The price to the home consumers is not being kept up by exclusion of cheaper goods and the dumping is not in any way at their expense. His rivals in other countries are being undersold only through his skill in adjusting prices so as to secure a maximum output; their remedy is to compete with him in his home market.

As to the second point, adjusting prices to the conditions of different markets so as to make the maximum net profit over all, disposing of surplus stocks at a sacrifice, selling for a time at a loss to make goods known to new customers, selling for a time at a loss in order to drive a rival out of business or bring him to an agreement, are all part of the technique of marketing, whether in domestic trade or in foreign trade. In so far as some of these forms of price discrimination are open to objection, *e.g.* temporary price cutting in order to establish and later to exploit a monopoly, the objection applies equally, whether the discrimination is within one country or between different countries. And the practical difficulty in each case is how to distinguish and check harmful price discriminations without stopping the wheels, or at least one of the wheels, of commercial progress. Appreciation of this danger usually leads to no action being taken to stop price discriminations within a country. The danger is just as real when the price discrimination is international.

It is unreasonable to object to all price discriminations between different markets. What are the forms of price discrimination between domestic and foreign markets to which objection may be taken rightly or with good show of reason? And what action, if any, can prudently be taken to stop them? It will be sufficient here to examine four leading cases. They may be described as sporadic dumping of casual overstocks, predatory dumping, monopoly dumping, and State-aided dumping.[1]

The disposal of casual overstocks of goods at a sacrifice is a universal and necessary business practice. It becomes dumping when the holder of the stock, in order to avoid ruining prices in his principal market at home, makes his sacrifice sale for choice in a foreign market. This is the commonest kind of what is usually called "sporadic" dumping. Its harmfulness lies in its essentially temporary

---

[1] This is not, of course, an exhaustive classification of dumping. For such a classification reference may be made to Professor Viner's work, cited above. In his second chapter, Professor Viner divides dumping under ten distinct headings according to motive, and groups these ten under three classes according to continuity, namely, "sporadic," "short-run or intermittent," "long-run or continuous."

character. Markets and production in the country receiving the dumped goods are upset, and since the continuance of dumping cannot be counted on, even the consumers who benefited originally by the cheap goods may lose in the end. In the casual character of this dumping, however, lies also the difficulty of dealing with it. The existence of a permanent tariff is no obstacle to it. When casual overstocks have to be disposed of somehow, the holders are often prepared to take prices that will defeat any ordinary tariff. Nor need the sacrifice be greater in dumping over a permanent tariff wall than in dumping into a Free Trade country. Prices in the protected country will normally be higher than in the Free Trade country—otherwise the tariff would be needless; if the tariff is just high enough to give the desired amount of protection and no more, the difference of the Free Trade and protected prices will be practically represented by the tariff. All that the dumper has to do is to undercut the normal market price in each case; he will be able to dump into either market at different prices, but at the same sacrifice to himself.

From one point of view, indeed, a manufacturer with a casual overstock may prefer to dump it into a Protectionist rather than a Free Trade country; the latter is more likely to be a permanent market for him and therefore one which he will least desire to spoil by flooding it with goods at unremunerative prices. The reason which may lead a manufacturer to dump rather than sell at a sacrifice at home will also lead him to dump for choice into a protected rather than an open market.

A really prohibitive tariff will, of course, stop dumping as well as all regular trade. But ordinary tariffs don't stop it and the idea that a Free Trade country is solely or peculiarly exposed to casual dumping is a delusion. This is shown both by historic instances of dumping into protected markets,[1] and, more convincingly still, by the fact that the most highly protected countries in the world have thought

[1] *See* Smart, *The Return to Protection*, pp. 165-6.

it necessary to add to their regular tariffs special duties against dumping. Thus Canada has had anti-dumping legislation since 1904, Australia since 1906, South Africa since 1914, and the United States since 1916.

The South African regulations are described and criticised in an article by Professor Plant reprinted on p. 248 as an Appendix. Their working may be taken as typical of the difficulties that arise in the application of additional duties to stop casual dumping. There is first the difficulty of time. If, as in the original South African Act of 1914, previous notice has to be given of the duties, goods will be rushed in during the period of notice; against sporadic dumping, this amounts always to closing the stable-door after the horse has been stolen. If the additional duties can be imposed without notice, crippling uncertainty is introduced into the importing business; for, as is noted just below, it is by no means easy for an importer to know beforehand whether any particular transaction will be treated as dumping. There is, second, the difficulty of determining the domestic price of the imported article in its country of origin, in order to see whether price discrimination has in fact occurred. Determination of what are strictly comparable prices in two widely different countries is, with modern complexities of marketing, always a difficult and sometimes an insoluble problem; that is to say, it has often to be solved in practice by giving a large amount of arbitrary power to customs officials. There is, third, the tendency continually to sacrifice general to sectional interests, well illustrated by Professor Plant, by the instances of cement and wrapping-paper. There is, fourth, the tendency of temporary anti-dumping duties to grow into additional general and permanent Protection, illustrated in Professor Plant's article by the case of wheat.

This does not show that special anti-dumping duties are always unworkable. One distinguished economist at least, Professor Jacob Viner of Chicago, who is among the strongest critics of tariffs generally, has expressed the view

I

that the anti-dumping provisions of the Canadian tariff have proved beneficial. But it does show that dealing with dumping by duties is far from simple, and is exposed to many risks. They are risks that should not be taken, except to deal with evils that are both certain and large. Sporadic dumping of casual overstocks hardly satisfies that condition. What of the other forms of dumping named above?

The harmfulness of predatory dumping, if it occurs, is undeniable. It is, moreover, a process necessarily taking some time, so that anti-dumping duties could be applied to check it. But is it the sort of thing that is likely to occur often? When the conditions that would make it a profitable proceeding are examined more closely, the chance of its occurring often is seen to be a small one. To make it worth while for manufacturers in country A to dump goods in country B in order to kill the domestic manufacturers there and then raise prices, they must be sure of a monopoly in B when they have accomplished their object. If a third country C is still in the field, the manufacturers of A, when they have killed those of B by a costly price war, will not be in a position even to recoup their losses by extorting monopoly prices in B. As soon as they try raising prices above a fair level, the manufacturers from C will come into the market. In other words, determined predatory dumping will only be worth while for manufacturers who already have in hand or in prospect a monopoly, not in their own market alone, but in all the world outside the country where they dump. If they are in the position of a world-wide ring, it will, nine times out of ten, be easier and more profitable for them to bribe the outstanding manufacturers into joining their ring, than to put them out of business by dumping. This does not mean that price wars between manufacturers of different countries do not occur; obviously they do and are an essential part of economic progress, of rival producers trying their strength and testing their markets. The danger is that this beneficial kind of competition, which is always going on, may be stopped, in the attempt to stop the much rarer cases of competition that is harmful.

What is to be said of dumping by a monopoly from behind a tariff wall? This undoubtedly occurs; it was a more or less systematic policy of the German Kartells before the Great War. Undoubtedly also, it may inflict severe losses on the rival industries of other countries. An industry in a protected country, practising this kind of dumping, may undercut a rival, either in his home market or in neutral markets or in both.

From some points of view, systematic undercutting in this way is indistinguishable from competition based on better resources or more efficient management or cheaper labour or any other advantage. The cheap goods, in themselves, are an advantage rather than a disadvantage to the country that receives them; if one trade suffers, others will be stimulated. The dumping is only a specialised form of that adjustment of prices to market conditions noted above as a reasonable business practice; the market conditions taken into account include the additional element of monopoly behind a tariff. This makes no difference from the point of view of consumers in the country receiving the dumped goods.

But, from other points of view, the additional element of monopoly behind a tariff makes all the difference in the world. The consumers in the country which dumps are exploited by a monopoly, in order to subsidise exports. Where the articles concerned are the raw materials of other industries, this soon leads to organised protest. German users of coal, iron and steel complained of being placed at a disadvantage in export markets, in competition with rivals receiving these dumped supplies from Germany; the Kartells found themselves driven to sell at lower prices to exporting industries. The exploitation of the domestic consumer, however, remained and was intensified. The rival producers in the country receiving the cheap goods have also more to complain of than the simple fact that they are being undersold. They are being undersold with the help of subsidies extorted by a foreign monopoly from its domestic consumers under protection of a tariff; they have not the possibility of reprisals by invading the home market of their opponents.

Monopoly dumping from behind a tariff wall is a form of competition which it is certainly desirable to discourage. It is an irritant all round, to the domestic consumers who are exploited and to the rival producers who are put out of business. It is, in fact, one of the strongest general objections to Protection that it makes this kind of thing possible. South African experience has been used in this chapter to illustrate the working of anti-dumping legislation. It could also be used to provide one of the worst examples of monopoly dumping; the South African sugar producers, organised into a close ring under the shelter of a high tariff, have at times sold sugar in the Union at a price nearly twice that at which they export.

Monopoly dumping from behind a tariff depends indirectly on State aid—in maintaining the tariff. It is only going one stage further for the State to aid dumping directly, either by bounties on export or in some less obvious manner, such as favourable rates, for transport on national railways, of goods destined for foreign markets. In the Middle Ages and later, when trade policy was governed by mercantilist theories, export bounties were almost as regular a feature of national policy as import duties or import prohibitions. To-day they are somewhat differently regarded. In principle there is, indeed, little difference between subsidising a domestic manufacture by import duties and subsidising exports by bounties, or between damaging the trade of another State in the one way and attacking it in the other way. Tariffs, however, are now by most countries accepted as permissible forms of State interference; logically or not, export bounties are not accepted. The difference is, of course, that by an import duty a State is primarily discriminating in favour of its manufacturers in its own market; by an export bounty it is openly carrying that discrimination into neutral markets. But it does this last also, if it permits a protected monopoly to use its protection to dump outside.

It is easier, however, to see the objections both to dumping by a protected monopoly and to State-aided dumping, than to devise a certain and safe remedy. A permanent general tariff, as has been pointed out, is of little avail. It will not always prevent dumping over the tariff into the home market, and it is of no use at all against dumping into neutral markets; all it can do is to help the producers in the country attacked to dump in revenge. Special anti-dumping duties, if they could be limited to cases of monopoly and State-aided dumping and could be prevented from developing into general Protection, might be effective and are not open to theoretical objection. But in how many modern states could these two conditions be maintained? It is significant that Professor Viner, in justifying special anti-dumping legislation, confines this approval to countries whose general policy is one of Free Trade. If Protection against competition in general were safely out of the way, it would be more possible to consider Protection against types of competition "whose benefits" in Professor Viner's words "are transient, but whose injury to industry is lasting."

Even so, anti-dumping duties are a poor device. Sporadic dumping hardly calls for a remedy. The essential harm of systematic monopoly dumping and State-aided dumping is the embitterment of international trade relations. The only satisfactory way of dealing with them, as the tangled history of the sugar bounties showed, is by international action. An international convention to deal with dumping might, it is suggested, contain at least two main provisions:

The first and most important would aim at the inclusion in the tariff of each country of a clause allowing re-importation duty free of goods originally made in that country. This would automatically limit the difference between the home and foreign price of any article to the amount of two freights, inward and outward. If the home price tended

[133]

to exceed the foreign price by more than that, it would pay to bring back goods after export.

The second provision should be a recognition of the right of each State absolutely to prohibit imports, when their price had been artificially cheapened by subsidies from another State, subject to appeal to some international tribunal.

It is easy to foresee the opposition that would be organised by powerful interests in some states against the first of these proposals. But it is not easy to see what even fairly plausible arguments they could use.

These suggestions, it will be seen, deal only with dumping in the sense of the economists—with price discrimination between national markets. Selling goods cheaply in a foreign market because one can make them cheaply is not dumping at all, whether the cheapness results from richer natural resources or from better management or from labour that is more efficient in relation to the wages it requires. Protection against such competition is just ordinary Protection. The case against that has been set out fully in earlier chapters. The case against that is one of the chief reasons for caution in adopting special measures against dumping.

CHAPTER XII

PROTECTION and preferential trade, though often treated as two halves of the same policy, are distinct policies and may in practice be inconsistent policies. The essence of Protection is the discouragement of imports. The essence of preferential trade is the encouragement of some imports rather than others, with a view to securing a market for exports. Protection negatives international trade. Preference aims at developing international trade by giving it assured channels. In their extreme form, of a customs union with a high tariff against the rest of the world, but no barriers within the union, arrangements for preference may be viewed as the most practical way of securing the largest possible measure of Free Trade. They may with flawless logic be supported by one who accepts all the arguments against Protection set out in the preceding chapters. They may be urged at this juncture as the only way of securing for Britain something like the place in the economic structure of the world that was envisaged for her by the founders of her fiscal policy.

In the past hundred years the population and industry of Britain have grown to suit a world of international trade, and no other kind of world. She has become highly specialised to manufacturing and commerce. Her density of population and standard of life are possible only on the assumption that she is a manufacturing and trading centre for a much larger area, from which she can draw food and raw materials, and to which she can supply in return manufactures, and trading, transport and financial services. This assumption, once so natural, has latterly become increasingly hard to realise. For this there are two reasons: the development by other countries of their own natural resources for manufacturing, and the spirit of economic nationalism.

The first of these developments is not in itself a new feature in the world. America and Germany, to say nothing of other countries, soon followed Britain down the industrial path. Nor, up to the end of last century, could the industrial development of other countries be described, with any regard to facts, as a threat to Britain's prosperity. On the contrary, it helped that prosperity by increasing population and markets; the principal manufacturing countries, specialising in those things for which they had greatest advantage, could become one another's best customers. But the new century has brought a new possibility before us. Britain's industrial position rests on her natural resources, above all, coal. If, after a century of working, these resources are no longer comparable to the resources of other countries—in coal, oil and water—the world's demand for Britain's services, at the price which her people have come to demand for their work, may prove insufficient to employ them all. This is the possibility to which the check to our material progress in the past generation unquestionably points.

Economic nationalism also is no new phenomenon. But it also is one which in the last generation has become more portentous for Britain's future. The passing over to protective policy of countries like Australia, South Africa and India dates from within the present century. The establishment of new countries, each with a policy of self-sufficiency, is one of the legacies of the Great War. The rising tariff of America and the programme of Russia are notorious.

In a world apparently bent on organising itself into units each as self-sufficing as possible, the position of one country remaining highly specialised may become precarious. Might it not be wise for such a country to seek to make itself definitely part of a larger unit which as a whole can be self-sufficing or nearly so? Britain is an enormous market for food and raw materials, and a producer of manu-

factures. If she can find another country or group of
countries which, in exchange for preferential terms in her
market for food and raw materials, will offer her a preferential market for manufactures, the deal may seem worth
while. When the suggestion of such a bargain can be associated with hopes of securing a better distribution of population and of capital resources throughout a commonwealth
of kindred nations, it has added attractions. It can certainly not be rejected off-hand on Free Trade principles.
It must be examined on its merits.

What are the prospects and conditions of making,
between Britain and all or some of the countries of the
British Empire, preferential trade arrangements of mutual
advantage? How far could such arrangements be carried?
A brief consideration shows that they could not be carried
far without a revolutionary change of policies, alike in
Britain and in the Dominions. An attempt to make the
Empire to-day into a close-knit economic unit would
conflict with major interests alike of Britain and the
Dominions—with the interest of Britain in its established
trade connections outside the Empire, with the interest of
Britain in cheap food and raw materials, and with the
interest of the Dominions in the development of their own
industries under Protection. These three points will be
taken in order.

The first point hardly needs emphasis. Britain's economic
structure has been built on a world-wide basis. She has
trading connections with South America, Scandinavia,
Denmark, even with industrial rivals like Germany, of
immense value to her. She obtains from them food and
raw materials and finds markets for manufactures, often
on better tariff terms than are allowed her by the Dominions.
She cannot erect a tariff barrier between herself and these
foreign countries, without weakening these connections
and risking loss or diminution of these markets. She cannot
prudently take that risk, unless a more than equivalent
gain is in prospect elsewhere—of assured new markets in
the Dominions. But this, as will be seen just below, is what

[137]

the Dominions do not offer her and cannot offer her, consistently with their view of their own interests.

The second point raises the highly controversial issues of food taxes. There is no question that any extensive preferential arrangement with the Dominions would mean, for Britain, the imposition of a tax on some at least of the essential foods that it now imports in part from foreign countries—on wheat, meat and dairy products among others. This was urged frankly by nearly all the Dominion Premiers at the Imperial Conference of 1930. An import duty would have to be placed on wheat and other foods from foreign countries, in order that a lower rate of duty or no duty at all might be charged on similar imports from the Empire. How far is it a valid argument against such arrangements that under them the price of food might be higher in this country than without them? There is a strong tradition against food taxes in Britain. Does the tradition rest on anything but prejudice or has it a solid basis in economics? It has a very solid basis indeed. Taxes on primary food are in themselves bad taxes, and they are particularly bad for Britain.

All taxes are evils, and though to have taxation of some kind is necessary, not all kinds of tax are equally evil. Some are worse than others and a tax on primary foods is among the worst of all. A poor man spends a larger proportion of his total income on food than does a rich man; a man with a family spends a larger proportion than does a bachelor. The burden of a tax on primary food, accordingly, falls most heavily just where it is most felt. It is like an income-tax graduated the wrong way round, say 5s. in the £ on the first £200 a year and 2s. 6d. in the £ on the rest, or like adding £25 to the taxable income for each dependent child, instead of taking it off. A rise in the price of primary food is more felt by the poor than by the rich. Conversely, a lowering of the price of food is a way of raising the standard of living where it most needs raising. A tax on food is a bad tax, to be avoided if possible.

Taxes on primary foods, accordingly, are objectionable

[138]

on general grounds. Britain's position as a trading nation makes them specially objectionable for Britain. In order to maintain so large a population in so small an island, Britain must sell exports in competition with other countries throughout the world; for that, the prices and the costs of production of the exports reckoned in terms of gold are vital. It is possible, of course, as the United States of America have shown, to combine high money wages with low costs of production. But it is an added advantage that any given rate of money wages should, through cheapening of food and other necessaries, represent higher real wages; it is one means of combining a high standard of living with low money costs of production; it means reckoning each transaction in fewer counters. To tax primary food is to add to the number of counters used in reckoning. To avoid, if possible, the taxation of food and raw materials is a primary British interest.

It is sometimes urged that taxing food from foreign countries need not raise the price of food in Britain; sufficient for all needs could come in tax free from the Empire under preference. It is true that in that case no tax would be paid on importation. But if the preference were necessary to preserve the British market to the Dominions, that could only be because the price being charged by the Dominions was higher than would be charged by foreign countries without the tax. It might even in some cases have to be higher than the Dominions themselves were charging outside Britain. In this connection, wheat, the food which figured most largely in the Canadian and Australian proposals at the Imperial Conference, deserves special notice.

The dominant fact about wheat is that the British Empire taken as a whole has a large export surplus of wheat. Britain and some other parts of the Empire import wheat; Canada and Australia export it. But what Canada and Australia export is, in all normal years, much greater than what Britain and the rest import, not only from Canada and Australia, but from the whole world. In other words, if by a tax, all foreign wheat were excluded and the whole British market were reserved for Canada and Australia, these latter would still, in all normal years, have to find a market for part of their crops outside Britain. They would still be in competition with the Argentine, in Greece, Italy and other neutral markets; they would meet there the supplies excluded from Britain by the tax. In these circumstances, so long as the Australian and Canadian farmers continued to compete among themselves, none of them could get a penny more for his wheat in Britain, as the result of the preference, than he would get in the world market outside Britain. If one of them began to get a higher price in Britain, others, in place of selling to foreign countries, would direct their supplies to Britain. The simple fact that the Empire as a whole is now an exporter of wheat transforms the situation. Dominion farmers cannot by any kind of preference in the British market, get more for their wheat than they can get without any preference at all, except on two suppositions: first, that they cease competing among themselves and form an export monopoly; second, that they use their monopoly power to sell more dearly to Britain than to foreign countries. The first supposition, perhaps, is not impossible. The second supposition is startling. If it were realised, it would mean that the Dominions were using the preference in order to carry out a scheme of monopoly dumping from behind the British tariff at the expense of the British consumer. It would mean that the British people were being taxed in the worst possible way to provide funds for subsidising, not any of their own industries or interests, but either the Dominion farmers or the trade competitors of Britain, or both.

It is hard to believe that Mr. Bennett, before making his proposals in October 1930, can have thought out their economic implications. For without this development of the Dominions selling wheat at a monopoly price in Britain, and at a lower price outside it, the only effects of imperial preference on wheat would be (*a*) to diminish slightly, by the tax, the British and so the total world demand for wheat, in favour of some untaxed substitute; (b) to diminish the satisfaction of consumers by changing the character of their flour; (c) (possibly) to increase the profits of some ship-owners in moving wheat over greater distances than before, at the cost of the consumers or the producers. On the other hand, with this development, the sacrifice asked for from British consumers in respect of wheat was almost ridiculously out of scale with the offers which the Dominions could make of markets for British manufactures. It presupposed a degree of economic unity in the Empire to which the Dominions were emphatically opposed.[1]

This leads to perception of the third and principal difficulty in the way of any far-reaching re-construction of imperial economic relations, namely the protectionist policy of the Dominions. The Dominions are among the new countries which in the last twenty-five years have most conspicuously and firmly pursued the policy of fostering their manufacturing industries by high Protection. This policy, whatever its merits from other points of view,

[1] The case of wheat has been discussed here on the assumption that, though foreign wheat was to be taxed, Dominion wheat come in free, that is to say, that there would be no protection for the British farmer. Some British advocates of preference for imperial wheat, however, combine with it a proposal to help British agriculture by taxing all imported wheat; the preference would consist of putting a higher duty on foreign wheat than on Dominion wheat. Except on the supposition of monopoly dumping explained above, preference for his wheat with free entry to the British market cannot improve the position of the Dominion farmer. Preference coupled with protection to the British farmer must make it definitely worse; in a world already tending to grow more wheat than it wants to consume, a stimulus to increased production in Britain must damage producers elsewhere. This is not an argument against the revival of British agriculture in strictly British interests, whether by protection or technical improvements or otherwise; the question of protection for domestic agriculture is dealt with in another chapter. But nugatory preference for the Dominions combined with real protection against them cannot rationally be advocated as part of a mutually advantageous imperial bargain. The fundamental inconsistency of protective and preferential policy is shown here from another angle.

[141]

limits rigidly the value of any markets they can offer to British manufactures in exchange for a preference on food or raw materials. To raise yet more against foreign countries a tariff wall already high enough to stop the importation, from Britain as from elsewhere, of anything that can be made in the Dominions is a nugatory preference. There are, of course, many articles which are not now manufactured in the Dominions; some of these are already imported from Britain; others are imported from foreign countries and could almost certainly never be got from Britain; for others a preference might lead to supply from Britain rather than from elsewhere. The preference here would be real. How large the range of this third class is will be considered later. Here the general difficulty has to be noted that, so long as the governing policy of the Dominions is one of Protection, they cannot guarantee that preferences, even where they are now real, will remain real in future.

More than one of the Dominion spokesmen at the Imperial Conference emphasised the need for stability in preferential arrangements. If reciprocal preferential arrangements were to be arrived at, said Mr. Havenga, for South Africa, they must be made "for sufficiently lengthy periods to give confidence and ensure stability." "A preference which cannot be regarded as enduring," said Mr. Bennett, "is worse than no preference at all." This is sound sense, but it is not consistent with Mr. Bennett's declaration, in the same speech, that the basis of his proposals for preference to Britain is adequate protection in Canada to industries now existent "or yet to be established." "Australia," said Mr. Scullin, "is firmly determined to encourage her secondary industries and to witness their development. We recognise, however, that there are some types of goods for which the size of our market does not yet justify the establishment of manufacturing plants." The precarious nature of the markets thus offered to British manufacturers could not be more fairly stated. The latter could have no ground of complaint if, as soon as the

Australian market became important, they were excluded from it in the interest of home producers; they must look forward to being shut out from Canada as one industry after another comes to be established. No clearer illustration could be given of the thesis with which this chapter opened, that Protection and preference, so far from being the two halves of one policy, are at bottom inconsistent with one another. The protective policy of the Dominions prevents them from offering to Britain any preference except that kind which is "worse than no preference at all," because its stability cannot be guaranteed.

No one who is prepared to face facts at all can advocate to-day an attempt to make of the British Empire a close-knit economic unit, comparable to the United States of America. The suggestion of a Free Trade Empire, that is to say, an Empire with Free Trade between all its constituent parts and a tariff against all the rest of the world, has been rejected, as neither practicable nor desirable, by the spokesmen of the Dominions. Reorientation of Britain's economic position by an extensive scheme of imperial preference is off the map. Survey of the actual trade of Britain and the principal Dominions shows how limited is the field in which preferences could possibly be worth while.

When the possible scope of imperial preference is being considered seriously, with regard to facts, two groups of articles must be excluded at the outset: those of which the Empire as a whole has now a substantial export surplus, and those of which the Empire supplies are able to satisfy only a small proportion of the Empire demand.

The reason for excluding the first group has been explained in discussing wheat. Where Empire production is already so great that, even if the whole Empire market were reserved for it by a preference, and foreign supplies excluded altogether, part of the Empire produce would still have to find a market in foreign countries, reservation of the Empire market would benefit the producing countries only on the supposition that they exploited a preference monopoly within the Empire and dumped outside it. The first group of articles includes not only wheat, which is the chief export of Canada and the second export of Australia, but wool, which is the chief export of Australia, diamonds from South Africa, jute and ground-nuts from India. If with this group is excluded also gold, on which a tariff is clearly inadmissible, there fall at once outside the scope of practicable preference by Britain, nearly two-thirds of the exports of Australia and South Africa, nearly a third of Canada's exports, more than a quarter of New Zealand's and one-seventh of India's.

The reason for excluding the second group is that where the Dominion supplies form only a small proportion of the whole imports to Britain, preference involves a sacrifice by British consumers out of all proportion to the benefit that can be conferred on the Dominions: tax is paid on large volume of imports in order to give an advantage to a small body of producers. This group of articles is typified by cotton from India and maize from South Africa. The greater part of the Indian cotton supply goes to the foreign competitors of Britain, and much the greater part of Britain's imports of cotton come from elsewhere than India; a duty on foreign raw cotton would damage British industry far more than remission of the duty could benefit India. So, too, a tax on the 85 per cent. of their maize that British farmers get from foreign countries would cause them harm out of all proportion to the benefit by preference to the South African producers of the remaining 15 per cent. Bacon, eggs and wood pulp are other important articles in this group.

After these two groups have been excluded on general grounds, other articles have still to be excluded, on grounds peculiar to each, from the scope of practicable preference. Thus beef, which is one of Britain's larger imports, comes in three forms, chilled (chiefly from the Argentine), frozen (about one-third from Australia and two-thirds from foreign countries), and canned (mostly foreign). It has not yet been found practicable to transport beef in the superior chilled condition from Australia. In these circumstances

[144]

chilled beef really falls into the second group named above; a tax on it, even with preference to the Empire, would not so much cause Empire supplies of chilled beef to increase, as compel British consumers either to change over from chilled to frozen or pay more for chilled. A tax on frozen beef, on the other hand, might simply cause the Argentine to concentrate more completely on chilled beef. Timber presents another class of difficulty—that of bulk. Canada has a large export and Britain a large import, but four-fifths of Canada's export goes to the United States as her nearest neighbour, and most of Britain's imports for the same reason come from Scandinavia; to deflect this trade by tariffs would obviously cause to all parties more harm than good. The case of cheese is different again. Here the Dominions already supply about five-sixths of Britain's imports. The residue consists mainly of specialised Continental cheeses, which would not be altogether excluded by a tariff; the scope for substantial advantage to the Dominions by preference is very small.

In one way or another, most of the larger exports from the Dominions go out of the picture, as soon as preference comes to be considered as a practical issue. They do not all go out. Canned salmon from Canada, mutton and lamb from Australia and New Zealand, butter from these two and from the Irish Free State as well, tea from India and Ceylon, and paper from Canada and Newfoundland, are the material of a substantial trade between Britain and the Dominions, which by a preference might be made more substantial still. There are a number of minor articles, for which preference in the British market would be helpful to the Dominions and not unduly burdensome to the British consumer. But preference on these minor articles alone would be little more than a gesture, while of the major articles listed above as within the range of practicable preference all but the last-named (paper) are important foods. It might be reasonable to give a preference on such foods, if Britain were going to tax them as a protective measure for agriculture. But this is an unlikely and, in the view here taken, a most unwise development. On the other hand, to tax such foods simply in order to give a preference to the Dominions might, by its re-action on popular feeling in Britain, do very poor service to the cause of the Empire. It would certainly raise acutely the question of how great were the reciprocal advantages that the Dominions could guarantee. That as markets they are valuable to Britain, both in themselves and as a result of existing preferences, no reasonable person would deny. That they could be made extremely valuable, by a lowering of tariffs against Britain, is also certain. But this, on the present policy of the Dominions, is not in prospect; at the Imperial Conference their Premiers spoke only of raising tariffs still higher against foreign countries. Is it going to be worth while for Britain to tax Argentine beef or Danish butter and bacon, in order that Australia may tax yet more American motor cars or Czechoslovakian woollens? That is the kind of calculation which practical preference involves.

Imperial preference as a practical proposition cannot be presented to-day as it was presented in theory at the outset of this chapter—as a means to freer trade; to lower, if discriminating, tariffs. It means that Britain should put import duties on food and materials that now come in free from foreign countries, in order that the Dominions may tax yet more highly foreign manufactures that they tax already. It is an addition to tariffs, not a reduction of them. It is, in the view taken in this volume, a step that, in the long run, is in the wrong direction. Does it offer any sufficient compensating advantages in the short run— either to British trade or to imperial unity?

Twenty-five years ago, in the days of Mr. Joseph Chamberlain, before the Dominions became so protectionist, there was far more scope for imperial preference than there is to-day. A hundred years ago a campaign for a Free Trade Empire might have succeeded. To-day it is hopelessly out of date. It was never, perhaps, very hopeful. The analogy by which it is often supported, of the United States of America, as a great Free Trade area within a tariff wall,

all but self-sufficing, secure against the chops and changes of commercial policy in other lands, is a false analogy. It is false geographically. The states of America lie close together; the states of the British Empire are spread all over the world, interspersed with foreign states, each with markets and supplies nearer than those of the Empire. The analogy is yet more false historically. The states of America have all grown up together, under one tariff with no possibility of a tariff between them; the states of the Empire have grown up separately and as they grew up their economic ways have diverged more and more. To seek to drag them forcibly together may lead only to a break.

For the danger that bargaining about preferences may lead to friction is real, not imaginary. If trade grows naturally by mutual advantage, between the peoples of two countries, friendly relations and good feeling grew naturally with it. But if trade has to be fostered by bargains between governments, and depends upon the nature of the bargains, bad feeling is as likely a consequence as good feeling. Suppose that the prosperity of Canada came to depend upon the price fixed for wheat by a Government Import Board in Britain, or the prosperity of Australia on the height of a British tariff against the Argentine? People with sufficient imagination to value the British Empire as it stands to-day—a free association of free peoples knit by blood or speech or institutions or ideals—may well shudder a little at that prospect.

CHAPTER XIII

THE CASE OF AGRICULTURE

THE foregoing chapters have been devoted to an examination of the general case for Protective Tariffs. The analysis they contain is general; that is to say, it is applicable to the case for any particular tariff. Unless it can be shown that the arguments for the protection of any particular industry are different in kind from the arguments here discussed, those arguments are invalid.

Now it is a matter of common observation that when any particular tariff is being put forward, its advocates always suggest that the circumstances are exceptional, that the arguments for the protection of that particular industry are different in kind from the arguments for the protection of other industries. Usually on examination these claims prove to be ill-founded. The capacity of the average protectionist for self-deception is apparently endless, but his originality is strictly limited; and the colossal literature of special pleading consists for the most part of the repetition in particular terms of the general arguments we have already discussed. It often happens, however, that people who are quite capable of refuting these arguments when stated in general terms, are bewildered and confused when it is a question of applying them to particular cases. They find it easy to see why it is inadvisable to protect *a* "given industry," but they find it difficult to apply this knowledge when it is a question of protecting *the* so-and-so industry. Their capacity for logical thought is paralysed by the impact of particular perceptions; they know so well that the wood must be distinguished from the trees, but once under the branches the distinction loses reality. For this reason, and because it will enable us to examine in greater detail matters which we have been

compelled to pass over somewhat cursorily in earlier
chapters, it will be convenient to devote a little time to
examining the case for certain particular proposals which
now figure very largely in public discussion in this country.
In this chapter we shall discuss Protection for agriculture.

Agricultural depression is a world phenomenon. Not
only in this country, but all over the world the producers
of agricultural products are in distress. In the Middle
West of the United States, in Canada, in Australia, in the
Argentine, agricultural depression is one of the main pre-
occupations of politics. Nor is this distress an altogether
recent phenomenon. It is true that the coming of the great
slump has been marked by a great intensification of the
difficulties of the agriculturalist, but throughout the years
which have followed the War it is true to say that relatively
to manufacturing industry most forms of agricultural
production have been depressed. This does not apply to
all forms of agriculture. Agriculture is a term covering
a great variety of enterprise and a few kinds of agriculture
have been doing quite well. But it has been one of the most
remarkable features of the recent economic history of the
United States, that while manufacturing industry has been
enjoying a boom of unprecedented dimensions, the farmers
of the Middle West have been in almost continuous difficulties. Even in France the complaint is often heard that
the prosperity of the towns has distracted attention from
the thoroughly mediocre condition of the peasantry.

Why is this?

If we were to judge by the verdict of public opinion in
each of the countries concerned, we should be disposed to
interpret the whole thing in terms which were highly
particular. In this country farming is inefficient. In that
country the merchants are grasping. Here the credit
facilities are deficient. There a marketing organisation has
pursued a reckless and ill-considered policy. In one country
peasant farming has proved inadequate. In another the
lack of a peasantry has been the ruin of agriculture. And,
no doubt, since something, if it is only the weather, is

nearly always wrong everywhere, there is *something* in nearly all of these local explanations. There is always room for improvement anywhere.

But when we are confronted with a consilience of local catastrophes in particular lines of industry, when most kinds of agriculture in most places are depressed relatively to most kinds of manufacturing industry, the economist who has not a particular axe to grind will suspect the existence of causes more general than those commonly cited. He will not necessarily dispute, without detailed examination, the existence of these other causes. But he will look round to see if there are not operative forces common to the whole group of industries concerned.

In the case of the main agricultural products, these forces are not far to seek. The production of the staple articles of food, particularly wheat, ministers to human needs which have very definite limitations. If a man doubles his income he may well double his consumption of many things, but he is extremely unlikely to double his consumption of bread. As Adam Smith pointed out, the capacity of the human stomach is limited: as modern economists would put it, the demand for the simpler forms of food is relatively inelastic.

Now this means that as the production of such things increases, their prices tend to fall more rapidly than the prices of commodities which minister to more expansible wants. A relatively small diminution of price may clear the market of a relatively large increase in motor cars. But it may need a relatively great diminution of price to carry off a relatively small increase in wheat. Hence there is, as it were, a continual squeeze on the producers of such products to transfer their efforts to some other line of production where demand is more expansible and where incomes rise more rapidly.

Broadly speaking, this is what has actually been happening ever since the beginning of history. In early times the proportion of productive power which was directed to satisfying elementary needs was very high. In modern communities, taken in the mass, it is very much smaller. And the proportion is continually diminishing. It is difficult to find a long period in history when agriculture was not relatively depressed and when contemporary writers did not lament the poverty of the country-side and deplore the greater attractiveness of the more opulent industries of the towns. This is not to say that agricultural incomes have always been falling. It is only to say—what is notoriously true—that they have failed to rise as rapidly as incomes in other branches of industry.

In recent times this secular tendency has been speeded up. The application of science to production which distinguishes the modern age from all others, though late in coming to agriculture, is beginning to show itself in increased productivity. The industrial revolution is spreading to agriculture. Nor does it seem as if this tendency were likely soon to be exhausted. We are only at the beginning of revolutionary changes. The application of methods of mass production to wheat farming which is being staged so skilfully by the Russians, is still in its infancy. The present slump in wheat and other agricultural products is undoubtedly due in part to the collapse in credit which has come with the great depression; but when the depression is over it is improbable that the average price, year in year out, will be as high as it has been in the past. The only cure for the relative depression of agriculture would be either in some way to make the production of such products *less* efficient, to slow up the spread of modern methods of cultivation—a hopeless task, if anyone were insane enough to recommend it, since, unless the diminution were the same all round, those groups which did not impose such restrictions would gain at the expense of those which did—or, by the removal of artificial barriers, to hasten the transfer of labour and capital from the production of necessities which are in relatively inexpansive demand to the production of things which are in relatively expansive demand—either agricultural products which are more in the nature of luxuries or to altogether

[151]

different kinds of products. The latter is unquestionably the plan which would be adopted in a rational world. At present by their policies of subsidies and tariffs the present governments of the world appear to be trying their best to imitate the former.

Such in broad outline are the world tendencies. It is notorious that this country has not been immune from their operations. But beyond the causes making for agricultural depression in general, in this country there have been local causes tending to intensify our difficulties. While here, as elsewhere, there have been particular branches of agriculture not producing for a world market which have not done badly in the last half-century, producers of the staple products, in particular the producers of wheat, have suffered relatively more than producers of similar products abroad. Save during the brief prosperity of the war years, there has been a gradual absolute decline in the home production of cereals. Not only have these farmers participated in the misfortunes of agricultural producers elsewhere; they have also gradually lost a part of the local market. The domestic consumer has come to procure a larger proportion of his consumption of these commodities elsewhere.

No doubt it is possible to exaggerate this aspect of the problem. As we shall be seeing later on, the greater part of our increased dependence on foreign food supplies has come about to meet the needs of a population *additional* to that which existed at the time when British agriculture supplied the home market. For the most part the foreigner has captured a market which the British farmer never had. But that there has been *some* encroachment it is impossible to deny.

In the face of these difficulties it has often been urged that agricultural production in this country should be protected. The form which this protection should take is a matter on which opinion has not been unanimous. Some have urged all-round protection, others protection of particular products. Probably the proposal which would obtain most support is the proposal for a straightforward

[152]

tariff on wheat. In any case, such a measure may conveniently be taken as typical of proposals for agricultural protection and for the remainder of this chapter it is this that will be chiefly in mind.

Now there can be no doubt that a tariff on the import of wheat would, for a short time, at any rate, be a benefit to wheat farmers. The price of wheat in this country would rise, the profits of wheat farming would increase, lands which by reason of the greater expense of cultivation have been abandoned to pasture would now once more pay to cultivate, and for the time being the decline of arable farming would be arrested. In the long run it is doubtful whether these benefits would be permanent. If wheat farming became more profitable, rents would tend to be adjusted upwards, it is not improbable that wages would absorb some of the increase and in any case there would gradually be an increase of competition which would bring profits in that line of industry down to the profits obtainable in others. It is a complete fallacy, fostered, it must be regretfully admitted, by the incautious statements of free traders, to suppose that in *the long run* the entrepreneurs in any particular industry can hold for themselves the gains due to discriminating Protection unless they have permanent monopoly. Landlords may tend to gain permanently if the tariff is such as to increase the demand for land as a whole. But profit-makers can only gain more than others until competition has had time to operate. Moreover, it must be remembered that, if the general tendencies described above still continue to operate in the world at large, it would be necessary continually to increase the tariff if the temporary fillip were not to be wiped out by fresh competition. Still, it may be admitted that in the short run agriculturalists would benefit, and it is clear that the amount of land under arable cultivation would be greater than it would have been without the tariff.

But would this be a good thing for the community? That, and not the question of the benefit to the particular industry, is the question which we have to answer.

[153]

Advocates of the view that it would be a benefit base their case upon one of three considerations. Firstly, they may urge that it would be an "economic" benefit to have agriculture made more prosperous by these means—by which we may take them to mean that the average real income of the community would be raised (or would be higher than it would otherwise have been). Secondly, they may urge that for reasons of defence it is necessary to have a larger domestic food supply. Lastly, they may urge that agriculture is a healthy industry or that it is æsthetically or "socially" desirable to have at least a certain proportion of the population of these islands engaged in arable farming. Usually, of course, these positions are hopelessly confused. Propositions involving the one are supported by arguments which relate to the other. People think that because it might be good for reasons of defence to have a larger domestic food supply, *therefore* real incomes in time of peace would be bound to be increased by measures designed to secure it—which is a palpable *non sequitur*. Still they are analytically separable and we will therefore examine them separately.

Let us turn first to the so-called economic argument—the argument that we should all, or most of us, be better off—that is to say, have higher real incomes if agriculture were made prosperous in this way.

Higher real incomes for the majority of the community can be conceived to come about in two main ways. Either by a redistribution of income in favour of the majority with smaller incomes or by an increase of the total real income available for distribution. That is to say, from this point of view we may judge such measures either as they affect distribution or as they affect production. Let us deal with these things separately.

So far as the distributive effects of a tax on a food such as wheat are concerned, it is safe to say that its effects are not likely to be such as to commend themselves to the majority of the community. The rise in price would go either to the agriculturalist in the shape of increased receipts or to the

Exchequer in the shape of the proceeds of the import tax. A slight fall in world prices might follow the adoption of Protection for wheat in this country[1] but in the main it is clear that both the higher incomes of agriculturalists and the new receipts of the Exchequer would come out of the pockets of British consumers. The consumers of bread would finance the increase of domestic agriculture and the new accession to the revenue.

Now when the matter is put this way—and there is no doubt this is the right way to put it—there can scarcely be two opinions that, from the distributive point of view, a tax of this sort would be thoroughly unpopular. The effects of such a tax would be steeply regressive. Expenditure on bread forms a much larger proportion of the poor man's budget than of the budget of the rich man. A rise in the price of bread to finance either the budget or increased arable cultivation would have the same effect as an income-tax which was graduated downwards. The poorest would pay proportionately most. It is true that one recent election has been won (in a rich district) on the cry of taxes on food. It is doubtful if this would happen frequently if these implications were clearly realised.

So much for the distributive effects of the tariff. On any democratic principle of tax-apportionment they are likely to be condemned. But are there any gains on the side of production? If the aggregate real income of the community were to be increased by such measures it is conceivable that on balance they might be deemed desirable.

But if there is anything at all in the arguments developed in the foregoing chapters, it should be fairly obvious that the aggregate real income of the community will not be increased. On the contrary there is every presumption that it will be diminished.

We can see this most clearly if we turn back to the broad historical developments we have already examined. Why

---

[1] On the possibility of taxing the foreigner, *see* Chapter XIV below. It is worth noticing that in so far as " the foreigner " was taxed, a substantial part of him would be a British subject in the Dominions.

is it that as time has gone on the inhabitants of this island have come to procure a larger and larger proportion of their wheat from abroad rather than procure it at home? Obviously because it was cheaper. They have paid less for their wheat by procuring it this way. And this cheapness is not merely a matter of money; it has a deeper significance than that. In the last analysis, it means that by using capital and labour to produce the things we exchange for foreign wheat we procure more wheat than we should if we used the same capital and labour to produce wheat at home. This is not to say that domestic labour and capital are absolutely less productive than the labour and capital by means of which the foreign wheat is grown. Probably they are not. It is only to say that domestic labour and capital are more productive if put to other uses.

Or to put the same thing yet another way. If the labour and capital, which are expended in procuring by way of exchange that part of our domestic food supply which comes from abroad, were put to domestic agriculture, we should lose a greater volume of potential real income than we should gain. If this were not so then relative prices and incomes would be different. There would no longer be a greater profit to be made elsewhere than in agriculture.

So that if we were to adopt the policy of agricultural protection we should be sacrificing this benefit which we derive from international specialisation. After what has been said already it should be simple to envisage the process. The tariff would be imposed. The price of wheat would rise. For a time farmers would benefit. But the relatively greater profit to be made in this line of production would cause production to be extended. As production was extended, costs would tend to rise—it should be clear that it is the lands which are *more* costly to cultivate which have been thrown out of cultivation. Eventually equilibrium would be established with wheat farmers making no more than was being made elsewhere, a greater proportion of the food supply produced at home, and a national income smaller than it would have been by the extra cost of raising that much more wheat at home rather than procuring it abroad by way of exchange. How much loss would be involved would, of course, depend on the height of the tax. A small tax would only cause a small extension of cultivation and a small loss. A high tax would cause a great extension of cultivation and a high loss. The tax that would be necessary greatly to increase the domestic production of wheat would have to be something terrific. In Germany recently the tax on certain imported cereals has been three times the world price. But still some imports have come in. In any case *some* loss would be inevitable.

Considerations of this sort, as we have seen in earlier chapters, are applicable to protective tariffs on the importation of any commodity. They are perhaps at their strongest in the case of protection for agriculture. This for three reasons.

In the first place the advantages of territorial division of labour are particularly obvious in the case of agricultural production. It is possible for reasonable men to disagree about the magnitude of the advantages to be obtained from territorial division in the case of certain manufactures. It is difficult to conceive any ground for such disagreement in regard to agricultural production. It is clearly advantageous that the bulk of the world's wheat should be produced in those parts of the world where the open spaces are most extensive, where land is plentiful and natural conditions are suitable. It is a tendency under Free Trade that a country should export the products whose production involves the use of a larger proportion of the factors of production with which she is relatively best provided and import the products whose production involves the use of a large proportion of factors with which she is relatively less well provided. Thus when we export manufactures, we are as it were exporting the services of our relatively lavish provision of capital and highly skilled labour. When we import wheat we are importing the services of the land with which the Canadians and Argentinians are relatively so well provided.

[157]

Secondly, it should be observed that so far as agriculture is concerned, the case against Protection is complicated by none of those short run difficulties which may arise when manufacturing industries having surplus plant which could be worked under conditions of diminishing costs are being considered. There may be a case for larger units in agriculture in this country. In spite of the fact that it seems to be the object of all political parties to foster smaller units, there are strong reasons for believing that there is. But there is no presumption that they cannot be introduced under competitive conditions. On the contrary, experience shows that those who have been boldest in this respect in recent years have usually been those who have suffered least.

Thirdly, in arguing against the case of protection for agriculture, we need be troubled by none of those difficulties which arise when we are considering the case for protection for manufacturing industries in which there exists a large volume of unemployment. The unemployment argument, ultimately unsound anywhere, is entirely inappropriate here. For supposing we did wish to absorb the unemployed into an industry which was protectable, we should most certainly choose an industry where wages were relatively high. Unless we were completely regardless of all considerations of economy, we should not try to absorb them into industries in which wages were relatively low. For the fact that wages were low in those industries would be a sign that the productivity (in value terms) of labour in those industries was low. It would be a foolish policy to create employment (if that, indeed, is possible) just where the price indication shows that employment is least remunerative. Now it so happens that agriculture falls into this second group of industries. Wages in agriculture are lower than wages in almost any other occupation. Clearly, unless we wish to abandon all idea of a "proper" apportionment of labour between different industries, this is almost the *last* industry in which we should wish to "create" employment.

[158]

If this analysis is correct, therefore, it should be fairly clear that no direct and immediate "economic" gain is to be derived from Protection either for wheat or for other agricultural products. On the side of production it would mean a diminution of the aggregate real income, and on the side of distribution it would mean that this real income would be less equally distributed. It would be hard to argue that such results would be "economically justifiable."

But now, it is sometimes argued, this is all very short-sighted. It may be very true that here and now we have nothing to gain from such a policy. Yet if we look a little further ahead, the balance of advantage is different. At the present time we may gain by procuring our food indirectly. But in a world in which the inhabitants of each national area are trying more and more to manufacture, this gain is likely to be transitory. Sooner or later we shall find that the world will not accept our products. We shall wake up and find our customers gone and the domestic estate neglected.

Such an argument sounds very plausible, and there can be no doubt that it is considerations of this sort which weigh with the more intelligent advocates of agricultural protection. The fear of a day when the forces of economic nationalism shall create a situation in which those countries which have depended on international trade the most are excluded from foreign markets is a very real fear to-day with many who before have been unmoved by such apprehensions.

Yet, in fact, there is very little in the argument. It is quite true that in time to come the terms on which we trade with the rest of the world may become unfavourable. This might come about because of economic Nationalism. It might come about as a result of a growth of population elsewhere so great as to involve a demand for the necessities of life which would only be satisfied at a relatively unproductive margin. So far as we have seen this tendency has not been apparent. So far from the terms of trade between

[159]

agriculture and manufacture moving against manufacture, the movement has been in the opposite direction. One of the main difficulties of the British export industries to-day is due to the fact that in return for a given bale of manufactures, we are getting so much larger a bale of agricultural products. Still it is conceivable that this tendency may be reversed, although the probabilities seem against such a supposition.

But supposing it was? What then?

No doubt we should be poorer in consequence. No doubt we should have to extend domestic agriculture. Capital and labour which before was more profitably employed in procuring food indirectly by manufacturing other things and exporting them would now find more profitable employment in producing the food at home. The prices of manufactures would fall, the prices of agricultural products would rise. To extend domestic agriculture *then* would be an advantage. We should be making the best of a relatively worse position.

But that is no argument for extending it *now*. On the contrary, to extend it now would be to forego tangible and obvious gains in the present, to guard against difficulties which if they arise in the future, will bring with them the appropriate re-adjustment. So long as the relative costs and prices make it advantageous for us to procure a large proportion of our food from abroad, so long is there a presumption that we are better off for doing so. If it should come about that we were worse off, that worsening in our position would show itself in a change in relative prices. The possibility of War apart, which we shall be examining below, there is no reason to suppose that the change would come anything but gradually. There is nothing in the technique of agricultural production which would lead us to suppose that the reorganisation of domestic industry which would have to follow could not take place at an appropriate pace. To anticipate such a change here and now, to forego all the obvious benefits of cheap food for a danger which may never come would be as foolish as it would be for a man to take to his bed now because he feared that in later years he might be overcome by some disease which necessitated such a change in his habits.

There is one case, however, in which such a procedure might have justification. If the provision of cheap food from abroad was conducive to the growth of a larger population, and if there were the possibility later on that such supplies might not be forthcoming, there might be a case for adopting measures which, while diminishing wealth in the present, precluded the possibility of greater needs which could not be satisfied in the future. Thus, if at the time of the repeal of the Corn Laws, there had arisen prophets who argued that the importation of food from abroad would permit an expansion of population which, if later on the terms of trade turned violently against us might find itself reduced to disastrous poverty, they could not have been said to be advancing arguments which were entirely foolish. There can be no question that if we had had to depend on domestic food supplies the population of this country would never have attained its present dimensions. There can be no doubt that if our food supplies from abroad were to become more expensive we might be placed in a position of grave disadvantage. Hitherto we have gained, and it has been argued above that it is improbable that we shall not continue to be gainers. But the argument that we should not gain in the long run would not then have been inherently ridiculous.

But at the present time it has no application. The population of these islands is rapidly approaching a condition of stationariness. Unless a complete change comes over the habits of the people, it is clear that a declining rather than an advancing population is the more probable tendency in the future. Hence this aspect of the problem need not concern us. Our problem is to provide for the present population as best we may. And so long as the population does not increase, the argument that has been developed is applicable. If the terms of trade turn against us, then the price mechanism will bring about the appropriate shift of capital and labour. Till that day to shift in advance is simply anticipating troubles that may never come.

So that from the point of view of increasing real income there is nothing to justify the artificial fostering of domestic agriculture. So long as it pays to get a certain proportion of our food abroad, it is desirable from this point of view that we should continue to do so.

But supposing our food supplies are cut off by war? Will not our greater wealth in time of peace have been bought at the price of a most terrible insecurity? Do not considerations of defence justify what considerations of mere opulence would suggest to be inadvisable? Would it not be wise to forego wealth now in order to guard against military insecurity later?

This is the second of the three main arguments for agricultural protection. And it may be admitted at once that as regards logic it is on altogether a different footing from the so-called " economic " arguments. It may be questioned straight away whether *if* it is thought desirable to attempt to make provision of this sort, the tariff is the best means of doing it. As we have seen already, a food tax is a regressive tax. It hits the poorest consumer hardest. If we want to foster domestic agriculture there are surely other and better means of doing it. Still, granted that the extension of agriculture is thought desirable and that the tariff is not ruled out for these distributive and administrative reasons, no economist will urge that there is anything inherently illogical or unreasonable in the proposal. If you propose to plan industrial life on the assumption that the danger of war is a permanently given fact, if you are to sacrifice opulence to defence, and if you are alive to the nature of the sacrifice you are making, there is nothing in economic analysis which would condemn such a choice as a foolish one. It is only if you say we are going to be better provided against war *and* better provided with the constituents of real income that the economist can call your logic in question.

Nevertheless, if the choice is to be made it is essential

THE CASE OF AGRICULTURE

that it should be an enlightened one. If agriculture is to be protected for this reason it is essential that we should realise the exact nature of the sacrifice and the other alternatives open. It is essential that we should realise the limits of probable gain.

At this point a few simple statistics will be useful. The following table shows the relative importance of the foreign and domestic supplies of certain staple articles of consumption.

AVAILABLE SUPPLIES OF CERTAIN AGRICULTURAL PRODUCTS

THOUSAND TONS

Average 1924-25 to 1927-29

Commodity	1 Imports	2 Domestic Supply	3 Domestic Supply as Percentage of Total Supply
			%
Wheat . .	5342	1418	21
Beef and Veal .	794	604	43
Mutton and Lamb	287	227	44
Pig Meat[1] .	623	294	32
Potatoes . .	522	3245	86

The magnitude of our dependence on foreign sources of supply is very obvious; 79 per cent. of our wheat supplies comes from abroad, and 60 per cent. of our main meat supplies. It is obvious therefore that our danger in time of war is considerable. The experience of the last war showed that it might become one of real peril.

But at the same time it is equally obvious that this dependence *cannot be remedied* save at a cost which is altogether

[1] *i.e.* pork, bacon, hams, live animals as meat, and lard.

[163]

prohibitive. To make this country self-supporting as regards food supply would involve a sacrifice of the material gains of a century. This is strong language to use in a scientific discussion, but it is not too strong for the subject-matter. On this point, the opinion of the late Deputy Director-General of Food Production is decisive.

"It has been asked," says Sir Thomas Middleton, "is it not possible for the United Kingdom to feed its entire population, or at least to supply all necessary foods, except the small percentage that could only be grown in tropical or semi-tropical climates? From the purely agricultural point of view it may be answered that there would be no special difficulty, if the people of this country were content to place themselves under the direction of some all-powerful food controller, who would feed them with what was necessary, as a farmer feeds his cattle. If they would be satisfied with the rations of protein, fat, and carbohydrate which their bodies must have, and if they would be prepared to pay for their food on a caloric basis, the farmer could, no doubt, supply the necessary protein and energy. But the public would not be content with rations of protein, fat and carbohydrate, and would not pay on a caloric basis. They must have bread, meat and many other things in certain customary quantities; and thus, under present circumstances, or under any circumstances that can be foreseen, there is no possibility of providing the foods they demand from the soils of the United Kingdom. It would require more than twenty million acres of land to supply the grain alone that is consumed in this country, and to secure this quantity of grain it would be necessary to plough every acre of land not subject to flooding and not too far above sea-level to prevent corn from ripening. The cost would be prohibitive, and the suggestion that we might furnish our people with their normal food supply may be dismissed as absurd."[1]

[1] *Food Production in War*, pp. 323-4.

If this is correct, and its substantial accuracy has never been challenged, we must resign ourselves to the fact that we can never altogether eliminate our insecurity. All that we can hope to do is at best to diminish the margin—to produce supplies at home for a few more days of the year. At the height of our effort during the War we raised the home supply (estimated on a rough basis of calorific content) from 125 days out of 365 to 155. This was in a period when the accumulative fertility of the soil was recklessly exploited in order to produce to the uttermost. To maintain such an increase indefinitely would have involved even greater expenditure. To-day to maintain arable farming at *its present* dimensions (if it were carried out by a tariff) would involve measures raising the price of wheat to at least 50s. per quarter—that is increasing the present price by more than 20s. To extend the area of wheat cultivation would involve even higher protection. Moreover, if the price of wheat continues to fall, if the improvements in agricultural technique which have been responsible for much of the present cheapening continue and take place at a more rapid pace abroad, then the protection would have to be continually increased. If this were not done after a short time the decline in cultivation would continue.

Nevertheless, it might be decided that such measures were desirable. Yet before such decisions were deemed ultimately rational we should wish to be sure not only that the cost had been adequately computed, but also that the alternatives had been properly weighed.

The extension of arable farming at home is not the only method of procuring greater security of food supply during war. It is conceivable that a greater degree of security could be obtained by expenditure on defences, by strengthening or maintaining the strength of the navy. The Tribunal of Economists which investigated the agricultural problem in 1924 came to the conclusion that, at the then existing level of prices and costs, to secure an extension of arable cultivation of some $2\frac{1}{2}$ million acres, an annual subsidy of some £7,000,000 would be needed. To-day that sum would be greater. It does not seem improbable that if it is really felt that the danger of a war in which our food supplies would be seriously menaced is imminent, a direct expenditure of this order would be more expeditious in securing the end in view.

This conclusion is reinforced considerably when we reflect that security in time of war for this country is not merely a matter of food supply. Modern warfare is a complicated technique, and demands a variety of materials for its successful conduct. If Great Britain were again to become embroiled in a conflict of world dimensions it would be just as essential that it should have a continuous supply of things like rubber and petroleum which *cannot* be grown at home as that it should have a continuous supply of wheat and mutton. To strengthen defence directly would secure all these ends, to foster agriculture only one of them.

Moreover, if we are thinking in terms of war and power, we must not ignore the fact that in modern times success in war is not only a question of equipment and food supply. General financial power is just as important. It is fairly safe to say that in the last war, at any rate, the great wealth and foreign investments of this country counted as much as anything in securing ultimate victory for the opponents of the Central Powers. If before the War our policy had been consistently to aim at self-sufficiency, to sacrifice trade and wealth for a fancied security, this power would not have existed. To achieve anything like self-sufficiency at the present day would, so far as financial power and international connection is concerned, involve relegating ourselves to the status of a second-class power.

For these reasons, it seems unlikely if the actual cost were fully realised, that it would be felt desirable to foster agriculture for purely defensive purposes. And even if it were, the distributive considerations adduced above suggest that a protective tariff would scarcely be the best means of doing it.

We come finally to the third group of arguments for agri-

[166]

cultural protection, the arguments, namely, that it is desirable to have a greater proportion of people employed in agriculture in order to preserve national balance.

Now it is clear from what has been said already that there is nothing in this notion of balance from the point of view of securing material real income. The best balance from this point of view, given the distribution of income, is that balance which the mechanism of relative prices is continually tending to bring into being. To suggest that from *this* point of view there is another "balance" which is desirable is meaningless. The only way in which the balance argument can be given meaning is to appeal to considerations of military security (which appeal we have just examined), or to considerations of the healthiness of rural life, or to considerations of its æsthetic desirability.

The argument that life in the country is healthier than life in towns is one which receives very shadowy support from statistics. It is true that in the past the death-rate has been rather higher in urban than in rural areas. But the rate of improvement in the towns has been greater than the rate of improvement in the country, and there is now very little in the difference. Moreover, if the disparity were greater than it is, this might simply be an argument for paying greater attention to the sanitary condition of towns. In any case, it cannot be made an argument for more agriculture. Agriculture is not the only industry in rural areas. And if it were decided that for reasons of health it were desirable to increase *rural* industry, the fact that some forms of agriculture are on the wane would be a strong presumption against stimulating this form of industry. In fact, of course, with the extension of electricity supply and the coming of cheap motor transport, many industries are at present migrating to the country.

There remains therefore only the æsthetic argument that there is a virtue in agricultural pursuits which makes it inherently desirable that whatever the value in price terms of agricultural produce, a certain proportion of the population should be engaged in some sort of farming. Here we enter the realm of mysticism. Intrinsic value is a matter of ultimate valuation about which scientific analysis can say nothing. But it is at least pertinent to observe that those who most loudly extol the virtues of agricultural labour are usually those who are not themselves under the necessity of earning their bread in this fashion. Unquestionably, food production is an honourable industry capable of calling for admirable virtues and demanding for its successful conduct intellectual qualities of a very high order. But it is clear that a great many people who are engaged in agricultural occupations are not unwilling to change their pursuits if opportunity presents itself. No doubt some of the drift from the land is due to the pressure of economic forces. But it is abundantly clear that some of it is due to the greater attractiveness for the people concerned of life in factories and towns. It has been well said, "It is all very well for sentimentalists to speak of contact with the soil and the ripe wisdom of Hardy's philosophical peasants, but the one desire of every young man in the country-side is to find work in towns where he can escape from the slavery of winds and weather and the solitude of dark winter evenings into the reliable and human atmosphere of the factory and the cinema."[1] This may be a good thing or a bad thing, but it is a state of affairs which only those who are blind because they do not want to see, can ignore. In a democratic country it is a grave responsibility to lay down canons of taste for the majority.

From this point of view fortunately there is one very simple test to which we can submit all such proposals. It is clear from what has been said above that the main burden of an agricultural tariff must be borne by the consumers of the products which are taxed. The luxury of more agriculture, however secured, is one which must be mainly financed at home. If therefore it is desired to increase domestic agriculture for "social" or "æsthetic" reasons, a subsidy is at least as good as a tariff. Indeed, as has been shown already, there are reasons for believing

[1] Bertrand Russell, *The Conquest of Happiness*, p. 152.

it to be superior. Moreover, judged as an engine of demo-cratic government, it has this advantage, that at every stage it brings home to the citizen as taxpayer the nature of the sacrifice he is making. If knowledge of the implica-tions of tariffs were as well diffused among the electorate as knowledge of the A, B, C, we might assume that, in voting for a tariff, he was as conscious of the nature of the sacrifice involved as he would be in voting for a subsidy. Unfortu-nately, such knowledge is not universal, and there is reason to believe that many who would resent an extension of agriculture financed by a subsidy would cheerfully welcome a similar extension brought about by a tariff which was at least as expensive and certainly distributively less equitable. To be consistent, therefore, the advocate of agricultural protection who claims that in fostering domestic agriculture he is giving effect to the ultimate decisions of the demo-cracy, must be prepared to implement his policy by a subsidy. If not, he must incur the grave suspicion of wishing merely to bamboozle the electorate.

CHAPTER XIV

I

AT the present day a substantial proportion of the revenue of most countries is raised by tariffs of one kind or another. A substantial proportion of our own revenue is raised by tariffs. In 1929-30 they contributed £118,000,000 to the Budget, which was 14 per cent. of the total revenue; in 1930, £121,000,000, which was 15 per cent. Many of the great powers are similarly dependent on the product of such indirect taxation. Indeed, generally speaking, we may say that in spite of the increasing resort to methods of direct taxation which is characteristic of modern democracies, customs duties still provide one of the most important methods of raising revenue. At the present day, so far as Great Britain is concerned, the problem of raising additional revenue is more urgent than ever before. It is, therefore, important to discuss in some detail the merits of this form of taxation. We must discuss the merits of import duties in general, and we must discuss the merits of different forms of import duties. We must then give some attention to particular proposals for tariffs for revenue purposes for this country.

II

Let us turn first to the general theory of import duties.

It is sometimes thought that it is an advantage of this method of taxation that it relieves the citizen of the taxing country, and throws the burden on the shoulders of the foreigner. Whether this is a particularly respectable argument, especially in a country whose inhabitants are very much better off than the majority of the inhabitants of the rest of the world, is fortunately not a question which it falls within our province to decide. Observation suggests that although the majority of the citizens of this country are becoming opposed to predatory wars against the foreigner, a substantial proportion are not yet averse from adopting measures which, in less crude ways, have the same effect. And in any case, while the foreigner himself adopts such methods, the ethical argument against their adoption here is not likely to carry much weight. Those who recognise most clearly our superiority in other respects would be loudest in denying our right to be superior in this one.

None the less, acquiescence in the view that it would be undesirable not to tax the foreigner if we can get at him, does not imply that this delectable relief from the most hateful of all the duties of citizenship is always open to us. Indeed, a very little reflection on the plain facts of the collection of such duties, unadorned by any theoretical subtleties, should do much to suggest to our harassed taxpayer that the possibility is by no means obvious. For, speaking broadly, customs duties are paid by importers. That is to say, the actual money is collected from the merchants who order the goods from the foreigner. Before they can take the goods out of bond, they have to hand over cheques to the customs authorities. Now, of course, some of these importers may *happen* to be foreigners. But it is not *quae* foreigners that they pay the tax. The English importer of wine, equally with the French agent domiciled in London, must pay the full duties on import. It is clear that, using terms in their actual factual significance, the tax is not paid by anyone *outside* the country.

But of course this is not the end of the matter. The importer pays the tax in the sense that he hands over the money. But, since he is not in business for his health, he is not likely to continue to engage in that kind of enterprise unless, in one way or another, he can get as high profits there as he can hope to get elsewhere. That is to say, speaking generally, we should not expect the margin between receipts and expenditure in any line of import to be permanently

[171]

lowered by the imposition of an import duty. Nor, of course, is it the intention of the Government imposing the duty that this should be the case. That would be contrary to all established ideas of equity. The importer is always regarded not as the ultimate *source* of taxation, but only as the *channel* through which it is paid. Whatever may happen when the tax is first imposed, it is known that in the long run, there must be adjustments which allow the normal margin in the taxed line of enterprise.

There are two ways in which this may take place. Either the amount charged to the consumer may be raised. If this happens, demand will fall off and some importers may have to go out of business, but eventually those who are left will be getting normal profits again. Or the amount paid to the producers may be reduced. Foreign producers may be induced to take less for their wares. In the first case we say the tax is "paid" by the domestic consumer. In the second, it is "paid" by the foreign producer.

Now it is sometimes contended by over-zealous Free Traders animadverting against import duties which have protective effects, that the adjustment is only conceivable in the former of these two ways. That is to say it is contended that the consumer must *always* pay. This is not true, and the Free Trade case which, as we shall see in a minute, is quite strong enough without the aid of bad theory, is only rendered suspect by such over-emphasis. It is indeed conceivable that the foreigner may be made to pay. If the article in question is one which is supplied by foreign producers who have few remunerative alternative occupations and few alternative markets, and is consumed by domestic consumers whose demands are easily satisfied by other things, then it is indeed possible that the unfortunate foreigner may be made to bear some of the burden of domestic taxation.

But while this is analytically possible, and while it is probable that actual cases occur at various times and at various places, it is fairly safe to say that in the case of a community such as ours, dependent for essential supplies

[172]

upon foreign producers who have many alternative markets, it is most improbable that any substantial part of the burden of import duties can be shifted in this manner. Where the foreign producer has alternative markets, and where the domestic consumer's demand is urgent, the effect of the imposition of an import duty will show itself much more in a raising of the domestic price than in a lowering of the prices on the world markets. Here and there it might be possible to pick out a commodity whose producers abroad could be squeezed if it were thought to be desirable. But in the great majority of cases the boot would be on the other leg. The tax would be paid by the domestic consumer. Contrary to the usual belief, which attributes theoretical subtlety to the Free Trader but practical sense to the other side, in this respect at least, pure theory offers a possible case for a tariff, but the horse sense of the matter is all for Free Trade.

For all practical purposes, therefore, it may be assumed that the hope of compelling the foreigner to share some of our budgetary burdens by means of import duties—however much it may appeal to some of us—is illusory. Import duties as a means for raising the wind must be judged as instruments for taxing our own co-nationals. The belief that, while we pay income-tax and other such direct taxes, taxes on imports are paid by the foreigner, is false.

Judged as instruments for raising revenue, import duties are subject to an important criticism. It rests not on economic analysis, but upon the interpretation of economic analysis in the light of assumptions with regard to equity commonly made in modern democracies. Indirect taxes, in so far as they are not imposed solely upon items of luxury expenditure, are likely to be "regressive" in incidence. They are proportionate not to income but to expenditure on the taxed articles, and since it is probable that the items taxed form a larger proportion of the expenditure of poor men than of rich, it may be said that they press hardest on those least able to pay. This is not a verdict which is justified by any generalisation within the corpus of economic science:

for there is no scientific method of comparing subjective burdens. But if we accept the canon that taxation should be in accordance with ability to pay, then it follows that *judged by themselves* import duties are open to some criticism.

But it does not follow from this that, judged as part of a general system of taxation, all import duties, all tariffs for revenue, are necessarily bad. That depends upon what other taxes are imposed. Few sane men are likely to interpret the democratic canons in such a way as to argue that poor men should pay no taxes. That way lies bread and circuses, and the drying up of the springs of capitalistic accumulation. It may well be that a few well-chosen indirect taxes are a better means of collecting revenue from the recipients of small incomes than more direct methods. It is not seriously proposed by any party in the State to abolish indirect taxation altogether.

And at the present time, when direct taxation is unprecedentedly high for what should be normal peace-time conditions, it is clear that if it is desired to strengthen the revenue side of the Budget some increase in existing tariff rates and some additional impositions are probably among the best means available. (In a later section of this chapter we propose to indicate further the nature of the possibilities.) No doubt this would be very unacceptable to certain people. But, acceptable or unacceptable, there is no doubt that, subject to the limitations set out above, tariffs for revenue purposes provide a tolerably efficient second line of defence for the national finances.

III

But this brings us to the very heart of our subject—the choice between import duties. For, so far in the course of this argument, we have been discussing import duties in general. What we have said is as applicable to duties on tea as it is to duties on imported wheat; we did nothing to take account of the important fact that some duties are protective in effect and some duties are not.

This distinction between protective duties and non-protective duties is fundamental from this point of view, as from so many others. For, as should be clear immediately to unprejudiced reflection, the criteria of duties as protectors for domestic industry, and as revenue-raising instruments, are necessarily different. *To the extent that a duty protects—that is, prevents foreign produce from coming in—it fails as a revenue-producing instrument. To the extent that it produces revenue—that is, taxes incoming produce—it fails as a protective agency.*

Now it is important to realise the implications of this argument. It does not mean that a duty which affords protection does not yield *any* revenue. It would be absurd to argue, *e.g.* that a duty on foreign wheat would not yield a substantial sum to the Exchequer. Clearly, a duty on wheat would both protect some home producers and afford some revenue: and it would be absurd to argue the contrary. But it is not absurd, indeed it follows from the very definition of the words, to argue that the measure of its effectiveness as a revenue-producing instrument would be the measure of its ineffectiveness as a truly protective tariff. We know that not all the wheat needed in Great Britain could be grown in the country, and we know that no government would dare to impose a duty sufficiently high to make profitable the utilisation for wheat farming of all the land which could be so used. In so far as land which could be devoted to wheat growing was not in fact devoted to that purpose after the imposition of the duty, we could say that the duty was not high enough to be protective of the cultivation of wheat beyond a certain margin. It would be the wheat which came in in spite of the duty (and thus yielded a revenue) which would be the effective competitor with these potential uses of the land. Protection—the exclusion of competing imports—and the raising of revenue are mutually exclusive ends, although one duty may perform both functions simultaneously.

But while a single import duty can only perform both functions at the same time by performing each function

[175]

imperfectly, it is of course perfectly possible for *a tariff schedule as a whole* to attain both objects. Given normal trading conditions with a great variety of types and grades of imports, it is generally possible so to differentiate in the tariff rates in one schedule that the securing of maximum revenue from some rates is not incompatible with others being made prohibitive. When we speak of *the* American tariff or *the* South African tariff, it is of course a structure of duties of this sort that we have in mind. And although, as has been shown in another chapter, the actual tariffs in vogue are very far from attaining even the limited respectability of the ideal "scientific tariff," as this kind of structure is sometimes called, yet it is clear that the thing is conceivable and is not ruled out by the logical considerations we have just been contemplating.

But it is essential to notice the condition of attainment—*infinite complexity in the tariff rate book*. Differentiation must be practised not only as between broad classes of commodities. It must also be practised between grades and qualities within these classes. One has only to compare the size of the present customs tariff of the United States of America or any of the Dominions with that of earlier versions to realise the degree of complexity which is necessarily involved by the pursuit of this dual aim.

But complexity is not the only drawback of the tariff which is designed both to yield revenue and to protect industry. Extreme uncertainty of yield is a further characteristic. This arises from two circumstances. In the first place comes the uncertain character of the object of assessment. Import duties are paid on trade as it goes on, and they are therefore necessarily imposed upon expectations of what may occur in the future. Direct taxes need not necessarily be imposed upon expectations of this sort. It is, therefore, easier to readjust them in the light of recent experience. This is not to say that such adjustments are always made. But it is obviously easier for a Chancellor who is adjusting his rates upon assessments of a year's income *which has been earned* to make an accurate prediction of yield,

[176]

than it is for a Chancellor who is adjusting rates on trade *which has yet to take place*.

In the second place, in practice the framing of the tariff is likely to be disturbed continually by extra-fiscal considerations. It will show too much flexibility one way, not enough another. It is no accident that the countries which place most reliance on this expedient are those countries which have exhibited the least capacity to adjust revenue to expenditure. The United States, for instance, very seldom succeeds in getting near a balanced budget. The late Professor Hoxie, after an elaborate study of the customs revenue of the United States of America, delivered the following impressive verdict:

"On the whole, it may be asserted without fear of contradiction that throughout the history of the Customs Revenue in the United States, the income from this source has been determined, not by government need, but, almost wholly, by the character of temporary industrial and, more especially, temporary commercial conditions.

"As a consequence, in war the current public income has proved utterly insufficient, unstable, and inflexible; in peace it has shown itself extremely uncertain, fluctuating with every crisis, and even with the changes in the policy and condition of foreign nations; in times of prosperity it has forced upon the Treasury embarrassing surpluses, leading to extravagant expenditure, speculation and crises; in adversity it has left the Treasury empty, necessitating the lavish use of public credit."[1]

On the other hand, tariffs for revenue purposes only on a few articles of staple consumption do not exhibit nearly the same instability.

From the technical point of view, therefore, the choice between tariffs is simple. If tariffs are desired for revenue purposes only, then a few well-devised rates on a small selection of commodities on the lines of the British tariff are

[1] R. F. Hoxie, *Journal of Political Economy*, Vol. III, pp. 43-64.

least costly and most efficient. If it is desired that the tariff should be both protective and productive of revenue, then, to be at all efficacious in fulfilling these requirements, it must be elaborate and extensive. This is not a speculative conclusion. Tariff-making is nearly as old as history, and there is not much to learn about the technique of import duties. All that we have said in this connection is supported by an overwhelming weight of experience in tariff - making whenever and wherever it has taken place.

IV

All this has a very important bearing on the present controversy in Great Britain. It has recently been proposed that the best solution of our difficulties would be the imposition of a revenue tariff which consists not of carefully differentiated duties on a restricted range of commodities, but of two flat rates to apply, with one or two exceptions and rebates, to the whole range of imports of food, and of raw materials and manufactures respectively. Such a tariff, it has been argued, would fulfil with peculiar appropriateness the double function of protecting our industries and affording relief to the Exchequer.

Now if there is anything at all in the considerations which have been adduced above, it is clear that the beautiful simplicity of this scheme has attractions which from the economic point of view are wholly illusory. No doubt from the political point of view it *sounds* very fine to say, " Let us get away from the infinite complexities of the revolting tariff systems of the unenlightened nations around us and have only two flat rates, one or two exemptions, and a few 'rebates' framed on 'broad and simple lines'"; and some very simple minds may be taken in by such a proposal. But, save as a means for bamboozling the electorate, its attractions are wholly æsthetic. Judged as an instrument either for raising revenue or for affording protection, the thing is pure folly; and the fact that distinguished economists have been found to give it support in defiance of all the teachings of theory or history, can only be interpreted in terms of regard for political expediency rather than economic efficiency.

These are strong terms. They must be justified in greater detail.

Judged purely as a protective tariff, the revenue tariff, as proposed, is laughable. It fails to protect at all adequately industries which are alleged to be most in need of protection. At the same time, it imposes unnecessary disabilities on certain industries using imported raw materials or semi-manufactures, which are themselves very sorely stricken. Mr. Keynes seemed to think that the case of industries such as shipbuilding and tinplate, agriculture and so on, could be met by a few "rebates" framed on broad and simple lines. It is difficult to believe that he gave very much thought to the concrete difficulties of this proposal. For if one thing is certain as regards the effect in practice of a decision to grant any exemplary rebates or drawbacks, it is that the system would inevitably become complicated. And quite rightly too—if the thing were not to embody the most ridiculous anomalies. But by admitting the principle of exemption and rebate, Mr. Keynes destroyed even the political attractions of this proposal—that it ruled out sectional privilege and sectional prejudice.

Nor does the proposal fare any better when judged as a revenue-producing instrument. For it should be perfectly clear from what has been said already that a general tariff rate is not the best way of raising a given amount of revenue. On the contrary, it is probably almost the worst. From the technical point of view it is a return to the Dark Ages. It is administratively extremely expensive and wasteful. It is productive of endless irritation to travellers and manufacturers: and it involves, as we have seen, all sorts of unfair differentiation as between industry and industry. If the collection of a given revenue by means of import duties is the end in view, what is required is a policy of taxing comparatively few commodities by means of differential rates, having regard to the elasticity of each type and quality imported. Nearly a hundred years ago Great Britain found out that it does not pay to tax a great variety of imports. Mr. Keynes is merely leading a return to early Victorian practices. But it is surely possible to admire Lord Melbourne without imitating his fiscal policy.

We can see this quite clearly if we examine a little further the probable yield of the actual rates proposed. As a matter of fact, it is possible to entertain vastly exaggerated ideas with regard to the sum forthcoming. No less an authority than Mr. Keynes himself originally estimated this at being in the neighbourhood of from fifty to seventy-five millions; and although with characteristic candour he has since acknowledged this estimate to have been wrong, it is conceivable that there remain a certain number of his followers who were so carried away by his original predictions, that they do not yet realise the much more modest claims which, in the light of further discussions, he now finds it possible to make.

It is easy to see how a hasty view of the figures might give rise to rosy optimism. The import totals for 1930 were as follows:

		£
(1)	Food, Drink, Tobacco . . .	452,000,000
(2)	Raw Materials	212,000,000
(3)	Articles wholly or mainly manufactured	283,000,000

Five per cent. on the first two categories, and 15 per cent. on the last, give exactly £75,000,000. It is impossible for a man of Mr. Keynes' intelligence actually to have arrived at his totals in this way, and one can only conclude that, writing in a hurry, he just made a guess. But it is easy to imagine unsophisticated laymen being very impressed with these figures.

Unfortunately, before these figures can be used even as a basis for computation, there is a correction to be made which most materially reduces their significance. The prices at which internationally traded goods have changed

Because

Three important changes occurred
in England . of the ...
apparent weakening of Britain
economic position retardation

2 - Growth of economic
interference by the State

3. Growing economic retarded period -
with economic ...
condition ...

1. Dependence on trade increase
... machinery

hands in 1931 are very considerably below the prices at which they changed hands in 1930, and this must curtail the totals contemplated as available for taxation. It is not possible to foretell with complete accuracy the total returns for the year. But on the basis of the trade which has already taken place, an estimate made in a spirit of generosity comparable to that of the estimate we are contemplating would suggest the following as a basis for discussion:

		£
(1) Food, Drink, and Tobacco	. .	379,000,000
(2) Raw Materials . . .	.	148,000,000
(3) Articles wholly or mainly manufactured		231,000,000

If we could persuade our unsophisticated layman to follow us thus far, he would no doubt unhesitatingly budget for a revenue of about £61,000,000.

But it was proposed to exempt raw cotton and wool, and it is doubtful whether in practice there would be excluded from this exemption such raw materials as iron and non-ferrous ores, wood and timber, hides and skins, paper-making materials, and rubber. To take account of these would very considerably reduce the revenue from Category 2, and bring down the original crude estimate to something like £55,000,000.

Nor must we forget that a range of foodstuffs and manufactures is already subject to duty. If we assume that Mr. Keynes would not increase the taxation of silk, motor vehicles, musical instruments, etc., already the subject of high Protection, nor those categories of food which already pay import duties, we must make a further allowance of about £10,000,000. And even then we are making no allowance at all for the "broad and simple" rebates which Mr. Keynes proposes should be conceded on imported material entering into exports, nor for the curtailment of demand for the taxed imports (which would certainly follow if the revenue tariff had any protective effects at all): still less for the probable demand for concessions to the

Dominions by way of Imperial preference, which would certainly follow if those strong supporters of Mr. Keynes' policy—Lords Beaverbrook and Rothermere—had anything to do with it.

So that in the end the relief to the revenue that would accrue from this precious innovation, destructive at once of the principles of Free Trade and of scientific tariff-making, would be a very modest figure. If manufactures only were taxed on the conditions proposed by Mr. Keynes, and with the subsequent inevitable modifications, it is doubtful if much more than £20,000,000 would be secured. If food and raw materials were included, £30,000,000. This is surely nothing to get very excited about.

It is worth while comparing the flagrant inefficiency of the so-called revenue tariff with the neat efficiency of a few clear-cut tariffs for revenue purposes on the lines traditional in this country. If we compare the customs revenue of 1922-3 with that of 1929-30, we find that the Exchequer has sacrificed something like £37,000,000 by reductions of the duties on *two commodities alone*, sugar and tea. In the former financial year, £100,000,000 was raised by import duties on sugar, tea, and tobacco. This huge sum was raised with the minimum of administrative cost and the minimum disloca-tion to the national economic structure. If additional revenue must be raised by tariffs to-day surely it is along these straightforward lines that the thing should be attempted.

Moreover, duties of this sort, as we have pointed out already, have the further merit of lending themselves to considerable precision in estimates of revenue yield. On our present system of restricting tariffs to a few selected commodities in the last few years, the estimates of revenue from customs compare with the actual yield as follows:

	Budget estimate £	*Net receipts* £
1923-4 . . .	117,000,000	120,000,000
1924-5 . . .	102,000,000	100,000,000

			Budget estimate £	*Net receipts* £
1925-6	.	.	102,000,000	103,000,000
1926-7	.	.	108,000,000	107,000,000
1927-8	.	.	112,000,000	112,000,000
1928-9	.	.	121,000,000	119,000,000
1929-30	.	.	120,000,000	121,000,000

Suppose Mr. Keynes had had his way at some time in the past three years. The Chancellor of the Exchequer would have had to estimate the results of a flat percentage imposition on import values which have fluctuated as follows:

		1929 *Actual* £	1930 *Actual* £	1931 *Probable* £
Food	. .	509,000,000	452,000,000	380,000,000
Raw Materials	.	286,000,000	212,000,000	150,000,000
Manufactures	.	305,000,000	283,000,000	230,000,000

No Chancellor could possibly be expected to foretell accurately fluctuations of such magnitude. It is safe to say that at the end of each year large deficits would have exhibited themselves, and Mr. Keynes would have had to think of new ways of raising the wind! Of course, Mr. Keynes obviously believed that his proposal would cure the slump. But, save on this improbable hypothesis, the revenue tariff does not come very well out of the comparison.

The revenue tariff, therefore, has the worst of both worlds. It is neither good for Protection nor good for raising revenue. Except on the rather dubious assumption, not foreign, however, to recent discussions of the way out of our present difficulties, that two minuses make a plus, it is difficult to see how it can satisfy anyone. If, by the vagaries of politics, it ever does come into operation, it can be confidently predicted that it will not be long before it is modified.

The moral of all this is that if tariffs for Protection are bad, so too are protective tariffs for revenue purposes. If we reject tariffs as protective instruments, there is no need to consider protective tariffs as instruments for raising revenue. But tariffs for revenue purposes only on lines traditional in this country may well provide a powerful aid in times of financial difficulty.

CHAPTER XV

In the earlier sections of this book an endeavour has been made to show that the broad theoretical case for Free Trade, in the form in which it was elaborated by the so-called "classical" economists, still remains unchallenged. Nevertheless, the refinement of methods of economic analysis has enabled some theorists to distinguish one or two hypothetical situations in which taxes on certain industries and bounties on others might conceivably increase the national wealth. The range of situations and industries coming within this field is very limited, and the possibility of basing concrete tariff proposals upon these ingenious discoveries is still more limited, for, to quote the words of Professor A. C. Pigou, "we are not able to say to which of our categories the various actual industries of real life belong."

Even if this last difficulty were solved, it does not follow that we should be wise to make the attempt, for between the refinements of tariff theory and the crudities of tariff practice there is a great gulf fixed.

Were governments in a position to confine their tariff practice within the limits that economists could approve, the range of the tariff weapon would be narrow indeed. But governments have never shown themselves to be either able or willing to do so. Particularly in modern democracies, they have failed conspicuously in their attempts to give precise effect, whether legislative or administrative, to expert proposals which involve sharp discrimination between the economic interests of large sections of the electorate. When, as with tariff proposals, the achievement of the intentions of their authors demands consistency of policy over a fairly long period of time, the ultimate performance of the parliamentary machine has rarely been either recognisable or acceptable to the promoters of the measure. And retreat from failure is at least as difficult as advance.

In consequence, a tariff proposal, no matter how ingenious and attractive in content, and how eminent and respectable in origin, must be counted an idle dream unless it is accompanied by a scheme of implementation adequate to overcome the weaknesses which have proved fatal in existing tariff-making systems.

A scheme has, in fact, been elaborated in connection with the tariff campaign recently launched in this country. It first appeared on 12th March 1931 in a memorandum issued under the title "Industry and the Nation" by the Federation of British Industries. Substantially the same proposals were put forward by Mr. Baldwin, as the leader of the Conservative Party, in a speech in Hull on 17th July 1931; they will be referred to below as the Federation of British Industries scheme. The difficulties have not been denied. "Mr. Baldwin was wise to insist," says a not antagonistic leader-writer in *The Times* (18th July 1931), "that the British Tariff Commission must be very different from any similar Commission which the world has hitherto seen." "I have made up my mind to this," declared Mr. Baldwin, "that in no circumstances am I going to be responsible for any Government of which I may ever be the head, making this country a profiteers' paradise or making the British Legislature a crooks' corner. . . . To know the dangers in time is the right way to guard against them. . . . We have, so far as we can, to make the tariff knave-proof, and it can be done. . . . It is essential in my view that the scientific adjustment and the adaptation of the tariff should be taken out of politics, taken as far from politics as you can. . . . Tariff adjustment must be taken away from ordinary politics"; and he proceeded to outline what he described as "the right way to achieve these things."—(*The Times*, 18th July 1931.) A scheme enjoying

[186]

such confident and authoritative sponsorship clearly demands the closest examination.

The authors of "Industry and the Nation" contemplate three distinct stages in the process of putting Protection into effect. Their scheme provides for:

(1) The immediate control of imports, under powers to be obtained from Parliament as soon as a Government assumes office prepared to adopt a policy of Protection. The principle to underlie control, and the machinery to be used, are not disclosed. Control is to last only until the second stage is ready. Mr. Baldwin apparently made no reference to this stage in his speech at Hull.

(2) The imposition by the Government of a temporary emergency general tariff under powers granted and within limits prescribed by Parliament. There would be power to modify the provisions at any time to rectify mistakes. Mr. Baldwin announced that the principles of the tariff had already been worked out and that the detail would be filled in after assuming office.

(3) A permanent tariff to be devised upon the recommendations of a permanent Tariff Commission. The Federation of British Industries suggests that its provisions should supersede those of the Emergency Tariff in stages, for large groups of commodities at one time, rather than in one step.

It is evident, before looking at any of the detail of the scheme, that the interval between the assumption of office by a protectionist government and the completion of the permanent tariff will be filled with uncertainty and anxiety for industry and trade alike. The construction of the permanent tariff schedule will admittedly be an intricate and lengthy process. The question at once arises whether an emergency general tariff, applied without resort to similar investigation, could possibly achieve anything beyond bringing grave dislocation into the economic life of the country. To answer that question, and at the same time to bring out the significance of the detailed proposals, it is necessary to be clear as to what is involved in drawing up a tariff which will achieve what is desired (and possible) with the minimum of undesirable repercussions.

The Construction of a Tariff Schedule

A distinction should first be drawn between the work of deciding tariff policy, of laying down the objects of tariff intervention, and that of interpreting policy in terms of tariff rates. Much, but by no means all, of the misplaced optimism in the efficacy of expert tariff boards has been due to failure to realise that the power to determine what shall be attempted by means of the tariff instrument has never been entrusted to experts. It has already been observed that if the determination of policy were left to a commission of economists the scope of the tariff would be narrow indeed. Rarely has the determination of tariff policy even been deferred until an expert commission has investigated the precise condition of industry. It is significant that the Federation of British Industries scheme, as published in "Industry and the Nation," completely ignores this distinction, whereas it is explicit in Mr. Baldwin's speech that "such a commission would not settle tariff policy. That must be the function of the Government."

The essential work which it is now universally agreed that experts with special knowledge and experience should undertake is that of investigating conditions of production and consumption, and of recommending tariff rates in the light of that information which will give effect to the general tariff policy. That experts will avoid many of the most flagrant blunders which inexperienced draughtsmen would make is of course undeniable. But the fact that the recommendations of the best-trained experts are no better than wild guesses is only now being dimly realised (except by the experts themselves, who have no delusions on the point) even in countries which have suffered decades of acute disappointment with the practical working of tariff systems.

[188]

Consider first of all an enormously simplified problem in tariff adjustment. Imagine an expert tariff commission instructed to fix a rate of duty on a single commodity which will make profitable a certain increase in the volume of production. It will need to estimate—

Firstly, by how much the market price must be raised before the additional output will be profitable, assuming no reduction in demand;

Secondly, by how much the demand for the product will be reduced if the market price is raised to that extent, for if the additional output were not taken off the market the higher price could not be maintained (the first estimate must be corrected accordingly);

Thirdly, how high the tariff must be made to secure the increase in market price necessary according to this estimate; for if foreign competitors found it impossible to sell more of their output elsewhere and inconvenient to reduce the scale of their output it would pay them to lower their export price, *i.e.* pay part or even the whole of the duty, and thus maintain their sales. To the extent that this happened, the Treasury would gain revenue from a tariff which failed to protect.

It may seem at first sight that the second estimate, relating to the possible effect on demand of a given rise in price will involve most guesswork. Little can be ascertained about the willingness or capacity of consumers to pay more for an article rather than buy substitutes or other things. Yet at least as great uncertainty is entailed in the other estimates of volume of output and costs of production. Home production will probably be carried on by many different firms, which will not all be induced to increase the scale of their output in the same proportion as the selling price rises, for their costs of production will not be composed of the same items in identical proportions. Every industrialist who has attempted to estimate production costs for a hypothetical expansion of output on the basis of cost records will realise the degree of inaccuracy involved where only one plant is concerned. How much greater is the amount of sheer guesswork in a composite forecast of the behaviour of many different firms (even if detailed cost figures were available), when allowance must also be made for the possible output of new producers whom the higher selling price would attract to this field of production. In the third place, enlightened guesswork would be a euphemistic description of the process of ascertaining the competitive position of all foreign suppliers (whose cost records, of course, would not be available), in order to estimate the likelihood of their paying part of the duty.

The example just taken is of course much simpler than the problems involved in the construction of a general tariff, which would extend over the whole range of different grades and types of product of every industry. When these complications are introduced, the conception of a "scientific" tariff becomes entirely ludicrous. In the first place, the demand for the different products of a major industry does not vary identically for each as the selling price is changed, nor does the supply of each product vary in equal proportions in each factory as the selling price is changed. Each grade of product will require distinctive treatment, and as several are manufactured jointly the ideal tariff-rate (if it could be ascertained) for one product will conflict with that for the others. Unsatisfactory compromises will have to be attempted. A second complication is, however, far more damaging. When a large-scale adjustment of tariff-rates is to be made, affecting most of the industries of a country, it becomes completely impossible to utilise any estimates of either costs of production or variations in demand. The various industries are so closely knit together in buyer-and-seller relationships, that the magnitude of every item in their costs becomes an unknown quantity varying upward with the degree of protection that may be accorded by the new tariff to the constituent raw materials directly or indirectly entering into their products; while demand for their products also becomes an unknown variable, dependent upon and itself in part determining the amount of the consumers' outlay upon other products. The number of unknown quantities becomes entirely unmanageable; the problem is indeterminate.

The conclusion is, therefore, that it is not possible to adjust a general tariff "scientifically." If a single commodity could be dealt with at a time, with an ample interval for supply and demand to readjust themselves to the new conditions before a further change were undertaken, some of the difficulties would be eliminated, yet the tariff-making process would still remain largely a matter of guess-work. But that procedure is exceedingly unpopular among protectionists, as the history of the safeguarding enquiries has revealed, for the "one-thing-at-a-time" method exposes the extent of the burden involved, and industrialists who are adversely affected oppose the proposed duty; whereas when all commodities are dealt with at the same time industrialists are more easily placated by counter-concessions, which obscure the real incidence of the burden of the tariff while placing it more certainly upon the ultimate consumers.

Expert tariff-makers, if they cannot foresee the evil repercussions of the protective rates they recommend, have at least endeavoured to confine them within the narrowest possible limits. The growing complexity of modern customs tariffs is in part a result of their efforts. By treating as a separate case every grade of a commodity that seems to warrant the application of a special rate of duty, the direct interference with international trade is reduced more nearly to the limits which the protectionist policy demands, and revenue is secured from rates which need not be prohibitive. The protective tariff applied in South Africa in 1925, for example, doubled the number of tariff items and enormously increased the number and intricacy of the different rates levied; but such refinements inevitably increase the costs of administration, of checking the description and valuation of commodities, and of preventing evasion or misrepresentation.

It is necessary to remind ourselves at this stage that the tariff schedule which an expert board finally recommends is rarely the same as that which the Government at a later stage places before Parliament, and is still less recognisable in the tariff which ultimately becomes law. The Treasury, for instance, is concerned to see that the tariff rates on imports from which the Exchequer derives revenue are not made really protective, and the Government will be compelled at least to make a compromise which will attain neither object completely. For the rest, political influences will not be idle at any stage. As will be seen in the following comparison of the Federation of British Industries scheme with modern tariff experience elsewhere, the existing universal dissatisfaction with tariff practice arises as much from the failure of the political machine to give precise effect to expert recommendations as it does from the failure of the expert boards to solve an unsolvable problem.

The Emergency Tariff

After the foregoing discussion it is possible to deal very shortly with the temporary emergency general tariff. In the first place its advocates are determined that the permanent impartial experts shall take no share whatsoever in drawing it up. The Federation of British Industries scheme does not reveal its own intentions as to the authorship (can modesty be the deterrent?); but Mr. Baldwin has disclosed the fact that "an immense amount of preliminary work has already been put into it by experts *under myself and my colleagues.*" The work has been commenced under political direction; the intention is to complete it under the same auspices after assuming office.

The emergency tariff is to be of a simple character. The Federation proposes several classes of *ad valorem* rates, ranging from free entry for some imports to an effective high rate of duty for others, the guiding principle to be in general "that the nearer a commodity is to a completely finished article the higher the rate of duty."

[192]

Comment is hardly necessary. The foregoing discussion makes it abundantly clear that a simple tariff and effective protection are incompatible ideals—unless, indeed, a thorough dislocation of foreign trade is to be regarded as effective protection. Great complexity is the price that must be paid for a combination of the appropriate degree of protection where it is desired with the maximum of relief from the burden of tariffs where they can achieve no object. A prolonged preliminary study of conditions of supply and demand is unavoidable if the tariff is to be free from rates on some commodities which simply destroy the effects which other rates are intended to produce. Few devices are more unsuitable than a tariff for dealing with an emergency situation. Its inevitable crudity must result in the dislocation of industry and trade, the loss of markets, and acute disappointment even to those who anticipate the greatest favours. Adjustment and relief are promised, it is true, after the damage has been done; but the industrialist or merchant whose business is being ruined must wait his turn until "some suitably constituted tribunal," "vested with power to hear and decide appeals by any responsible body of traders or other persons directly interested," has time to investigate the facts and make up its mind whether "British interests are thereby being prejudicially affected."

What can have persuaded the Federation, and Mr. Baldwin, to put forward this proposal? Have they simply yielded to insistent pressure from strong sectional interests bent on immediate favours? Or have they reasoned ingeniously with themselves that after the chaos of emergency tariff conditions the introduction of the permanent tariff, with all its inevitable shortcomings, will seem to industrialists and traders alike the dawn of a new era of Free Trade? Can it be, even, that the proposal first of all to control imports by arbitrary government action is made in the hope that thereafter the emergency tariff itself may come in the guise of a liberating instrument?

It will be opportune at this juncture to examine for a

N   [193]

moment the guiding principle which is suggested in the Federation of British Industries scheme, viz. "the nearer a commodity is to a completely finished article the higher the rate of duty." Its attractions are obvious (although on first thoughts one might have imagined any one stage of production likely to make as strong a claim for Protection as any other). In the progress of crude raw materials through the various stages of manufacture to the final state in which the ultimate consumer uses the product many distinct businesses may be involved, the "finished" product of one being a "raw material" for another. If each stage receives protection more than sufficient to compensate for the increased cost of its protected "raw material," one serious conflict of interest may be avoided. Moreover, producers are generally organised in associations to protect their group interest, whereas "final consumers," as a group, are not; and a tariff which passes on as much as possible of the burden of higher prices to the final consumer has the best chance of becoming law. Further, the more completely finished the article, the greater is the amount of employment that has resulted from making it.

Carry the analysis a stage further, however. The wisdom of using a tariff to "make employment" has already been discussed in the first part of this book and need not be examined again here. But do the considerations just enumerated necessarily imply generally higher *ad valorem* rates of duty on the relatively more finished articles?

Firstly, if the object of imposing a tariff on the later stages of production is merely to compensate for the increase in the cost of raw materials which are to be protected by the tariff, a rate of duty *lower* than that imposed on the raw materials will be adequate. If, for example, in the final price of an article which formerly sells successfully in the home market at £4 the cost of certain raw materials is £1, and a duty of 50 per cent. on the raw material raises its cost to (say) £1. 10s., then a rise in the price of the final product to (say) £4. 10s. will be sufficient to compensate, and in a simple case a duty of about 12½ per cent. will bring about that rise. The costs of other raw materials, equipment and labour entering into the finished article are not necessarily affected.

Secondly, there is no justification *in general* for the belief that the later stages of industry are more in need of protection than those branches which manufacture the crude and semi-finished products. Indeed, there is strong reason for believing that in this country, with its specialised skill and technique, the contrary is the case. It is noteworthy, for instance, that in the iron and steel industry foreign competition has been most severe in the crude and semi-finished stages, whereas exports of finished products have been maintained; but the Federation of British Industries proposal would give least protection in the case of iron and steel where its present costs are least competitive.

Thirdly, and here the tariff experience of other countries is illuminating, attempts to fit the countless products of industry into a series of distinct stages, from "raw materials" at the one end to "finished articles" at the other, reveal a host of unexpected difficulties in tariff-making. Articles of the most finished appearance, such as wire-netting, motor lorries and tractors, glass bottles and corks, are discovered to be essential "raw materials" for the crudest and earliest stages of production, such as agriculture, which would be seriously handicapped by higher tariffs on these "finished articles." Finished textile products are used as materials in the electrical and rubber industries; and so on. The net effect is that in so far as the "earlier" processes of one industry involve the use of the more "finished" products of later stages of any industry there arise the most unanswerable reasons for further increases in their protection. During the three years, 1921-1924, the first South African advisory Board of Trade and Industries encountered so many conflicts of interest of this nature (although a general revision of the tariff was not then in progress) that it appended a long list of them to its final report.[1] The Australian Tariff Board has been troubled

[1] *The Journal of Industries*, South Africa, 1925.

by the same problem from its inception, as its annual reports disclose.[1]

Finally, in this connection, it must not be assumed that even if a tariff were finally evolved which successfully placed the main burden upon final consumers industrial conflicts would thereby be overcome. Where labour is strongly organised, the trade unions have not been slow to defend the interests of their members when tariffs have been raised. In Australia and South Africa, for example, when employers (supported sometimes by the employees) have succeeded in obtaining an increased tariff, the workers have at once applied to the Arbitration Court or Wage Board, or pressed through their trade union, for a share of the benefit, and have pointed to the effects of increased tariffs on the cost of living in support of their demands. The Australian Tariff Board, seeing "nothing but economic disaster ahead," protested in vain that such tactics "can only result in an ever-increasing wage rate and an ever-increasing tariff." The South African Board of Trade (Report No. 28 of 1928) could not "lightly contemplate a condition of industrial affairs under which the manufacturer would be compelled to run shuttle-wise between the Wage Board and the Board of Trade and Industries." Wherever workers are well organised a tariff which places its burden upon the final consumer will inevitably lead to wage disputes and threaten to raise the wage costs of industry.

Not without reason do the advocates of this "guiding principle" anticipate "temporary but serious dislocation or inconvenience to some branch of industry," unless prompt relief can on occasion be given from the operation of the emergency tariff.

The Application of a Permanent Tariff

The distinction drawn earlier in this chapter between the work of deciding tariff policy and that of interpreting policy in terms of tariff rates provides a convenient basis

[1] See, for example, those for 1922 and 1923.

for an analysis of the powers and duties of the permanent Tariff Commission, which is to be concerned, according to the Federation of British Industries scheme, with the task of constructing a permanent protective tariff.

(a) The Determination of Tariff Policy

For a judgment on the merits of the proposed tariff machinery, the answers to two questions are vital. In the first place, by whom are the general lines of tariff policy to be determined? Is that fundamental power to be entrusted to the expert, impartial Commission? Or will the Government of the day take the decision?

Secondly, on what evidence will that decision be based? If the expert commission decides general policy, it may be assumed that it will base it upon a thorough investigation of the actual conditions and needs of the country's industries. But if the Cabinet is to lay down the general lines of tariff policy, will it defer its decision until the permanent Commission has made its investigation and submitted its recommendation? Or will policy have been determined on other grounds, in advance of any expert and impartial enquiry?

Quite clearly it is impossible to protect *the whole* of a country's industry. In the first part of this book it has been shown that the benefits conferred by Protection are essentially sectional in character, the protected sections gaining at the expense of the remainder. Unless an expert and impartial investigation is to be conducted in an endeavour to ascertain the general lines of tariff policy which would associate the maximum amount of benefit with the minimum of loss, and the recommendations of the Commission are to be made the basis of any tariffs that are subsequently imposed, the scheme forfeits all claim to have been designed to further the national interest as a whole.

In this connection the disclosures of the present Chairman of the South African tariff commission (The Board of Trade and Industries) concerning the protective tariff of

1925 are enlightening. In an article in the Johannesburg *Star* (Financial Supplement, March 1926), he says, "The Board is as free to act according to a certain policy as to have certain aims. In both matters, however, the Board has to be modest and careful. If the 'policy' of the Board is not acceptable to Government and the majority of the community, then that policy is not of much practical use." Writing of the actual work of drawing up the tariff, he adds, "The next question was to decide what course to pursue. The opinion was expressed on the one hand that the Board should creep into its shell and then later emerge with an 'ideal' tariff to be presented to the Government for acceptance or rejection. Fortunately the more practical view of getting from the Government its general views of fiscal policy, and then framing the tariff and tariff legislation accordingly, prevailed in the end." It should be added that the Board had only just been re-constituted at the time by the new Government, and had made no investigation of the condition of the industries of the country.

In the case of the recent tariffs of the United States, the rate-fixing authority has endeavoured to interpret a general slogan of the governing political party, such as the Republican "true principle of protection" which made its appearance in the case of the Payne-Aldrich tariff of 1909 —"the equalising of the costs of production at home and abroad."

The memorandum of the Federation of British Industries is strangely silent on the whole question of responsibility for general policy. It contemplates an *executive* board, however, and lays down duties and instructions of a very general, slogan type, such as a board of economists could interpret only on Free Trade lines, but which a board of protectionists would take as a justification for a high tariff.[1]

---

[1] 1. "B. *Duties of Board.*

(17) Their principal duty should be to investigate the requirements of industry, preserving a due balance between industry and industry, and between the interests of industry and of the country as a whole, and on this basis to construct a full and

The vital problem of the relationship of the Tariff Commission to Parliament is side-stepped altogether.

But not by Mr. Baldwin; he leaves no doubt about the matter. "Such a commission would not settle tariff policy. That must be the function of the Government." The general lines of tariff policy would, in fact, be settled before the Board could begin its investigations; for an emergency tariff, the principles of which have already been worked out, would have been put into operation by Mr. Baldwin, and a reversal of policy by the same Government, as the result of subsequent expert advice, is hardly to be contemplated.

According to this scheme, then, there is no room left for doubt that the work of the Board would be confined to an attempt to interpret, in terms of tariff rates, certain general lines of policy which might be inconsistent in themselves and contrary to the national interest as a whole; for they would be determined by political considerations in advance of any expert, disinterested and non-political endeavour to ascertain the economic needs of the country.

> detailed tariff, which would provide fully effective protection for British industry.
>
> (18) In considering the framing of the Tariff the Board should have regard to the following considerations :
>
> (19) (a) The level of duties necessary to enable British industry to provide the greatest possible amount of employment, and by this increased production to cheapen prices, and thus not only benefit the home consumer but assist in the expansion of the export trade. These rates of duty may well be higher than those contained in the Emergency Tariff.
>
> (20) (b) The necessity of ensuring that where a tax is placed upon the importation of any commodity which is the raw material of any industry, the interests of such an industry are fully considered, and a due balance struck by the Board between the interests of the industries either as producers or consumers.
>
> (21) (c) The need in the interests of the great export industries for elasticity in the tariff to enable treaties to be concluded with other countries on terms favourable to the British export trade."—*Industry and the Nation.*

(b) *The Procedure for fixing the Tariff Rates*

The general lines of tariff policy are fundamental, and
yet the really crucial test of any tariff-making scheme
applies to the machinery for putting into effect the tariff
rates on each commodity which impartial experts decide
are most appropriate. Is the decision of the Tariff Board
to be final? Does the Government reserve the power to
reject its proposals, or the even more significant power of
amendment? Will the Tariff Bill as finally presented to
Parliament be subject to the ordinary legislative process?
Will any single authority possess the power subsequently
to modify the tariff schedule as it finally emerges from the
Tariff Board, embodying, as it is intended to do, a nice
balance of countless opposing considerations and con-
flicting interests?

It is upon this rock that every existing tariff-making
scheme has foundered.

Consider, firstly, the evolution of a tariff item in the
hands of the impartial and expert Board. What procedure
should it adopt?

It has been found necessary, for example, to lay down
precise rules in order to maintain unimpaired the reputation of the board for disinterestedness and determination
to base its decision upon all the relevant information. The
recent Canadian Tariff Advisory Board was particularly
well (if not adequately) protected in this way. Its investigations were conducted in part by means of public
hearings of evidence; the sittings were well advertised, so
that interested persons could come forward; the proceedings
were promptly published, so that evidence could be
refuted by subsequent witnesses; representatives of consumers' organisations, as well as of groups of industrialists,
were admitted to the public hearings; and in addition the
Board had powers of private enquiry into the costs and
producing conditions of affected businesses to enable
them to supplement the necessarily incomplete evidence

which was voluntarily tendered. But the Canadian Government abolished the Board after only four years' work.

The Australian Tariff Board is avowedly protectionist in its attitude, but its powers are similar. Since 1924 it hears evidence given on oath under public examination and can also obtain confidential information. The reputation of the South African Board of Trade and Industries, however, has not been safeguarded in this way. It was appointed by the Nationalist Government in 1924 immediately after its assumption of office, and the political sympathies of its members were not in doubt. Rarely is it made known that the Board is contemplating the amendment of a tariff item; rarely is evidence invited; no public sittings are held; and the whole proceedings are in camera. The Board in an annual report[1] has made it known that the Canadian procedure does not appeal to it. Critics, knowing that the

---

[1] Annual Report, South African Board of Trade and Industries (No. 95, dated 15th Feb. 1929).

" *Board Procedure.*

30. On occasions in Parliament and elsewhere, it has been urged that the Board should sit in public when evidence is taken in connection with applications for Customs Tariff assistance. Therefore, the working of the Canadian Tariff Board system has been observed with interest by the Union Board. In Canada applications are heard in open sittings. Evidence for and against is led by counsel, and counsel are also present who hold watching briefs on behalf of interested parties, and this practice is followed by local manufacturers, an anti-protectionist league, and overseas exporters. In short, the procedure followed is similar to the routine of a court of law, although apparently the atmosphere is less formal. But the Press is nowise bound to abstain from daily comment on the proceedings, and thus propagandist matter is circulated to the Government on behalf of the particular interest journals may serve. Much time and money are expended on consideration of Tariff applications under these circumstances, and the process is extremely involved and cumbersome. The Canadian procedure does not appeal to the Board. In South Africa the Board takes all evidence in camera, but, whenever supplementary information appears to be desirable, enquiries are addressed to parties who may be affected by the favourable consideration of any particular application. On the whole, this method appears to have given generally satisfactory results."

Board regards itself purely as an instrument of government policy, right or wrong, deny the likelihood of its suspecting the existence of, and taking steps to seek out, evidence which might prove government policy to be mistaken, and which would be presented if advertised public sittings were held.

The reputation of the Board for impartiality and competence will depend mainly, of course, upon the personal reputations of its members. Freedom from strong political sympathies, and skill in economic enquiry are outstanding requirements. Confidence in their impartiality will be most widespread if their tenure of office is long and certain, and their remuneration evidently adequate to free them from motive to placate either a government or a potential subsequent employer. It is curious how rarely these obvious requirements have been forthcoming in practice. In the United States the first Tariff Board, set up by President Taft as a result of the 1909 Act, consisted of three Republicans. Although no doubt competent and impartial, their reports were ignored (after 1911) by a Democratic House of Representatives, which abolished the Board in 1912. In 1916 a two-party Tariff Commission was set up, the salary of members to be $7500 and their term of office twelve years. (Such terms raise expectations. We shall see in a moment what use has been made of their work.) The Tariff Act of 1930, however, abruptly terminated the tenure of office of the then existing members, with but three months' notice, although their contract terms had not expired. In South Africa, as we have seen, the Nationalist Government reconstituted the Board of Trade immediately it assumed office in 1924, re-appointing only one of the former members. The present members do not disguise their political sympathies. Their salaries are lower than those of senior permanent officials, and their tenure of office (unless re-appointed) is only three years. Uncertainty of tenure inevitably reacts upon both the calibre of experts who will accept appointment and the attitude of members to their work.

Both the Federation of British Industries [1] and Mr. Baldwin [2] stress the importance of securing men of high standing, and of preserving their independence from political or industrial influence by the terms and character of their appointment. These sections of their proposals, taken alone and so far as they go, embody unexceptionable ideals. Whether men of the experience and quality envisaged would be prepared to devote themselves to the sort of work which the Board would be called upon to perform is, however, a very different matter. What is to be their relationship to Parliament?

It seems to be no exaggeration to say that the more independent a Tariff Commission has shown itself to be of

[1] *Industry and the Nation*, p. 6. " A. *Character of Board* (16). For the construction of a permanent tariff a Tariff Board should be set up of a permanent and executive character. It should be composed of men of the highest standing and ability, and should include members with commercial and technical knowledge and administrative experience in the important industries of the country. The members should be required to devote their whole time to their duties, and to relinquish any commercial or other interests which might in any degree impair their complete impartiality. They should be removed as far as is humanly possible from political influence by the terms and character of their appointment. In general, their position and freedom from external influence should approximate as closely as possible to that of His Majesty's Judges."

[2] " Now the right way to achieve these things would be to set up a permanent Tariff Commission, non-political, upon whose recommendations tariff variations would be made, subject only to the assent of Parliament. The status of the Commissioners ought to be lifted as far above the stress of party politics as is that of His Majesty's Judges. Our Courts of Justice have a world-famed tradition of impartiality. The Tariff Commission should set itself to emulate that tradition. They ought to be sufficiently remunerated to be absolutely independent and able to give their whole time to the task. I do not think they should be appointed as sectional representatives in any sense whatever. They want to be widely experienced men, selected solely on their personal qualifications with a view to composing the strongest possible body, and the chairman should be a man accustomed to the weighing and sifting of evidence, and Labour should be represented upon that body. (Cheers.) The aim should be that the Commission as a whole will command the fullest confidence of the general public and of all branches of industry and commerce, employers and employed alike."—*The Times*, 18th July 1931.

the Government in power the less effect has it had upon tariff legislation. In the United States the two-party Tariff Commission appointed in 1916 had six years of active work before the passing of the Fordney Tariff of 1922, and placed voluminous reports covering the production costs of several thousand commodities before the Ways and Means Committee. The Chairman himself has recorded his view of the result. "The Tariff Commission had little influence in determining the duties in the present law. . . . Occasionally, it is true, the Commission reports were used in debate with sufficient effect to influence the result. But with rare exceptions national economic considerations yielded as on former occasions to political, factional and sectional pressure. . . . Many of the duties therefore diverged widely from those shown to be reasonable by the data of the Tariff Commission. . . . Almost daily both while the Bill was in committee and later on the floor, decisions were reached and revoked, changes were made in rates and classifications, and all the symptoms of a perfect turmoil of indecision were manifest." [1] In the middle of 1929, again, a special session of Congress was called by President Hoover to reconsider the customs tariff. Professor Taussig has provided an informative account [2] of the proceedings, from which emerged the Hawley-Smoot Tariff of 1930. As before, tariff rates were debated in committees of both the House of Representatives and the Senate. Since 1922 the Tariff Commission had "continued to make investigations and to maintain a portfolio of informational data. Much had been hoped from work of this kind. . . . All such hopes seem to have been disappointed by the ten years' experience since the War, the period during which the Tariff Commission has had a real chance to function. Nothing has been achieved toward improving the essential character of tariff legislation. . . . Congress has gone the same old way in 1929-30 as it did in 1922. Congressional Committees have indeed utilised the material of

[1] T. W. Page, *Making the Tariff in the United States*.
[2] *Quarterly Journal of Economics*, Feb. and Nov. 1930.

the Tariff Commission, and have borrowed copiously from its documents and from its experts. But it has been done chiefly for making points in debates or in Committee hearings, or for enabling a Congressman to see just what the figures mean for his party or his constituents." The rate proposals of the House and Senate went to the usual Conference Committee for final adjustment. "The innumerable cases in which the two houses differed were settled there. The Committee sessions were necessarily compressed into a few days. Every one was weary and in a hurry to get them through. . . . The nature of the outcome—whether in the end a rate higher or lower than the corresponding one of 1922—depended on compromise, 'trading,' accident, and not infrequently on the persistence or dominance of some individual member."

American politics may, of course, be regarded as a very special case. The Australian position at first sight appears more promising; for the Tariff Board, first established in 1921, has, like the Government, been protectionist in sympathy throughout, and no tariff amendment may be enacted before the Board has reported on the proposals. Yet its annual report for 1927-8 records that "as regards some of the most important subjects investigated by the Board either the Minister of the day or the Parliament has seen fit to act otherwise than in accordance with the recommendations of the Board. The method adopted by interested parties to influence departure from the Tariff Board's recommendation is worthy of study and deserving of strong comment. It has happened, after the Tariff Board has held an enquiry, at which over a hundred witnesses were publicly examined on oath, has carefully studied the whole of the public and confidential evidence, and has presented a recommendation to the Minister, that a few men, parties to the application, have made representations to members of Parliament and to the Government which have resulted in the setting aside of the weight of public evidence and the studied recommendation of the Board.

"Different industries have developed to a particular

degree in the different states of the Commonwealth. It has been a practice of persons working in Parliamentary lobbies on the interests of their concerns to procure assistance for their project by bargaining for reciprocal aid—one State group with another. This practice has been rather successful to the parties, but it has proved one of the strongest factors in preventing the enactment of a well-balanced tariff. Undoubtedly the principal object of the enactment of the Tariff Board requiring evidence to be publicly given and on oath, was to put an end as far as possible to the use by interested individuals of unfair influence exerted by the presentation of a one-sided view of the case under circumstances which allow of no considered answer from the opponents."

On recent occasions the Australian Government has not even waited for an expert opinion. In November and December 1929 and again in April and June 1930, for instance, additional duties and prohibitions were imposed without prior report from the Board.

The Canadian Tariff Advisory Board, with its more effective machinery for investigation, evidently proved too hampering to the Canadian Government in its tariff policy, for it was abolished in 1930 after four years' work. As for the South African Board, the special reasons why it has not run counter to the governmental wishes have already been explained.

It may now well be asked what there is in the Federation of British Industries scheme to prevent a similar treatment of expert tariff recommendations in this country.

The Federation of British Industries avoids the issue. It envisages an *executive* rather than an *advisory* Tariff Board, and deprecates parliamentary interference, without suggesting an alternative. "The procedure," it says, "for effecting the necessary legislation is a matter for constitutional and parliamentary experts rather than industrialists, but the experience of other countries has shown that discussion of the details of a tariff by Parliament is in the highest degree undesirable." Students of political institutions have pressed without success for satisfaction on this vital point.[1] Mr. Baldwin's pronouncement in July ruled out the Federation's proposal of an *executive* Board and at the same time disappointed those who hoped for a new political invention.

[1] A notable example is the following letter from Sir Chas. Grant Robertson in *The Times* of 25th June 1931.

" To the Editor of *The Times*.

SIR,—The mechanism of Tariff Reform, to which Sir Edward Grigg has recently drawn attention in your columns, interests all students of our institutions and their working. If I understand aright the process proposed, it is to be as follows :—An emergency general tariff will, first of all, be imposed, presumably after a mandate given at a General Election, and after it has been proposed by the Government and approved by the House of Commons. Behind this, a ' scientific tariff ' will be constructed by a special and impartial tribunal, which will give ample opportunity to producers, distributors, and consumers to state their case. This tribunal, I infer, will report its recommended scientific tariff to the Chancellor of the Exchequer and the Cabinet. (Concurrently, I presume, the Government will have negotiated with the Dominions the scheme of reciprocal preferences. Whether the results of these negotiations will be sent to the Tariff Tribunal to be incorporated in, and to be reckoned for, the ' scientific tariff ' is not clear. Perhaps they are to be sent from the Government direct to the House of Commons for approval, and quite distinct from the tariff drawn up by the Tariff Tribunal.)

What is to be the next stage ? Will the Cabinet be pledged to accept, without review or modification, the recommendations of the Tariff Tribunal ? Will they then be incorporated, *en bloc*, in the Finance Bill of the year, and be subject to detailed modification and amendment by the House of Commons, which may in the play of party, regional, or industrial forces, completely upset the scientific character of the tariff schedules determined by the Tariff Tribunal after elaborate investigation of the economic evidence ? Or will they be presented in a separate Bill presented to the House of Commons, like ecclesiastical measures under the Enabling Act, simply for acceptance or rejection but not susceptible of amendment ?

In a word, are the Cabinet and the House of Commons to surrender both their responsibility for, and their power to deal with, the proposed tariff as a whole or any part of it ? Or is the work of the impartial tribunal which frames the scientific tariff to be analogous to that of a Royal Commission, the recommendations of which, based on its independent examination of the evidence, can be adopted in whole or in part or not at all, by the Government and the House of Commons ?—Your obedient servant,—CHARLES GRANT ROBERTSON.

All Souls College, Oxford. (25th June 1931.)"

[207]

"Tariff adjustment," he said, "must be taken away from ordinary politics. By this I mean that government action must be founded on full and impartial information—information available not only to the Government but to every citizen of the country who cares to study it, so that it is not being done in secret." The duty of the Commission "would be to advise authoritatively the Government of the day and [on ?] the detailed applications of the tariff as it affects one commodity or another."

Hungry seekers for crumbs of comfort will find but one tantalising morsel in that announcement to appease their craving: when the Government decides to act, the report on which it acts will be published. Possibly *all* the reports issued by the Tariff Board would be published immediately they are submitted to the Government. If that course were adopted it would certainly be more difficult for the Government to ignore the expert advisers, and less difficult for it to resist external pressure if it wished to adopt their recommendations. Even that, however, is not to be inferred from Mr. Baldwin's pronouncement. If the Government finds it for any reason inconvenient to take action, the public need not know that a report has been presented. The work of the Tariff Board would then be less effective even than that of a Royal Commission.

The conclusion is inescapable that the recommendations of the Tariff Board would carry no more and no less weight than any other expert opinions which are put before the Government. The same influences which cause Ministers at present to press for the amendment or rejection of expert proposals on other economic questions will operate with at least equal force when tariff rates are before the Cabinet. The Tariff Bill which the Government introduces into Parliament will be subject at every stage to "the play of party, regional or industrial forces." What is likely to remain, at the end of that process, of the complex and delicate structure of rate schedules in which the expert Tariff Board may hope to have reconciled the protectionist wishes of the Cabinet and the revenue requirements of the Treasury? There is not one proposal in the Federation of British Industries scheme which justifies the belief that tariff practice in this country would be one whit more successful than it has been in the Dominions or in the United States.

CHAPTER XVI

QUOTAS AND IMPORT BOARDS

TARIFFS are only one of the forms of Protection. If a Government by any measure imposes restrictions on the import of a commodity from which the home-produced article is free, that measure is protective. The arguments which have been advanced in previous chapters against Protection hold against such measures, just as much as they hold against tariffs.

It is quite true that in the past much the most important method of protection has been the tariff. Other methods have been used, but they have generally been of minor importance. The reason for this is obvious: tariffs may be primarily protective, but they yield revenue as a by-product. The other methods, far from bringing money into the Treasury, generally cost money. Between two methods of reaching the same end, a harassed Chancellor will usually prefer the one which brings money in to the one which takes it out.

But in particular cases, where consumers are politically powerful, and feeling against tariffs is strong, this consideration may be overborne by others. Realising that the electorate is unlikely to consent to the imposition of a tariff, the Protectionist resorts to indirect methods to gain his ends. It is obvious that protectionist opinion has for some time been drifting in this direction with respect to wheat. Of all the arguments against tariffs, one only seems to make any impression on the protectionist politician: "Your food will cost you more." He has learnt by bitter experience that the electorate has a natural repugnance to taxes on food, and so he has sought to gain his end by other means. The devices to be considered in this chapter—the quota and the import board—are largely the result of his cogitations. Although these proposals will be discussed more specifically with respect to the case of wheat (since that is practically the most important case), very similar arguments hold for other commodities.

A Quota for Home-produced Wheat

The principle of the quota proposal is simple, though its detailed administration would be less simple and straight-forward. The object is to ensure that the quantity of im-ported wheat consumed in this country does not exceed a certain definite proportion of the total consumption. A certain minimum proportion is reserved for the home product. The means by which this would be achieved would be a control of the millers. The milling industry (as a whole) would have to give evidence that it was using at least the fixed proportion of English wheat. It is agreed that it would not be feasible to lay this obligation on each particular miller. The milling of imported wheat is generally done at the ports, while English wheat is milled inland. This system brings about obvious savings in transport. If it were laid down that each miller had to use his fixed quota of English wheat, English wheat would have to be carried to the ports to be milled, and this totally unnecessary transport would obviously lead to a pointless but highly undesirable rise in the prices of flour and bread. In conse-quence of this difficulty it has been suggested that millers would only be compelled to produce certificates showing that the appointed quota of British wheat had been used by someone, not necessarily by the particular miller him-self. Those millers who specialise mainly upon British wheat would be at liberty to transfer certificates of purchase in excess of their own necessary quotas to other millers. By some such means as this (and there can be little doubt that something of this kind would be adopted) the milling industry as a whole would be compelled to purchase the fixed quota of British wheat.

Another administrative difficulty arises out of the importation of flour. Unless this was restricted there would be a danger of the scheme being evaded by the importation of increased quantities of flour. The quota would therefore have to be extended to flour imports. This could be done by making it compulsory to hand over one of these miller's certificates of the purchase of British wheat before it became legal to import flour.[1]

Thus the scheme is administratively feasible; but what would be its effects? These would naturally depend on the figure at which the quota was fixed. If the quota was no higher than the proportion of British wheat to total wheat milled would have been under Free Trade, then the scheme would be simply inoperative. It would have no effect on prices; but it would not help the farmer. However, since we may reasonably assume that no government would be foolish enough to set up an expensive machinery of inspection to have no effect at all, it is reasonable to suppose that the quota would be higher than this figure.

In that case, port millers would find it impossible to secure sufficient certificates to match their imports so long as they continued to pay the nominal price for certificates which would no doubt be required under any circumstances to cover the clerical costs of transference. Either they would have themselves to enter the market for British wheat; or, more probably, they would offer higher prices for certificates. Those millers who were favourably placed for milling British wheat would increase their demand for it, since in addition to the direct return got from selling the flour, they would also secure a by-product, in the form of the valuable certificate. Thus the demand for British wheat would rise, and the price would rise too. The farmer would be directly benefited.

On the other hand, not only would the price of flour made from British wheat rise, so that the consumer of

[1] For a discussion of these administrative provisions, *see* the Report of the Committee on Economic Co-operation set up by the Imperial Conference.

that flour, and of the bread or biscuits made from it, would suffer, but at the same time the cost of the certificates would be an addition to the costs of the miller of imported wheat. Since imports of flour would also be restricted, there would be no competition to compel such millers to sell below cost. They would add the cost of the certificates to their selling prices, so that the price of flour made from imported wheat would also rise.

There would thus be a general rise in the price of bread, just as there would be under a tariff. Whereas a tariff would cause a scarcity of imported wheat by taxing its admission and so discouraging importation, the quota would reduce imports directly. The effect on the price of bread would be exactly similar.

It is possible, however, that the rise in bread prices might be less under the quota than it would be under a tariff. A tariff (in effect) takes money out of the pockets of the consumer and hands over some of the proceeds to the home producer. The rest goes into the Exchequer as revenue. But the Exchequer gets no revenue out of the quota. Everything that is taken from the consumer goes to the farmer. Thus the quota makes it possible to confer a given amount of benefit on the farmer at a smaller sacrifice from the consumer than would be entailed by a tariff. The argument against protecting agriculture by a tariff—that it means laying a burden on those who are least able to bear it—holds with less force against the quota. It does hold, since the quota would raise prices. But if the quota would raise prices less than the tariff, it holds to a lesser extent. So far the contention of quota enthusiasts is valid; it does to some extent get round the sound popular objection to taxes on food.

But it does not altogether escape this objection, and it does not in any way escape the general arguments against Protection which have been advanced throughout this book. The quota is protective—there can be no doubt of that. And it is only true it would let off the consumer much more lightly than a tariff, so long as the farmer is content to derive the same amount of benefit from a quota as he would have received from a probable tariff. The fact that a given benefit can be conferred at smaller consumers' sacrifice is only too likely to lead the farmer to press for greater benefit.

The actual amount of benefit conferred on the wheat farmer, and of sacrifice imposed on the consumer, depends on the figure at which the quota is fixed, in relation to the level at which the proportion of British wheat milled would have stood under Free Trade. The most definite of recent proposals about the size of the quota is that which was brought up at the Imperial Conference, when a quota of 15 per cent. was discussed. (Mr. Baldwin has talked about a guaranteed price of 50s. a quarter, but since he has never made it clear how far this is to be attained by a quota, and how far by a subsidy, his proposals do not offer a very firm basis for discussion.) If reference is made to the adjoined table, the origin of the Imperial Conference proposal is evident. It is generally assumed that only about two-thirds of the British crop is actually milled; the rest (of inferior quality) being used mainly for poultry food. If, then, we adopt this assumption, and calculate the proportion of British wheat milled to total wheat milled for each of the last nine years (assuming also that all imports are milled), we find that up to 1927 a quota of 15 per cent. could have been enforced just comfortably without causing any appreciable change in prices. If there had been a quota of this size in force up to 1927 it would have had very little effect. Sometimes it would have been necessary to import wheat at less favourable moments than actually proved to be possible, but on the whole no one would have been greatly affected except the inspectors who were employed to administer the scheme.

WHEAT—GREAT BRITAIN

	Home Production (million tons)	Acreage (millions)	Yield (cwts. per acre)	Imports (million tons)	Quota
1922	1·74	2·03	17·1	4·82	19·4
1923	1·59	1·80	17·6	5·04	17·4
1924	1·41	1·59	17·7	5·87	13·8
1925	1·41	1·55	18·3	4·85	16·2
1926	1·36	1·65	16·5	4·82	15·9
1927	1·48	1·70	17·5	5·52	15·2
1928	1·33	1·45	18·3	5·18	14·6
1929	1·33	1·33[1]	19·1[1]	5·59	13·7
1930	1·13	1·35[1]	15·9[1]	5·25	12·5

Quota = $\frac{2}{3}$ Home Production as % of $\frac{2}{3}$ Home Production + Imports.

Since 1928, however, the acreage under wheat in this country has shown a decided tendency to fall, and (even if we leave out of account the bad harvest of 1930) the normal proportion of British wheat milled cannot, on the same basis, be much more than 13 per cent. Further, the very low prices of 1930-1 have not yet exercised their full effect on acreage, so that it is reasonable to expect even lower percentages to be realised in the near future.

A 15 per cent. quota would thus be definitely protective. Its object would be to preserve in this country the same amount of wheat farming as was profitable a few years ago —more than is likely to be profitable in the future with the great expansion of wheat-growing overseas, particularly in the British Dominions. The average price of British wheat would be raised and the present contraction of wheat farming prevented—at the expense of the consumer.

Although the average price would be raised sufficiently to preserve wheat farming, and to insulate it from the shocks due to increasing world production, it does not follow that wheat growers would make just comfortable profits every year. Harvests vary considerably, and ex-

[1] Estimated.

[215]

ceptional harvests, whether they were exceptionally large, or exceptionally small, would cause a good deal of trouble. If the harvest was exceptionally bad (as in 1930) and the quota was maintained unaltered, the price of British wheat would rise very sharply indeed—for short supplies of British wheat would bring with them an artificial shortage of all kinds of wheat available for milling. The only way in which it would be possible to avert a famine (total supplies 8 per cent. below normal would be famine conditions) would be to draw on the wheat generally used as poultry food. This inferior wheat would have to be milled in order to get permits for the importation of wheat from abroad. The shortage of wheat for non-milling purposes might become distinctly serious, though of course it would be possible for farmers to import foreign wheat if it was not to be milled. However, the foreign wheat would be more expensive than the cheaper grades of English wheat normally are.

The result of this state of affairs would be, on the one hand, to start a demand for assistance to poultry farming—a demand which it would be very difficult to resist. Probably we should get a tariff on eggs; since eggs are not milled, and so do not pass through a "bottle-neck," a quota would be impossible. On the other hand, public opinion could hardly fail to be roused by a situation in which bread was expensive and bad, while the children's wheat was cast to chickens! There can be very little doubt that the quota would be revised.

If the quota was revised downwards in bad years, it would be very difficult to avoid revising it upwards in good years. In good years the normal quota would cease to place any check upon imports; for the proportion of British wheat milled would naturally exceed the quota. The quota would become inoperative, and British wheat prices would fall to their normal Free Trade figure, rather below the price of imported wheat. Now if farmers were prevented from securing the gains which would come to them from an invariable quota in years of scarcity, they would have a strong case for demanding protection against the losses the same quota would bring in years of plenty. There can be little doubt that the quota would be revised in this case too—upwards.

That the quota would have to be adjustable is admitted by some of its advocates, and is amply borne out by Continental experience (for example, by the history of the German quota). The dangers of an adjustable quota are even greater than those of a fixed quota. If farmers knew that the quota would be raised in the event of a good harvest, they would have a strong incentive to have good harvests: that is to say, to invest more and more in the production of wheat. If the acreage under wheat rose, it might be possible to prove that the quota, instead of merely preserving the industry, was stimulating it to an unhealthy and expensive expansion; and to refuse on that ground to change the quota. But it is rather much to expect that all governments would do even this. If the output rose through more intensive cultivation, it would be more difficult to distinguish chance from intention. And the more the quota was raised the greater would be the sacrifice of national wealth.

Thus, when we compare the tariff and the quota, we must grant to the quota certain real initial advantages. It does avoid placing taxes on a necessity of life, and benefits the farmer at a smaller sacrifice by the poorer classes. But against these initial advantages it has grave drawbacks on a longer view. After all, a tariff is a limited liability: prices cannot rise above the world level by more than the amount laid down publicly and openly in the tax. But the quota is not limited in that way; and if it contains, as it probably does, a self-expanding principle, the ultimate sacrifice which it entails may be very heavy.

A Quota for Dominion Wheat

If the home production of wheat were protected by a quota, it is obvious that Dominion producers would also demand some kind of protection; and it would be difficult to refuse it to them. A quota for Dominion wheat has, in fact, been demanded by Canada and Australia as an essential measure of Imperial Economic Co-operation; if it were to be granted to them, what would happen?

A Dominion wheat quota raises different questions from a home wheat quota, mainly for the reason which was discussed above (in Chapter XII) that the Empire has an export surplus of wheat. However we try to protect Dominion wheat, whether by a tariff or by a quota, we are faced with the same dilemma—though perhaps the quota raises it in an even stronger form. On the one hand the Dominions may sell their wheat in a genuinely competitive manner through the ordinary grain markets; and in that case, no quota, however high, would benefit the Dominion farmer, nor indeed would it appreciably damage the home consumer. Even if the quota were fixed at 100 per cent. (that is to say, if the import of foreign wheat were *prohibited*) the price of Dominion wheat in England could not rise appreciably above the world price of wheat. It would be kept down by the competition of that Dominion wheat which could not gain an entry to the British market and had to accept the world price abroad. As soon as the price in England showed any tendency to rise, dealers in Dominion wheat would sell in England rather than elsewhere. There would be no restriction of supply and therefore no rise in price.

On the other hand, there can be very little doubt that the quota would give an immense stimulus to the revival of that system of controlling sales which has been practised in recent years by the Canadian pools. As things have been, the pools have practically broken down; but a quota for Dominion wheat would offer new advantages to be gained from that kind of organisation. If the Canadians could come to an arrangement with other Dominion producers, they could refuse to sell to British dealers below a fixed price, and dump the rest of their crop abroad for what it would fetch. Of course, exactly the same possibility would arise with a tariff on foreign wheat and Imperial Preference; but with a quota the danger is much more serious. The tariff would limit the extent to which the price of wheat sold to Britain could be raised above the world price; but with the quota there would be no automatic limitation at all.

Thus the Dominion quota runs a grave risk of falling between two stools; either it would be totally ineffective or it would be so dangerous that even a protectionist government could hardly face it. The authors of the report to the Imperial Conference were certainly not biased against the quota; but it is clear that they had some inkling of the true position. The United Kingdom delegation obviously set their faces firmly against any scheme which would enable the Dominion producers to fix the price of wheat on the English market; any guarantee was to be subject to the condition that the quota wheat must be supplied at world prices.

At first sight this condition would appear sufficient to prevent the price of wheat to the English market being fixed at Winnipeg; it appears to destroy the dangers of the scheme, though of course this would imply at the same time doing away with any advantage which it could confer on the Dominions. But Mr. Bennett did not turn down the scheme in this form; and it is possible that he was right to consider it. For everything depends on what is meant by "world price." If by "world price" it is meant that the Dominion pools must sell their quota wheat at a price which does not differ from the prices at which other kinds of wheat are available by more than the normal difference, then this would be a perfect guarantee to the British consumer. But if it means (and the chances certainly are that it would be interpreted in this way) that the price of Canadian or Australian wheat sold to England must not exceed the price of Canadian or Australian wheat on the outside market, then the "world price" clause is not watertight. The Dominions would not be allowed to sell on the Continent at lower prices than they sold in England; but there would be nothing to prevent them selling in England at any price they liked, however high, provided they were prepared to accept the consequence that such prices would prevent them selling wheat elsewhere.

This suggestion looks fantastic; but it looks much less fantastic when the recent history of the pools is borne in mind. In the winter of 1929-30 the Canadian pools did attempt to hold up prices: for a few months they refused to sell at the market price and the export of wheat from Canada was largely shut off. The reason for this conduct was partly the fact that the market price was unremunerative and partly that the pools were acting on a blind faith that prices would recover. Prices did not recover; and in the spring of 1930 Canada was forced to resume selling, since the pools could afford to hold on no longer. It is very interesting to speculate what would have happened during these months if Canada had had the guaranteed market in Great Britain which would be secured to her by the quota. Her attempt to dictate prices would not have broken down so speedily, for although she would still have been unable to sell to foreign markets, England would have been forced to go on buying at the price demanded. Since receipts would have been coming in for these sales, the pools would not have got into financial difficulties so early; nevertheless, stocks of wheat would have been piling up, and ultimately there would have been a breakdown. Yet this breakdown need not have taken the form it actually did take, of a resumption of sales at a competitive level. There would have been an easier and more attractive way out: prices could have been raised further on the British market!

Of course, the precise conditions of 1930 will not recur; but it is not at all unlikely that the same sort of thing may happen again. Up to the present the British consumer has been protected against manipulation of the grain market by the presence of ample supplies which were not under monopolistic control. The Dominion quota is only too likely to deprive him of this safeguard; and the condition about "world prices" would be a very poor exchange indeed.

Import Boards

A quota involves more radical interference with imports than a tariff does; import boards are more radical still. This is not necessarily an objection; we have seen that abnormal conditions on the market might easily lead a quota into difficulties; if imports have to be arbitrarily restricted, it is clearly better to try and foresee trouble, making adjustments to it in advance, rather than to make adjustments by a procedure which is only used on exceptional occasions, and which might not come into action until the damage had been done. In practice, a quota would probably mean fairly frequent governmental interference on the grain market; from that it would be only a step to complete State control—importation by a State monopoly—and it would be a step that under these circumstances might not be undesirable.

But of course the import board scheme has a very different origin from that of the quota; it is specifically a Socialist proposal, and has been put forward by sections of the Labour Party as the Socialist alternative to tariffs. And we can distinguish in the scheme two sides—the Socialist and the Protectionist. It started as a purely Socialist device, little stress being laid on its possibilities as a method of protecting the British farmer. It was contended that governmental operation of wheat imports would actually be cheaper, over a period of years, than the competitive system. The consumer would get his bread at a lower price, owing to the superior efficiency of Socialism.

More recently, however, there has been a change of tune. We are now told that "wheat and cereals present special circumstances at the present moment," and the import board now emerges as a means of protecting the home producer against low prices. In its modern shape the import board would not only buy imports: it would buy home produced supplies too. A fixed price considerably higher than the world price would be guaranteed to the British farmer, and this subsidy would be paid by raising the whole level of wheat prices to the consumer, in exactly the same way as they would be raised by the quota.[1]

Now these two sides of the scheme raise distinctly different questions. There is first the question of the economy of State management of imports—is it in fact the case that the competitive action of dealers on the grain and other markets is wasteful, so that unified control could effect economies, and supply the consumer more cheaply? This is the question raised by the import board in its first form. It is not one which has much directly to do with Free Trade. As long as the board did not attempt to give the home producer higher prices than it gave to the foreign producer, it would not be acting in a protective manner. Its actions might be or might not be for the good of the community, but it would not be liable to criticism from Free Traders as such. But as soon as its policy changed, as soon as it began to regulate imports so as artificially to raise the price of home products, then it would be protective. Now it is conceivable that an import board might not act in this way; but it is overwhelmingly probable that, in fact, it would do so. The rapid conversion of the import board prophets to protectionism as soon as agricultural prices started to fall, is an unfavourable indication of the policy their creation would be likely to adopt.

It is unnecessary at this stage of the discussion to enlarge upon the evils of such a policy. An import board by so acting would become an indirect means of Protection; its action would bring all the particular evils of Protection. It would not be supplying consumers by the cheapest way which lay within its reach; instead it would be utilising its privileged position to bolster up an industry where resources were being used in a wasteful manner.

However, this is far from being a final argument against

[1] This development of the import board scheme can be seen very clearly by comparing the evidence given in 1925 by Mr. E. F. Wise and other Labour representatives to the Royal Commission on Food Prices, with Mr. Wise's article " An Alternative to Tariffs " (*Political Quarterly*, April 1930), and with the propaganda of the Mosley party.

import boards. Even if the import board led to national loss through its protectionism it might bring sufficient gain through its socialism to balance the account. An import board which did not discriminate between home and foreign producers would be better than one which did; but if it can be shown that any sort of an import board would be better than an unregulated market, then even a bad import board would be an improvement on the present situation, though of course a good import board would be better still. Are the advantages of State control sufficient to outweigh the dangers of accompanying Protection? This question must now be examined.

The direct trading advantages which are claimed for the import board—those things which, it is hoped, would enable it to cheapen the supply of bread to the consumer— seem to fall into three groups. First, it is held that it would secure certain direct economies from trading on a large scale. These are not usually made very precise, but presumably they include lower freight rates for large orders, and economies in personnel owing to a reduced number of transactions. Second, great gains would be made by eliminating speculation, and reducing the fluctuations of prices. Third, it would reduce the danger of the British buyer being squeezed by the formation of large co-operative selling organisations, such as the American Farm Board, the Canadian pools, and the Russian export monopoly. These three arguments raise rather different issues, and had best be examined separately.

The first argument, about direct economies, can probably be admitted. The obvious direct costs of transport and distribution would probably be somewhat reduced by buying on a larger scale. Nevertheless, the fact that economies in a particular direction can be made by a change does not necessarily mean that the change is desirable. These economies might be offset by other disadvantages. It must be remembered that this sort of economy does not need an import board for it to be realised. It is perfectly open to private buyers, in particular to millers. If there are very large economies to be got in this way—economies which can be reaped without any compensating disadvantage—it seems impossible to believe that the large millers would not be exploiting them to the full. And there is quite enough competition to ensure that they will be passed on to the public.

Not even this very qualified approval can be given to the second argument. This is much more important than the first: it is the very heart of the import board proposal. And it is wholly fallacious, arising from a complete misunderstanding of the way speculation works. It seems to be considered that the continual fluctuations in the price of wheat on the markets are due to the action of speculators: that these fluctuations, which make production so difficult for farmers, are simply the result of speculators' endeavours to make an utterly unearned profit. The large fortunes sometimes made by speculators are simply an addition to the price of wheat, bringing therefore a loss to the consumer, and intensifying the difficulties of the producer.

But a little reflection on the problem confronting the wheat markets shows how radically wrong is this conception. The supply of wheat is derived from a large number of different sources, producing under different conditions and with harvests at different times. Since it is impossible to be certain how much new wheat will be coming forward in any particular future month, stocks have to be kept to avoid a shortage. But the keeping of stocks is an expensive business, and if costs are to be kept down, stocks must be kept at a minimum. As soon as the probability that future supplies will be sufficient increases, it is desirable that stocks should be reduced; as soon as the first signs of a shortage appear on the horizon, stocks ought to be increased. The day-to-day fluctuations of prices do thus have a most useful effect: they ensure that enough wheat is kept back to meet the most probable future needs, and not more than enough.

Even if there were no speculators on the market—even if all buyers bought wheat because they wanted to use it and all sellers sold wheat which was actually in their possession—these fluctuations in prices would still take place. As soon as holders began to anticipate a future scarcity they would demand higher prices before they released their stocks; as soon as they had cause to expect that prices in future would be lower than they had expected, they would release wheat on more favourable terms. Prices would still be tossed about, varying with each new piece of information which came in about the prospects of future demand and supply—and so large is the number of different influences which may affect these prospects that the changes in price would be very frequent.

Price-fluctuations serve another purpose quite as important as the regulation of stocks. If there is a prospect of a short harvest in one part of the world, prices will rise, and this will encourage the planting of more wheat in other regions where the season is later. It is sometimes suggested that the relative steadiness of the demand for wheat, and the fact that the world's annual supply does not as a general rule show very large variations, indicate that these price fluctuations are unnecessary. But the truth is the exact opposite. It is the price fluctuations which prevent excessive divergences between demand and supply.

Now, of course, these fluctuations give an opportunity to speculators. Anyone who thinks that the market has not estimated the future course of prices correctly can buy or sell forward and get a profit if he is right. His action will influence stock-holding, and if he is right it will influence it in the right direction. Skilled speculators who are better informed than the average dealer confer an advantage in the shape of a general reduction of costs to set off against the profits they make.

All speculators, however, are not skilled. Ignorant speculators influence prices, on balance, in a direction which is not desirable. Yet the professional speculator is always ready to counteract this; if prices fall for no sound reason, a well-informed person will buy; if they rise for no sound reason, he will sell; and in either case pocket an easy profit. But he is making this profit out of the ignorant speculator, not out of the producer or out of the consuming public. It is as a matter of fact unquestionable that professional speculators make the bulk of their profits out of their less careful brethren. The average price of wheat in this country, over a period of years, seems actually to be below the obvious costs of bringing wheat here. Even if we refuse to believe (what the statistics suggest, and what is quite possible) that the skilled speculators gain less than the unskilled speculators lose, there can, at any rate, be no doubt that the net profit of all speculators taken together is so small that it is not discernible statistically. On the other hand, the social gain from speculation is clear and undeniable. Stocks are reduced; and the public's need for wheat is satisfied from those sources which, in the particular circumstances of the year, can supply it most cheaply. Certainly this does not look a very hopeful field for economy.

The import board, it appears, would eliminate speculation by making long-term contracts with Dominion and foreign producers. For example, Great Britain would arrange to take a considerable proportion of the Canadian crop (say 40 per cent. of normal production) at a price fixed in advance for periods of five years or so. Certainly this might make it possible to effect economies in transport. But how would the price be fixed? It would be impossible to foresee the future course of wheat prices for so long a period as five years. The fair price would simply have to be guessed. Instead of purchasing at a price which is the result of informed estimation of all the factors in the situation, the import board would buy in the dark. It is not a method which appeals to one as an advance in economic organisation.

It is true that events might conceivably come to the rescue. There might develop an unsuspected tendency for prices to rise. If we had been buying wheat on long contracts in the early days of the War, a price fixed in peace-time would have been very satisfactory indeed to this country when the inflation of prices began. But this would have been sheer luck; and the chances of a similar rise in prices are not now very great—nor is the event very desirable. (The rise in prices which is probable as we recover from the present depression would no doubt be thoroughly discounted by sellers.) It is far more likely that the downward trend of recent years will, on the average, be continued; and in this case luck would be heavily against the import board. It would steadily be doing a great deal worse for the consumer than the free market would have done.

Even if we leave out of account this probability, it is still true that long-term buying would be unwise. For since there would be no objective criterion by which to fix prices, the price would have to be what the seller regarded as "fair." And it is notorious that in a risky trade sellers have generally rather ambitious notions of what constitutes a fair price. If the price was considerably below what they might expect to get in favourable years, they would not agree to it. But if the price was not considerably below, it would be unfair to the buyer.

Taking all these things into account it is most unlikely that an import board, supposing (as we may suppose) that it was composed of sensible and competent people, would be inclined to purchase much of its wheat on long-term contracts. If it did so, it would perhaps make certain savings in freights, but the risk of making bad bargains would be so great that it would not be worth while to try and get those savings. On the whole, a sensible import board would buy through the ordinary grain markets. By so doing it would avoid serious risks; but it would also lose the possibility of making any economies. It is hard to see that such a board would have any *raison d'être*.

Thus, on examination, the first two arguments for the economy of import boards prove empty. Is anything else to be said of the third—the fear of sellers' monopoly? At the time when the import board was first proposed, this was the most respectable argument put forward in its favour. Co-operative pools, which in practice were selling monopolies, did seem to be spreading throughout the more important grain-producing countries. It was not unreasonable to expect that their power would grow, and that there would soon be a real danger of overseas producers endeavouring to dictate the price of wheat, themselves abolishing the free market. Against so serious a danger some defence would be highly desirable; and it did not seem impossible that national negotiation might lead to better results than individual trading.

Nevertheless, it is just as well that Great Britain did not act on this view, and set up an import board five or six years ago. For these expectations have been totally falsified by events. The co-operative pools did attempt to control prices, but their action has been unsuccessful. Excepting for the case of Russia, they could not effectively control production, and this has been their fatal weakness. (Russia, on the other hand, has shown no desire to restrict production, though she might have been able to do so had she wished!) Any attempt by a selling organisation to maintain prices by holding back supplies only provided an additional incentive to farmers to produce more. The stocks in the hands of the pools increased, and their expenses naturally increased at the same time. This has been a very effective check on their activities.

It is, of course, conceivable that if an arrangement were made between the various exporting countries, so that a world control was introduced, then the consumer might be seriously penalised. But the recent meeting of representatives of the principal wheat exporting countries in London (May 1931) did not suggest that this danger is very pressing. The obstacles to such an arrangement are obviously immense. It does not appear at all probable that they will be overcome.

The truth of the matter to-day is evident: the British consumer has nothing to expect from any sort of an import board. In 1925 it could be suggested with some show of sense that an import board would serve as a protection to the consumer against exploitation. It cannot be seriously suggested in 1931. An import board would be far more likely to bolster up those failing overseas monopolies against which it was originally intended as a means of defence.

The economic arguments against the import board are thus overwhelming. It is impossible to see (at least in the present juncture) how it could be more efficient than the present system. Probably it would be much less efficient. And beyond this direct question of efficiency come its protectionist tendencies. It is quite clear from the writings of those who favour the proposal that they do not expect the board to buy where it can get wheat on most favourable terms, but that they expect it, and wish it, to be influenced by political considerations. Inevitably this must lay a burden on the consumer, of exactly the same kind as he would suffer from a tariff.

And—apart from these economic arguments—how grave are the political objections to such a policy! Imagine Canada demanding that the contract should be revised in her favour. Should we not have our Imperialist Press insisting that we must not exploit the Dominions, and then (only too probably) when the British public found it had been exploited, countering with an injunction to the board to squeeze some foreign country? The maintenance of peaceable international relations when the livelihood and the comfort of large sections of each people were directly and obviously concerned in disputes, would not be easy. Can we be sure that our Pact of Paris, or even our British Commonwealth, could stand up to such a strain? If we desire a socialist policy, surely we might begin with changes more hopeful and less dangerous.

CHAPTER XVII

THE CASE REVIEWED

THE many projects of fiscal change now current and the arguments supporting them have been examined. The first point emerging is that these various projects, though often praised by the same persons, under the general title of Tariff Reform, are different in aim and working, and are often diametrically opposed. Those who criticise the present fiscal policy of Britain are at one in that; otherwise they are divided, though often unconsciously, into hostile camps; their prescriptions do not blend.

Protection and preferential trade, for instance, though habitually combined, are at daggers drawn. It is the protective policy of the Dominions for their industries which, more than anything else, blocks their proposals for preference; they cannot, consistently with a policy of developing under Protection every industry which Protection can make possible for them, offer to Britain assured markets for manufactures; nothing but assured markets could compensate Britain for a sacrifice of trading connections and interests elsewhere. It would be as difficult for Britain to combine a policy of Protection for her agriculture with one of giving markets to the Dominions. Statesmen who describe the pouring in of foreign goods into Britain as if the goods were a destructive pest to be kept out by defences, and in the same speech urge development of imperial trade as a mutual enrichment, may not be conscious of how much mental agility they have. But the agility—and inconsistency of thought—are there, and the inconsistency is fundamental.

Protection and revenue are aims as diverse as Protection and preference. In so far as a tariff keeps goods out, it cannot bring in revenue; in so far as it brings in revenue, it does so by letting in goods. This does not mean that the same tariff may not, to some extent, accomplish both objects; give some Protection and bring some revenue. But the kind of duty that is best suited for one purpose is ill suited for the other; any actual duty will either be peculiarly harmful or useless as Protection or peculiarly oppressive as taxation.

Protection and retaliation are yet more opposed. The prospect that, in the course of commercial bargaining between governments, tariffs might be alternately raised and lowered, would destroy the confidence which is the basis of enterprise.

This diversity of aims does not mean that each kind of tariff reform is exclusive of any other. But it would clearly be impossible to achieve to any appreciable extent all these aims at one and the same time. In fact, as the argument of each successive chapter has shown, little, if anything, can be gained along any one of them. Nothing can be gained commensurate with the harm that is risked. Selective Protection can only change the channels of trade, and benefit one trade by a tax on consumers or on other trades. General Protection, in the long run, can only benefit trades in the home market at the expense of exports, or, if combined with systematic dumping, can maintain some export trades at the expense of others and of the home consumer. Defence of "infant industries" is an economic theory now exploded by facts; the infants never grow up, or if they do, use their manly strength to maintain Protection. For maintenance of the standard of life of any high-wage country against competition from low-wage countries, Protection is either unnecessary or unavailing; in the particular country of Britain, with a high standard dependent on specialisation, large exports, and cheap imports, Protection means an attack on the standard of life, not a defence of it. The economies of mass production in certain industries are undoubted, but a guarantee of the home market to home producers is neither necessary nor sufficient to secure these economies; the mass production argument is just another stalking horse for Protection in its crudest form. Defence of particular industries on political grounds, such as preparedness for war or maintenance of a peasantry, must be judged on other than economic reasonings; in general the game seems worth less than the candle. "Dumping" in any reasonable sense of the term is a rare process. In the exceptional cases in which dumping is an evil to the country receiving goods below cost, remedy by tariffs is a cure worse than the evil. In the still rarer cases in which at a particular juncture a tariff might, by affecting the export surplus or the price-level or the supply of gold, produce a net advantage to the country imposing it, some other method is more effective and less dangerous because less permanent. The case for a revenue tariff, so long as it is a revenue tariff and nothing else, with no protective influence or purpose, stands on a different footing from other tariff proposals. But the weight of argument is still against looking to a great extension of taxes on imports as a means of balancing our national budget. Import boards and quota schemes, in so far as they are instruments alternative to tariffs for covertly serving the same purpose, have the same vices, and other private evils of their own.

To say, therefore, that the different projects of fiscal change now current are inconsistent with one another, is not to say that some are good and some are bad. They are all bad. They are also mutually inconsistent.

Another and more general inconsistency underlies the thought of most of their advocates. In relation to business matters, nearly all those advocates, to borrow the words of the late Lord Balfour,[1] would regard the incompetence of Parliament not only as a plausible working hypothesis but as a fundamental axiom. Nearly all of them would cordially

[1] *Economic Notes on Insular Free Trade*, by A. J. Balfour, p. 6 (1903). Lord Balfour, it may be noted, only urged that *Parliament* could hardly assume its own incompetence as a fundamental axiom. He said nothing of the National Confederation of Employers or the Federation of British Industries, who can and generally do make this assumption. The statements made here do not apply of course to Protectionists who are also socialists.

agree, moreover, that a nation cannot make itself prosperous by Act of Parliament. Yet they are prepared to
trust to Parliament or rather to thrust upon Parliament the
most delicate economic task of all, that of guiding the
industrial development of the country.

Material prosperity depends, not on Acts of Parliament,
but on applying to best advantage the brains and labour of
the country to its natural resources. How is "best advantage" to be judged? In a Free Trade country it is left to
be determined by results; if the business men of a country
left to themselves secure the necessary supplies of a particular article A in a country, not by making A, but by making
more than the country wants of B and selling B abroad for
currency with which to buy A, they can and will do this
only because it pays best; because thus the labour and
resources of the country are being used with least friction
and least effort in relation to output. In a Free Trade
country development of industry is guided by business men
sticking to their business, applying capital and labour so
as always to get, over industry as a whole, the maximum
result from the minimum of effort; the separate industries
of the country compete with another in economic efficiency
alone. In a protectionist country the development of
industry is guided by politicians, or by business men
become politicians, by business men organising press cam-
paigns and lobbies, getting secret or open representatives in
Parliament; the separate industries compete with one
another, not in efficiency of production, but in political
influence and in the technique of pulling wires. This is the
worst effect—and an inevitable effect—of abandonment of
the general policy of Free Trade; the framing of tariffs
brings business men out of their offices and factories into
politics, and clogs the burdened political machine with
unfamiliar business; it is a misuse alike of business ability
and of political machinery. Of the United States of America
it is fair to say that it is a country prosperous in virtue of its
Free Trade, and badly governed in part at least through its
Protection. For the United Kingdom it is also fair to claim

that Free Trade leaves its government still one of the most truly national, least sectional and most honest in the world.

The judgment to which examination of tariff proposals leads to-day is therefore the same as the judgment pronounced in this country, when the issue was last fully debated, twenty-five to thirty years ago. The changes which have affected Britain's economic condition since then do not affect that judgment.

The first of the three principal changes noted in the opening chapter of this volume was the apparent decline of British prosperity. That is fundamentally due to difficulties cramping the growth of international trade, and cutting down Britain's share in such trade. It would be aggravated, not lightened, by the fresh obstacle to international trade with Britain, which a British tariff would present. The prolonged heavy unemployment which is the most conspicuous symptom of our economic ill-health to-day arises from diseases for which Protection is no cure.

The second change noted above—the development of economic nationalism—has been a contributory cause of British troubles. But a tariff is no answer to a tariff. The answer to foreign tariffs, which some have hoped to find in spreading Free Trade within the British Empire, cannot be made; the newer countries of the Empire are leaders of high Protection.

The last of the three changes is the growing activity of the State in the economic sphere, and its more frequent interference with private enterprise. It is arguable that this interference and the taxes needed to support it are a handicap to the power of British industry to compete with industry in other lands. Whether or not this is ever so, the handicap, so far as it cramps British industry as a whole, is not one which a British tariff can remove. It is arguable, again, that the State to-day is not only more active in the economic sphere, but also, through growth of administrative technique, more competent to act now than ever before. That may be so in general, but is, of course, no argument for the State's undertaking, by tariffs, the direction of industry and trade. Each particular form of State action must still be justified and judged on its merits.

It is against the particular form of State action known as tariffs and against alternative devices for the same purpose, that the arguments in this volume are directed. They are not directed against all action by the State and are not arguments for *laisser-faire* in general. Still less are they arguments against all change in existing industrial methods and in the policies of those who organise production or are leaders of labour. They are based, not on the view that all is now well with Britain, or will become well by going on in the old ways, but on the view that, while many things are now going ill and need remedy, tariffs are the wrong prescription. One of the greatest dangers in the prominence now given to proposals for fiscal change is that they stand in the way of more accurate diagnosis of our maladies and may delay application of true remedies. Though prescription of such remedies lies outside the scope of this volume, the need for some remedy is urgent and can be stated shortly.

One of the cardinal facts of Britain's economic position among nations is that she started first in the race of industrial development. At one time this was an advantage; her industries, her shipping, and her commercial connections became established without serious competition; in providing other countries with the products of a new industrialism, she reaped for a while the advantages of something like a monopoly; even after others began to follow down the industrial path, she played a large part in providing them, both to their profit and her own, with equipment and with financial resources. By helping others to become rich, she made for herself richer customers.

But Britain's early start held also another possibility—of disadvantage later. Other countries began their industrial careers at a higher stage of technical progress; they could profit by British experience and her pioneering errors; they could lay out mines and factories and towns and railways and roads with later knowledge. Britain also could modernise herself, but not so easily or always so completely. Mines and railways and even towns can hardly be laid out afresh. Moreover, in so far as industry is based on coal, the country which starts first works soonest through its easiest coal; with the main alternative sources of power—oil, natural gas, water—Britain is less well supplied than many others. From being pure advantage Britain's early start has become more and more a liability.

By its psychological reactions also this early prosperity has now become a source of weakness. Britain has become accustomed to a standard of life in advance of all her neighbours. That was easy and inevitable for the time. But it is not clear that there is anything in the material resources or other permanent features of Britain to maintain, for her people, an advantage over the rest of Europe. She now has to face as well the competition of low-standard countries in the Far East and elsewhere learning to work the same machines. She has to face that competition in export markets, and cannot escape it by a tariff.

To these secular causes of growing strain on Britain, must be added causes arising in the War and its aftermath. They have been so admirably described in the Report of the Committee on Finance and Industry[1] that here a few sentences suffice. The world as a whole has been disordered; there has been a growth of tariffs and other restrictions on international trade; Britain, merged in the world economy more completely than any other great nation, has been the chief sufferer. The War and its aftermath have called for changes and re-adjustments; Britain has always been slow to change. To those general causes of difficulties, British policy since the War has added two specific causes. By the return to the gold standard in 1925, British costs of production were raised in relation to costs elsewhere; her export trades were handicapped. Whether or not the advantages of this policy in other directions outweighed this loss, it is needless now to discuss; Britain in the past has depended not only on her export trades but on her standing in finance,

[1] Chapters V and VI.

[236]

and for that the return to gold may well then have seemed worth while. But the return to old ways with gold was not accompanied by the return to old ways that it called for in other directions; there was no re-consideration of money incomes and costs of production. Instead, with the return to gold, has come a second policy, of an insurance system for unemployment, fostering rigidity, alike of money wages and of occupations, where flexibility was the one salvation.

By these specific policies Britain's position has been made more hard. It would not have been easy in any case; she cannot now afford to do anything but make the fullest use of all her powers. That she has not yet learned to do. This could be shown in many ways; two illustrations here suffice.

There are two points on which the thinking of our leaders of industry, on each side of the wage bargain, is definitely and harmfully behind the times. There is the attitude of many trade unionists to rationalisation and machinery, and there is the attitude of many, if not most, employers towards the educational system.

The first of these has been sufficiently illustrated by the dispute on the six or eight loom system in Lancashire. The high standard of living in America is related directly and obviously to the use of machinery there. A workman digging out foundations with a spade, has in that day added less to the wealth of the world than one who has dug out six times as much with a machine; what he adds to the wealth of the world each day is the upper limit of what without cheating any man can claim for his day's reward. The Americans, as a friendly observer has said, are too wisely lazy to do anything themselves that a machine can do as well for them. The English workmen, so long as they oppose replacement of men by machines and other lightenings of human toil, must be content with the rewards of drudgery. The world as a whole is much richer now than in Britain's heyday. It may, as Mr. Keynes has suggested, be destined, in a few more generations of technical progress and birth control, to find itself startlingly, almost embarrassingly

[237]

richer than to-day.[1] But the embarrassed grandchildren of Mr. Keynes' fancy do not seem likely to be found living in Lancashire.

The desolating influence of restrictions on efficiency is a commonplace. The second point mentioned above is less familiar. For two generations the recruiting of men for public administration in Britain has been based on the educational system of the country and has followed its developments; the principle of the Civil Service has been to skim off for the various types of work to be done—clerical, executive, administrative—the best fruits of the educational process at each stage as they mature. Recruiting for business administration has paid little or no attention to the educational system; it has continued to be based on the practice of coming in at the bottom and working up; in doing so it has neglected, unfortunately for business, that particular development of the educational system known as scholarships. In the days of closed universities and restricted scholarships, recruiting from the bottom did not prevent business from getting its share of men of high natural ability; such men, if born in poor stations, were forced to begin earning as soon as possible; entering business life at the bottom they might, with luck, rise to be captains of industry. Now, however, high natural ability, wherever it crops up, earns scholarships—which take the clever boy from elementary school to secondary school, from two years at secondary school to four years, from school at last to the university. The abler he is, the further he rises up the educational ladder—and, the further he rises, the less likely is he nowadays to go into business, because the immediate offer that business makes to him, if he has nothing but ability to commend him, will seldom compare with what he can get in teaching or the Civil Service or other professions. This does not apply to technical posts; it does not of course apply to all firms. But it does apply very widely; many firms, even of those who take university men, make offers

[1] " Some Economic Possibilities for Our Grandchildren." (*Nation and Athenæum*, 11th and 18th October 1930.)

that cannot attract any but the weaker men; the tradition of beginning trained men and untrained alike at the bottom stands in the way of their getting the best of the trained ones. For a generation and more of growing secondary education and scholarships, the educational system has been steadily draining natural ability away from business, giving to university teaching, to school teaching, to the Civil Service, journalism, law and other professions more than their fair share of this rare quality. In that same generation the need of high ability highly trained has become greater in business than ever before. The quality of brains and training that made easy money for Britain in Victorian days will not keep her abreast of her Georgian competitors.

These are illustrations only, given here because they can be stated shortly, of ways in which Britain to-day is behind the times, is not making the best of herself. There are much larger and more difficult issues, on which decision and action are needed, but on which, within the limits of this chapter, no firm conclusion can be stated.

There is, for instance, the problem of price stabilisation. The years since the War have been a period of extreme instability of money and prices. There have been violent upward and downward swings of the general level of prices. There have been as notable changes in the relative prices of particular commodities, largely as a result of advances in the technique of production. These movements of prices have given rise to proposals to prevent or limit them—as regards particular articles, by schemes restricting the supply, as regards the general level of prices, by plans of monetary or banking reform. Is this price stabilisation a good policy or a bad policy? Here general prices and particular prices stand on a different footing.

For the stabilisation of general prices, if that can be achieved, there is much to be said, as it is said forcibly and persuasively, in the Report of the Committee on Finance and Industry; though there are also things which can be said forcibly and persuasively against it; the issue is one calling for full discussion by economists. Stabilisation of individual prices is almost certainly a will-o'-the-wisp leading to misfortune. The restriction schemes for particular articles have for the most part broken down, and in breaking have been a further cause of instability.[1] Their experience raises the doubt whether the present economic system will work if the price mechanism is taken out of it. Demand and supply in the long run are adjusted and production is directed only by movements of prices; if what should be flexible in the economic system is made rigid, there comes disequilibrium and a breaking strain. Is not that what is happening with labour and its price in Britain to-day—a rigidity of money wages out of accord with economic conditions, leading to incurable disequilibrium? It is a rigidity which along with other rigidities—of occupation and place of work—is dangerously fostered by our insurance system. In the early days of the East India trade, half the spice crop was sometimes burned to keep up the price of the rest; some modern restriction schemes have resorted to the same device. It is not altogether fanciful to see in the trade unionism and the insurance system of to-day a restriction scheme for labour, in which manhood is burned in the fire of unemployment.

There is again the general issue of what has come to be called "planning" as against *laisser-faire* in industry. So far as "planning" involves price regulation, a judgment on it has already been suggested. So far as it involves greater unity of purpose and co-ordination of resources in allied businesses, broader views, concentration of power, there is much to be said for it. This is essentially a matter for the leaders of industry. But the help of the State, though views may differ as to the nature and extent of this help, must not be excluded.

These larger problems of planning and of prices have been named here because it is vital that they should be discussed

---

[1] *Report of Committee on Finance and Industry*, p. 136. As is stated here, restriction schemes have been applied, "either in particular areas or over the world, to rubber, sugar, zinc, coffee, nitrate, copper, iron and steel, tin, wheat, cotton."

and settled. The weaknesses of Britain's economic position have been named, because it is vital that they should not be forgotten. Full discussion either of the weaknesses or their remedies falls outside the scope of this volume; its subject is tariffs, not the whole economic problem of Britain. But the general considerations here briefly set out do furnish one fresh general argument against a policy of tariffs. The causes of Britain's exceptional chronic unemployment from 1922 to 1929, as has been said elsewhere, "may nearly all be summed up under the general head of growing rigidity —of wages and occupations—in a world of increasing changefulness." "Adversity has replaced prosperity in Britain, not because we in Britain have changed, but because we have not changed—to meet a new situation."[1] Protection is at bottom always a policy of resisting change, of accepting and condoning rigidities.

This volume is concerned with tariffs, not with the whole economic problem. It is concerned also with Britain, not with the world at large, with permanent policies, not with expedients for an emergency. Little has been said in it, accordingly, of the slump of 1930 or of how to cure or prevent such calamities. The slump of 1930 is a calamity common to all the world. It is a calamity for whose passing away in due course we may fairly hope.

But just as consideration of the whole economic problem for Britain furnishes a standpoint from which a policy of tariffs can be judged and must be condemned, so consideration of the world slump of 1930 leads to a similar conclusion. The world slump has shown how closely the fortunes of all countries are now linked. If such disasters are to be prevented or lightened in future, that can be done only by growing international co-operation in the economic sphere. To help such co-operation tariffs can do nothing. They can and must do much to make it harder. For tariffs designed to stop trade are a form of compulsory non-co-operation and boycott.

[1] *Causes and Cures of Unemployment*, pp. 50, 58, by Sir William Beveridge (Longmans, 1931).

Q

The examination of tariffs in this volume began with a citation from the leader of British economists in the last generation. The examination leads to a conclusion which cannot be put more forcibly than in a citation from his most brilliant successor in this generation: "We must hold to Free Trade, in its widest interpretation, as an inflexible dogma, to which no exception is admitted, wherever the decision rests with us. We must hold to this even where we receive no reciprocity of treatment and even in those rare cases where by infringing it we could in fact obtain a direct economic advantage. We should hold to Free Trade as a principle of international morals, and not merely as a doctrine of economic advantage."[1] This was one of Mr. Keynes' three "dogmas of Peace" in 1923, a life-line through the dangers and disorders of the post-War world. Though in later days it has at times lost its appeal for Mr. Keynes himself, it has not done so for many of those to whom his outlook on international affairs was then an inspiration. It is a life-line to-day, as it was eight years ago.

To many this seems to be Britain's dark hour. She has built a world-wide Empire; to-day in one high Conference after another she must ask herself what Empire means and to what end it leads. She has built a world-wide commerce, and been a pillar of world finance; to-day she finds commerce slipping from her, and her financial structure still rocks from a blast which threatened its foundations. In these anxieties two things are certain. Britain's later place in the political structure of the world will depend less on constitutional forms and phrases than on how far she is able to keep alive, in the constituent nations of the Commonwealth, a sense of unity in ideals, and a common faith that the purpose of government is not the power of governors but the freedom of citizens. Her place in the economic life of humanity will depend at last, not on any fiscal device,

[1] "Reconstruction in Europe: The Underlying Principles," by J. M. Keynes (*Manchester Guardian Commercial Supplement*, Section Twelve, 4th Jan. 1923).

but on her efficiency, on how completely she can slough off bad habits and keep young in the changing world.

Whether she can do that completely or little or not at all, whether the great underlying economic forces work for her or against her, the fiscal policy that still suits her best is not doubtful. If her future be dark, it will be less dark, and if her future be bright, it will be more bright, with Free Trade than without it. The policy that to-day still serves best the material interests of Britain is one that keeps her where the founders of her prosperity strove to place her—in the van of all movements towards international goodwill and co-operation, an eager partner in every effort to show by precept or practice the folly and the dangers of economic war between nations.

CHAPTER XVIII

THE BALANCE OF TRADE

STERLING is no longer linked to gold. It has become an inconvertible and independent currency, linked to nothing. Its rate of exchange with gold-standard currencies can now vary, and has varied, freely. It follows that the prices of goods, expressed in sterling, can now move quite differently from the prices of the same goods expressed in, say, dollars or francs. This, too, has happened: during the last few months sterling prices have risen while gold prices have fallen. How do these changes affect our arguments or conclusions?

The gain to a country from specialising in certain branches of production, and exchanging goods and services with other countries, remains as great whatever the monetary mechanism by which these exchanges are effected. The gold standard is a device for maintaining practically fixed rates of exchange between countries which adopt it. Our departure from gold is a misfortune, for fluctuating rates of exchange increase the risks of international trade and investment. Yet it has simplified the mechanism. Payments between countries are still made in the ways described in Chapter III. But if more cars and so on are bought from abroad than our exports, in the widest sense, can pay for, the discrepancy is corrected simply through an alteration in the rate of exchange. The devices necessary to keep sterling pegged to gold are no longer needed for that purpose. The bank rate may have to be raised at times to prevent internal inflation, but movements of the bank rate are no longer necessary to prevent or check a loss of gold. It follows that this simplification of the mechanism in no way weakens our arguments or conclusions.

Chapter VII, however, deals with an argument for Protection based on the assumption that Great Britain would remain on the gold standard. Great Britain has not remained on the gold standard, so that for the present that argument has lost all force. It has no relevance to present conditions. Nevertheless, in one form or another, it has played a leading part in recent tariff discussion. We have been told that Great Britain's adverse trade balance constitutes a grave national emergency and that the most imperative task of the National Government is to redress it. This was, indeed, the most prominent argument for the Abnormal Importations Act, for the Horticultural Products Act, and for the recent ten per cent. tariff. It is the same argument as that discussed in Chapter VII, although it is sometimes confused with side-issues arising from the free exchange rate of sterling. We suggest that it must be misunderstood by those who put it forward, for sincere and reasonable men would not use a weapon which has no application whatever to the needs and realities of to-day. The present chapter is an endeavour to clear up these misunderstandings.

To begin with, "the balance of trade" is a phrase with several possible meanings. Since this can best be shown by an example, let us consider the relevant figures for this country for 1929.

Imports of merchandise amounted to £1,221,000,000, and exports to £839,000,000. Sometimes it is the difference between two such totals which is meant by "the balance of trade." In 1929, it would then be said, there was an "adverse" or "unfavourable" balance of £382,000,000.

Imports of gold coin and bullion amounted to £62,000,000 and exports to £78,000,000. The second possible meaning arises from adding the gold to the merchandise. In this sense, the adverse balance in 1929 amounted to £366,000,000.

The Board of Trade estimates that the net credits or receipts of this country in 1929 from the so-called invisible items, on income account, were as follows:

	£
Estimated excess of Government receipts from overseas	24,000,000
Estimated net national shipping income .	130,000,000
Estimated net income from overseas investments.	250,000,000
Estimated receipts from short interest and commissions	65,000,000
Estimated receipts from other sources .	15,000,000
	£484,000,000

The third possible meaning arises from adding these invisible items to the merchandise, thus turning an adverse balance of £382,000,000 into a "favourable" one of £102,000,000; and the fourth arises from adding them to the merchandise plus gold, giving a favourable balance of £118,000,000.

Capital transactions, however, have not yet been taken into account. It is difficult enough to make estimates approaching accuracy of such items as the net national shipping income or the net income from overseas investments. It is still more difficult, indeed, probably impossible, to make reliable estimates of capital transactions. One figure only, in this case, is known with certainty. In 1929 £94,000,000 of new issues for overseas were floated on the London market. Clearly non-residents might have brought sterling in order to subscribe to these issues and clearly British residents might have lent abroad in other ways. Such items, moreover, as the sale of foreign securities by Englishmen who transfer the proceeds to England, the withdrawal of sterling balances by foreign banks, and the purchase of English real estate by non-residents, to give only three examples, are not known. Let us suppose, however, that they could be ascertained, and included in our list of debits and credits. It is often urged that over any period of time, however long or short, a year, a week, or an hour, the two sides of the account would exactly balance, provided that we included only the payments and not the transactions which gave rise to the payments. Thus, for 1929, exports made in 1929 but not paid for until 1930 would be excluded, but payments made in 1929 for goods exported in 1928 would be included. This merely means that for every amount of sterling bought the same amount is sold. "The Balance of Payments always balances."

Yet this is a somewhat empty truism. It can perhaps be evaded by distinguishing between deliberate capital transactions on the one hand and an induced change in foreign balances on the other hand. Suppose that, as a result of all the operations of a given year, foreign banks, without willing it or desiring it, found their sterling balances in London increased by £50,000,000. In fact, they do not keep such balances in the form of gold in their vaults; they buy Treasury Bills, lend to discount houses, and invest in other fairly liquid ways. Thus the £50,000,000 might be termed an increase in Great Britain's foreign short-term indebtedness, and this is the course often adopted. Nevertheless, a clearer picture of what has happened is obtained if such a sum is distinguished in thought, even if it cannot be distinguished in fact, from other capital transactions. For it is important to bring out the point that if more sterling is required by foreigners than can be supplied by foreigners, then the foreign banks act as buffers and supply the deficiency from their sterling balances in London, while in the opposite case these balances absorb the difference. Of course this is true, to a less extent, of British banks and similar institutions which have balances in foreign currency abroad. When they are paying out more sterling in London than they are receiving on account of international transactions, their foreign balances increase; in the opposite case they diminish.

This induced residuum, then, which arises, if banks and similar institutions remain passive, as the result of the year's deliberate, willed operations between this country and the rest of the world, is the "balance" in a fifth possible sense.

We have now to consider the connection between the

balance of trade, in one or other of these senses, and a tariff upon imports.

Before 21st September 1931, when sterling became divorced from gold, there was undoubtedly an argumentative case for a tariff in order to redress the balance of trade.

In 1930 this country's excess of imports of merchandise was £386,000,000. There was a net import of gold of £5,000,000, giving an adverse balance in the second sense of £391,000,000, as compared with £366,000,000 in the preceding year. Moreover, the net receipts from "invisible" items had fallen. They were estimated at only £414,000,000, giving a favourable balance in the fourth sense of only £23,000,000, as against £118,000,000 in 1929. Capital transactions remained unknown, but new issues floated for overseas amounted to £109,000,000, so that it seems very probable that the balance in the fifth sense was negative or adverse.

In 1931 these tendencies were accentuated. The gap between imports and exports of merchandise became no smaller, there was a net export of gold, income from shipping and from overseas investments was known to be falling heavily. Whither were we tending?

Every transaction in international trade, to recall a famous phrase, is an independent transaction. If consumers find imported goods cheaper or more suitable, they will buy them. If investors find foreign outlets for their savings more attractive, they will use them. Neither consumers nor investors may even have heard of the balance of trade. Yet foreign sellers and borrowers must be paid, and in their own currencies, although by hypothesis there is not enough foreign currency available from British exports and other credit items to meet their claims. Thus foreign banks will find their sterling balances piling up and British banks will find their foreign balances diminishing.

This will not go on indefinitely, since foreign banks, as a rule, can use their excess balances (over and above what they need for making sterling payments) more profitably at home, while English banks require foreign balances adequate for their foreign exchange transactions. The banks, therefore, will tend to quote lower prices for sterling in the exchange market.

But Great Britain was on the gold standard. This meant that the rate of exchange between sterling and other gold-standard currencies could vary only slightly. When, for example, the price of sterling fell below 123·93 francs (the par being 124·21) it paid to convert sterling into gold at a fixed rate and ship the gold to France. Thus bullion brokers, or the banks themselves, would export gold.

But let us look ahead, as the advocate of a tariff on these grounds, in 1931, would have looked ahead. The export of gold alone will not be a solution. The real problem is to convert the negative balance, in the fifth sense, into a positive one; to equalise the flow of debits and the flow of credits; to make the payments into the London balances of foreign banks equal the payments out. The export of gold *per se* is like pouring bucketfuls of water into a tank from which the outflow is greater than the inflow. The real problem is to equalise the two flows.

Nor is raising the bank rate *per se* a solution. For a time the higher rates on short term investments may prevent or check an external drain of gold by making London a more attractive centre in which to hold liquid funds. Foreign banks, for a time, may retain or increase their London balances. The penalty will be to render Great Britain's position as a gold standard country more vulnerable, since a desire on the part of foreign banks to have more resources in a liquid form at home, or a fear that sterling may be driven off gold, will lead to heavy withdrawals. Even so, it will be necessary to attract a constantly growing volume of foreign balances, to keep the two flows equal; and it will be increasingly difficult, in the face of a growing supply of short-term capital, to make a high and rising bank rate effective. The remedy is not permanent.

The orthodox solution, of course, is that the loss of gold and the higher bank rate will have further consequences. It is important to realise what these are.

The problem is to raise the total value of exports or diminish the total value of imports, or both. Great Britain cannot force other countries to purchase the same quantity of goods at a higher price per unit. But a small reduction in the price per unit will probably lead to a considerable expansion of their demand, at the expense of her competitors, and will therefore raise the total value of her exports. To make this reduction possible, the costs of export industries must be reduced, and this means that costs must be reduced all round.

Similarly, Great Britain cannot force other countries to lower the prices of her imports. In order to reduce the total value of her imports, therefore, she must reduce the total value of all money incomes. But costs appear to their recipients as income. The same remedy serves for both exports and imports.

This remedy is a reduction of what may be termed "internal"[1] prices. Given free import and export, and fixed rates of exchange, the prices of goods which have a world market—of wheat or coal or motor-cars—cannot rise or fall much in Great Britain unless they move correspondingly elsewhere. But the prices of internal products, such as the services of railways or houses or labour, can do so. Transport charges or rents or wages can come down considerably in Great Britain, and yet remain the same elsewhere. The difference between internal and other prices is merely empirical. The two merge into one another. Labourers, and even in the last resort houses, will move between countries, or purchasers will migrate towards them, if price differences are sufficiently large. But, for convenience of exposition, the distinction can be drawn. In so far as it overstates the facts, it overstates also the case for a tariff.

The loss of gold or the higher bank rate, then, can re-

---

[1] "Sheltered" might be a better term, if it had not already been used to denote industries not in competition with those of other countries. In that sense the wages of workmen making for export are not "sheltered" but they are "internal" in the sense used here.

store international equilibrium only by reducing internal prices. Of these, the most important is the price of labour. Wages and other incomes from labour may be reduced. This will have a double effect. On the one hand, wage-earners and others will have less to spend on everything, including imports. On the other hand costs will be reduced in all industries, including export industries. Imports will be checked and exports stimulated until the two flows once more balance.

Now comes the crucial point. Suppose that wages, and perhaps other internal prices, in Great Britain in 1930 and 1931 were completely rigid. What then?

With Great Britain still on gold, both the costs and the selling prices of export industries would remain unchanged. Thus exports would not be stimulated. All adjustments would fall upon the imports side. Each person in employment, however, would receive as much as before and presumably would spend as much upon imports as before. The necessary curtailment of expenditure upon imports would have to be made through unemployment, by reducing some incomes to *nil*.

There are two reasons to suppose that exceptionally heavy deflation, involving widespread and growing unemployment, would have been required to restore equality between the two flows. First, the demand for imports, which include foodstuffs, is probably less elastic among wage-earners than the demand for home products. Second, unemployment benefit involves a transfer of spending power to the unemployed. Thus, on the assumption of rigid wages, a staggering amount of unemployment might have been necessary to curtail imports sufficiently.

The reader will remember that we are repeating the case for a tariff as it might have been stated, and was stated, before September 1931, and, upon the assumption of complete rigidity, the case was at least plausible. Rather than face such drastic deflation and unemployment, it was urged, let us devalue the currency, or restrict foreign investments, or grant export bounties, or in some way *make*

[251]

the two flows balance. One obvious way, it was said, was through a tariff. With a tariff we could remain on the gold standard, at the old parity. Import prices would be raised and imports checked while, by hypothesis, internal prices were rigid, so that if raw materials were not taxed the costs of export industries would not rise. Surely, on these assumptions, a much better solution!

Our answer to this line of reasoning is given in Chapter VII, but a few main points may be restated briefly here. Even on these assumptions, we believe that a less harmful corrective than a tariff could be found. But there is no need to elaborate this aspect of the matter. For these assumptions were not true. The recent experience of countries in three continents has shown that they were false. Rigidities greater even than our own have melted under a frontal attack. The real solution, and the only permanent solution, was to reduce our costs and to restore flexibility not only to wage-rates but to our whole economic organisation.

A possible retort is that by the late summer of 1931 it was too late to turn to these long-run measures. The crisis was already upon us, and something had to be done at once. Even so, we cannot believe that a tariff, which distorts production, sets up obstacles to trade, and creates vested interests which tend to make it permanent, would have been a wise remedy for a temporary emergency. But this question, too, need not be discussed. For it is clear that the exchange crisis was too violent for any tariff imposed then to have saved sterling from its fall. And, with that fall, both the "emergency" case and the long-period case have completely disappeared.

The problem considered in the preceding paragraphs was due to two factors. It was due, in the first place, to the assumed rigidity of internal prices, especially wage-rates. It was due, in the second place, to Great Britain's desire to stay on the gold standard. Remove either of these two factors and the problem vanishes. Remove the first, and it is solved by reducing money incomes and costs. Remove the second, and it is solved by a free exchange rate. Countries such as Germany, at the moment of writing, are still facing such a problem. For various reasons they wish to remain on the gold standard. Wage-rates and the like, although by no means rigid, cannot readily be reduced sufficiently to make the two flows balance. Hence the resort to such measures as tariffs, import quotas, exchange restrictions, and export bounties. Possibly a departure from gold would be better for them, and for the world, than these measures. But Great Britain *has* departed from gold. Whether this solution was ineluctably thrust upon her is a matter for debate. That it *is* a solution, and a complete solution, of the problem of restoring external equilibrium, is beyond dispute. The case for a tariff on these grounds is dead. Banks and similar institutions can now quote lower rates for sterling to prevent their London balances from becoming unduly high, or, in the case of British banks, to prevent their foreign balances from dwindling and disappearing. Since sterling is no longer tied to gold at a fixed rate, there is no obligation on the Government or the Bank of England to borrow abroad or to raise the bank rate or to take any action whatever to keep foreign exchange rates fixed. The exchange-value of sterling is determined from day to day, like the price of wheat or cotton, by the free play of supply and demand.

The exchange-value, or price, of sterling, moves to the point which equates the supply of sterling and the demand for it, whereas on the gold standard steps had to be taken to make the supply and demand equate at some point very near the fixed price of 4·866 dollars. On the supply side, of course, are British importers, and all other persons who wish to part with sterling in order to get foreign currencies. During recent months, these others have included the Bank of England, which has been accumulating dollar balances to repay its debt in New York, and the Bank of France, which has been withdrawing some of its sterling balances. On the demand side are buyers of British exports and all others who wish to part with foreign currency in order to get sterling.

These others include, for example, British residents who wish to sell foreign securities and—if exchange restrictions permit—to transfer the proceeds to this country. Foreign banks, and other institutions, can thus equalise the two flows simply by altering the price at which they will sell drafts on London.

As this price rises, some would-be buyers of sterling fall out: the higher price does away with their potential profits. On the other hand, new sellers appear, since foreign currency can now be bought more cheaply. An exchange-value of sterling well below the old level restricts the flow of debits and stimulates the flow of credits. It raises the price in sterling of foreign goods and services and securities. Thus consumption of imports is checked. It lowers the price, in foreign currencies, which British exporters need ask in order to get a given amount of sterling. Thus exports are stimulated.

These effects have been somewhat masked during recent months. Gold prices have fallen, so that the sterling wholesale prices of imports have not risen, as compared with September 1931, by the full extent of the depreciation of the pound in terms of gold. Many countries have left the gold standard and their currencies remain near their former parity with sterling. It is sometimes said that we can therefore buy as cheaply from these countries as before. That is not quite true. If the chief supply of a commodity comes from gold standard countries, and the gold price remains the same, then other countries will demand the equivalent of the old gold price. Britain is such an important market, however, that in some cases all sellers might lower their prices somewhat, even with unchanged costs, to prevent their sales to this country from being drastically curtailed. Possibly, to some extent, this has happened. If so, it implies that under our tariffs "the foreigner" may in some cases pay part of the duty. But it will be noted that exactly the same "advantage" has been obtained under a free exchange-rate and would have been obtained by remaining on gold and deflating.

[254]

A further reason why the cost of living has not risen in proportion to the fall in sterling is that internal prices have not increased, so that the portion of a retail price representing British labour in any form, remains unchanged.

On the credit side, the great decline in world trade has tended to reduce the total volume of British exports, although Britain's *share* of the world's export trade has risen.

Nevertheless, the effects, although masked, are present. No steps need to be taken to preserve international equilibrium. It will be achieved, and has been achieved automatically, by a free exchange rate.

Some readers may remain unconvinced. They may feel that our analysis is correct but incomplete. Will our conclusions hold if other countries go off gold or raise their tariffs? Will not a continuous depreciation of sterling be necessary? Is not a tariff needed to "defend" sterling?

The course of events since September makes these doubts look singularly unreal. Other countries have gone off gold, they have imposed new tariffs or quotas, nearly thirty countries have exchange restrictions, and yet, without a tariff, sterling has not continuously depreciated and shows no symptom of needing defence, while there is no sign of an adverse balance in any relevant meaning of that term. Nevertheless these questions demand some consideration.

Let us take an extreme case, in order to test our conclusions. Suppose that every country goes off gold. Will not our trade balance, in the fifth sense, again become adverse?

If it does, this means that foreign banks will be accumulating undesired sterling balances. They will, therefore, quote lower rates for sterling until this accumulation—our adverse balance in visible form—ceases and disappears.

Suppose their Governments wish to keep their currencies at the old parity with sterling, or below it. Then they must keep up the price of sterling by purchasing, day by day, these excess balances. This may continue for a time. Some may term the result an "adverse" trade balance of Great Britain. We prefer to call it an over-valuation of the sterling exchange, arising from the deliberate acquisition of funds in London by other countries. But the point is that this cannot last for long. As capital accumulates in London and becomes scarcer elsewhere, interest rates will fall in London, and rise elsewhere. Foreign Governments will either abandon their task as too expensive or will be driven to inflation. This will raise their money incomes and costs, so that imports from Great Britain will be encouraged and exports to Great Britain discouraged, until, at their chosen exchange-rate, the two flows are equal. It will be noted that what foreign exporters gain on the exchange, they lose on their costs, unless their Governments or banks are deliberately accumulating funds in London which they could use more profitably at home.

The view that our adverse balance cannot be redressed if other countries impose tariffs is also incorrect. The exchange-value of sterling would fall, assisting exports to surmount the tariff barriers and cutting down imports until the flow of credits equalled the flow of debits. We should suffer in that fresh tariffs elsewhere would still further contract trade, but we should have no adverse balance.

Will only a continuously depreciating exchange-rate solve our problem? If British wages and other costs rise sufficiently to counteract the exchange-bonus on exports, and to enable wage-earners and others to purchase as many imports as before, the problem reappears, to be solved only by a further depreciation of the exchange, and so *ad infinitum*. True: but what does it imply? It implies inflation —otherwise how can the total of money incomes continuously rise? If we refuse to inflate the problem is "solved," upon these assumptions, not by a depreciating exchange-rate but by greater unemployment. In fact, experience has already shown that these assumptions are not true: money incomes have not risen appreciably despite the depreciated exchange; and if they were true, they would apply just as strongly to a tariff. The tariff

[256]

would need constantly to be raised. The point is that a rise in money incomes not due to greater productivity will lead to unemployment unless counteracted by increased receipts of employers. A free exchange-rate, in such circumstances, tends to prevent such unemployment by raising the receipts of exporters at the cost of consumers of imports.

In what way does sterling need defending, now that the terms "favourable" and "unfavourable" have ceased to have any meaning, since there is now no need to take steps to prevent a drain of gold? A tariff will not make our exchange-rate more stable. It will not prevent temporary over- or under-valuation due to deliberate accumulation or withdrawals of capital. It will not prevent speculative movements due to anticipated changes in our exchange-rate. The remedy here is to return to gold, when conditions become favourable, at the most appropriate level. The preliminary to such a return should be the restoration of flexibility throughout our economic system, to prevent our being driven off again if conditions change. In these directions a tariff will not help. The only way in which it might "protect" sterling is by keeping our exchange-rate somewhat higher, and presumably that is what those who use such phrases mean.

A tariff checks imports. By reducing the purchasing power of other countries and raising the costs of export industries, it also checks exports. It is possible that imports will be checked more than exports—much depends on the extent to which wages rise—and in that event our exchange-rate will be higher than without a tariff. Is this desirable?

Less than half our foreign investments are fixed in terms of sterling. If our debtors continue to pay in full, a higher value of sterling will mean that our income from such investments (or our receipts if we sell them) will purchase more dollars or goods on the world's markets. On the other hand, as compared with the lower rate which would prevail without Protection, export industries will suffer and yet, owing to the tariff, the cost of living will not be lower. Both a high rate and a low rate bring gains to some sections and losses to others. The rate required is simply the rate which comes about naturally, without tariffs or restrictions. Sterling needs no defence.

In so far as those who wish to redress our adverse balance are thinking of the excess of merchandise imports over merchandise exports, they are restating in different words an opinion they might have expressed at any time in the last hundred years. They want Great Britain to be more nearly self-supporting. Cheap foodstuffs and raw materials from abroad have so far saved us from the worst consequences of the world depression. Yet ancient fallacies are still repeated, wrapped in new phrases.

The effect of a tariff resembles that of a depreciated exchange in cutting down imports. But there are dangerous differences.

A tariff does not leave consumers free to select which imports they can best do without. It makes the selection for them, or, at least, strongly influences their choice. This may be thought wise. We think it a loss. Nor is a tariff as flexible an instrument as a free exchange-rate. It creates vested interests and can only be readily altered in an upward direction. Further, by reducing imports it tends to make the rate of exchange higher than it would otherwise be. This places export industries at a disadvantage, even if wages and other internal costs do not rise. As the Tariff Advisory Committee will discover, even imported semi-finished and finished articles, as well as obvious raw materials, may form part of the costs of some export industry. Unless such goods are exempt from duty, or adequate drawbacks given, the costs of export industries will to that extent rise by the exchange depreciation *plus* the duty. If their other costs, notably wages, rise also by this amount—to the full extent, that is, of the increased cost of living—export industries will be in a worse position than before our departure from gold. Finally, the repercussions of a British tariff upon world trade must inevitably be harmful. A great trading nation does not gain by the impoverishment of its neighbours.

What then should be our policy, now that sterling is divorced from gold? First of all, in our view, we should guard against inflation. Under the gold standard insular inflation was impossible; it would have been stopped by the export of gold. To-day there is no such check. The danger of inflation is that it inevitably leads to a crisis when it stops, if not before, and that, in the meantime, it adds a depreciating exchange-rate to the risks and uncertainties of international trade. It can be prevented by keeping the bank rate sufficiently high and the note issue at its present level.

Next, we should do our best to restore the free flow of international trade and investment, from which, as a nation, we gain so much.

Finally, we should try to make our whole economic system more flexible, better prepared to adjust itself to changed and changing conditions. A free exchange rate solves the problem of maintaining external equilibrium. It does not abolish the rigidities which have been, and are, responsible for much of our heavy unemployment and for our lost ground among the manufacturing nations of the world.

In all these spheres a tariff will do harm. It will strengthen the demand for a lower bank rate and an increased note issue, to help industrial expansion. It will deal international trade a blow perhaps more severe than our departure from gold. It will tend to confirm and strengthen existing rigidities. Thus if we return to gold, either at the old parity or at a lower level, we shall be in constant danger of being driven off once more.

We shall not comment upon the new duties, existing or proposed, at this stage. The fact that tariffs have been imposed in no way weakens the arguments against them. Those arguments remain as strong as ever. We deeply regret that they will now be confirmed, in our own country, by the hard teaching of experience.

NOTE

THE Table on page 20 has been left unchanged, although revised estimates for 1929 and 1930 have been made by the Board of Trade, since the discussion in the text is not affected by these revisions. The most recent estimates, published in the *Board of Trade Journal* for 18th February 1932, are shown below in the form adopted on page 20.

INTERNATIONAL TRADING ACCOUNT OF THE UNITED KINGDOM IN 1929, 1930 AND 1931.

	(In millions of pounds.)		
	1929	1930	1931
Due to United Kingdom:—			
For Exports of Goods produced in United Kingdom . .	730	571	389
For Exports of Bullion . .	87	90	140
For Shipping Services . .	130	105	80
As Net Income on Overseas Investment . . .	250	220	165
As Short Interest, Commissions, and for other Services . .	80	70	40
As Excess of Government Receipts from other Governments	24	19	16
Total . . .	1301	1075	830
Due from United Kingdom:—			
For Goods imported and retained	1112	957	798
For Bullion Imported . .	71	95	107
Total . . .	1183	1052	905
Net Balance due to (+) or from (−) United Kingdom . .	+118	+23	−75

APPENDIX

A. THE ANTI-DUMPING REGULATIONS OF THE SOUTH AFRICAN TARIFF[1]

BY ARNOLD PLANT

(Reprinted, after abbreviation, from *Economica*,
February 1931)

THE first and main object of this paper is to examine the origin, the technical form, and the economic nature of the anti-dumping regulations which have been introduced into the South African tariff. Secondly, the question is considered whether the regulations, which differ only in minor technical detail and in the degree of wisdom with which they have been administered from those in operation elsewhere, are adequate to eliminate the business practices which they are intended to combat; or whether they are not really undesirable, except as part of a more comprehensive interference with discriminatory price policies, both domestic and international.

(1) DEFINITION OF DUMPING

It is fortunately unnecessary to give a general account of the nature of international dumping and of the attempts which have been made, during this century, more particularly by some of the sister nations of the British Commonwealth, to suppress it. That ground has been adequately covered by Professor Jacob Viner.[2] Economists are now

---

[1] Substance of a paper read before the British Association at Cape Town, July 1929.

[2] *Dumping : A Problem in International Trade* (University of Chicago Press, 1923), and *Memorandum on Dumping*, submitted to the Preparatory Committee for the International Economic Conference held

generally agreed as to what constitutes "dumping," and will not quarrel with Professor Viner's definition of it as "price discrimination between national markets," if qualified by the proviso that it is almost invariably understood in the sense of "selling at a lower price outside the national boundary."[1] Whether the fact that the price discrimination takes place across a national boundary provides any economic justification for peculiar treatment (as seems to be the view held by Professor Viner), will be considered later. Professor Viner regards it as essentially "A Problem in International Trade."

(2) TYPES OF DUMPING

Clarity will be introduced into the discussion by the adoption, with slight amendments, of Professor Viner's analysis (p. 23), classifying dumping according to the duration of the dumping and the motive of the dumper:

Sporadic.	(i) To dispose of a casual overstock.
	(ii) Unintentional.
Short-run or intermittent.	(i) To maintain or develop a market.
	(ii) To eliminate or forestall competition.
	(iii) To retaliate against dumping in the reverse direction.
Long-run or continuous.	(i) To secure economies from larger scale production than domestic market can absorb without cutting domestic price.
	(ii) On purely mercantilistic grounds.
	(iii) To counter a protective duty in the export market.

under the auspices of the League of Nations in 1926 (publications of the League of Nations ; II, Economic and Financial ; 1926, II, 63). Where in the course of this paper I take a somewhat different stand from that of Professor Viner, the disagreement must not be taken to imply any lack of appreciation on my part of the general excellence and comprehensiveness of Professor Viner's account and analysis.

[1] Cf. Taussig : " The disposal of commodities in a foreign country at one price, and to domestic purchasers at another and higher price."

International dumping may take various technical forms. In "ordinary" dumping, the price discrimination is revealed simply by a comparison of the invoices of identical sales to a domestic buyer and to a foreign buyer. In "sales" dumping, the invoice prices show no price discrimination, but the goods exported are sold by traders, or from stocks held "on consignment" by agents, in the receiving country, at lower prices. The term has also been extended to cover "bounty-fed exports," "freight dumping," and "exchange dumping," each of which may or may not involve price-discrimination between the domestic and foreign markets. These will be described and examined later.

(3) ANTI-DUMPING MEASURES

The student of economics, having regard for the welfare of the community as a whole rather than for that of a sectional interest without consideration of repercussions on the rest of the community, will always experience an initial difficulty in viewing the sale of goods to a community by a foreign seller at a price which does not represent the full cost of production, or which is lower than the price charged in other markets, as harmful to the community receiving the goods sold at the lower price. The conditions in which the proposition is true will be examined later. For the present it is only necessary to point out that the evils which accrue from discriminating selling do not arise from the fact that the seller is situated outside the national boundary, and are consequently in no way peculiar to international dumpings. In fact, for reasons that are not economic and are not difficult to understand, international dumping has been singled out for special regulation by certain countries receiving the goods at the lower price. Dumping may or may not be objectionable; and recognition of this fact is responsible for the regulations being made permissive in some countries, though mandatory in others. The measures taken to prevent dumping are generally of four main forms:

(i) A sufficiently high rate of customs duty against all imported goods of the "dumped" type, whether dumped or not, to offset any reduction in price.

(ii) Countervailing duties against bounties, although the bounties may not involve "dumping" as defined.

(iii) Prohibitions or restrictions on importation of goods, where intent is proved on the part of the exporter to destroy or injure a domestic industry. Australian legislation has followed this form since 1906.

(iv) Special anti-dumping duties, intended to equal the amount of the price discrimination between the domestic and foreign market, as provided for, *e.g.*, in Canadian legislation since 1904 and in South African legislation since 1914.

(4) COMPLAINTS AGAINST DUMPING IN SOUTH AFRICA

Judging by references in official publications, complaints against unfair competition and dumping have been loudest and most numerous in South Africa, as elsewhere, during periods of falling prices and trade depression. It is instructive to examine the protests which have been recorded (*a*) in the published evidence and reports of Commissions in the coastal colonies of the Cape of Good Hope and Natal in pre-union days, and in the Union of South Africa since 1910, and (*b*) in the official *Journal of Industries*; for it was the impression created by these complaints that made it possible to pass the legislation of 1914, first making provision for counter-measures, and the subsequent amendments.

The agitation for government intervention against dumping into the four colonies now forming the Union of South Africa can be studied in the Reports and Evidence of the Natal Industries and Tariff Revision Commission of 1905-6; the Customs Tariff Commission of Cape Colony, 1907-8 (G. 10 and 11 of 1908); and the Commission on Trade and Industries of the Union of South Africa, 1910-11 (U.G. 10 of 1912; U.G. 9 of 1913).

Classifying the complaints on the basis of the type of evidence adduced, we may distinguish three main groups.

(*a*) First, in the majority of cases, there is no evidence of actual dumping at all.

Thus the Natal Commissioners refer to doors and windows as "dumped" apparently because prison-made; and to cement as dumped because the ordinary duty has been removed. The Cape Commissioners record evidence of a straw-hat manufacturer who complains of the competition of dumped hats from Luton because the price is lower; of sugar "dumping" from Australia because the price is "in no way regulated by 'world values,'" meaning thereby the price of "88 per cent. Beet f.o.b. Hamburg"; and quotes the complaint of a Cape Town furniture manufacturer of the dumping of furniture from the East End of London made by sweated labour working "at least ten or twelve hours or more every day for small wages." The Union Commissioners report without evidence that dumped leather and adulterated leather are injuring the leather industry. As late as January 1921 the official *Journal of Industries* in an editorial comment calls attention to the "dumping" of low-priced goods made in Germany by American and British firms "on the American and other markets at prices which the native industry cannot meet," but does not allege that the export prices are lower than the prices in Germany.

None of these examples in fact shows any evidence of discriminating charging of the type known as "dumping."

(*b*) Secondly, a number of cases occur in which the sale of imported goods by auction is regarded as "dumping."

Thus the Natal Report describes as dumping "the consignment of goods for sale by auction at whatever price they will fetch"; the Cape Commissioners quote evidence of a Cape Town manufacturer concerning the dumping of cheap furniture to be sold by auction, of a Port Elizabeth jeweller concerning "indiscriminate dumping of jewellery, watches, silverware, and electro-plate through the local auctioneers," and a petition of thirty-five Port Elizabeth trading firms complaining of injury "caused by the frequent auction sales of new goods . . . specially imported for disposal by auction sale." The Union Commissioners of 1912 still coupled together the dumping of furniture, and importations of cheap furniture consigned to auctioneers for sale. Yet in none of these cases was it argued that the auction price of the goods was lower than the selling price in the exporting country.

(c) Thirdly, a few instances are recorded of allegations that selling prices of "dumped" goods were lower than the domestic price; or at least lower than the cost of production, implying actual price discrimination.

Thus the Cape Commissioners report dumping of surplus production at prices "very often less than the cost of production, which is possible owing to the preservation of their home markets by high protective duties"; and quote evidence of an East London miller which correctly describes "dumping" transactions, as generally understood. The Union Commissioners refer to sales at a loss to the exporting manufacturer, and in their report on the sugar industry refer to Javanese sugar refined in Australia and exported at prices considerably below the Australian price.

These instances show an understanding of what constitutes dumping. If the allegations could be substantiated the only question would be whether such dumping were detrimental to the South African public as a whole.

(5) MOTIVES ASCRIBED TO DUMPERS INTO SOUTH AFRICAN MARKET

It is somewhat surprising to find that the complaints against dumping before the 1914 Act was passed rarely alleged that the dumper had any ulterior motive beyond the desire to dispose of occasional surplus production. The Cape Commissioners, referring to the dumping of flour from Australia, remark that "it is admitted not to be a continuous practice, but one depending on the state of the market in the country of export." They did not bring out the point that the strength of their argument for anti-dumping regulations lay precisely in the fact that the dumping was not continuous and therefore capable of being anticipated in making contracts, but fitful and consequently disturbing to local production, although in the evidence of a Port Elizabeth miller the inconvenience of *spasmodic* dumping is stressed. The Union Commission of 1912 defines dumping as "the off-loading of the surplus products of manufacture of one country into the markets of another country," and only one witness, giving evidence concerning candle-making in the Transvaal, alleges that "predatory dumping" might take place, *i.e.* that the overseas manufacturer might dump in order to maintain his export market in the face of growing local industries and "play a losing game until he has succeeded in cutting out the South African manufacturer": but he makes no allegation that such dumping was taking place in the candle industry. Yet the Minister who introduced the dumping clause in the 1914 Bill (*Hansard*, 3rd June 1914) definitely described as the object of the dumping which the clause was to obviate "a temporary reduction for the purpose of raising the price ultimately." No evidence had been led that any overseas firm either was practising predatory competition or had such a control over overseas sources of supply as would make possible an ultimate raising of price.

(6) PREVENTIVE MEASURES PROPOSED IN SOUTH AFRICA
BEFORE 1914

It is clear from the published documents of the three Commissions that from the date of the Canadian legislation of 1904 there was a persistent clamour in South Africa for the application of a similar dumping clause. Many of the witnesses who advocated the adoption of such a clause before the Natal and the Cape Commissions had only the vaguest idea of its nature, and as has been shown their evidence suggests that in only one or two instances could they have secured any concession had it been applied at that time. The Natal Commissioners as early as January 1906 unanimously recommended the adoption of the Canadian Dumping Clause "amended to better suit, we think, South African circumstances and conditions." The Cape Commissioners in 1908 also recommended a Dumping Clause on the Canadian model, adopting the proposals of the representatives of certain of the milling and furniture businesses.

Two proposals other than the dumping clause were also made in the report and evidence of the Cape Commission. Some members of the Commission were impressed by the special pleading of the opponents of the sale by auction of new imported furniture, and recommended a special surtax on all furniture so imported at the rate of 20 per cent. *ad valorem*. Secondly, three witnesses before the same Commission, who had made much of the dumping of furniture, flour, and straw hats without appreciating the real connotation of the term, advocated higher permanent protective duties as the only possible method of securing relief. The Commission was clearly anxious where possible, however, to avoid unnecessary increases in the permanent duties.

In 1912 the majority of the Union Commission adopted as a recommendation with very few variations a form of dumping clause which had been modelled for them by the manufacturers' associations on the Canadian Act, the adoption of the clause being again urged by the representatives of the furniture, milling, sugar, and leather industries. Two members of the 1912 Commission, in separate minority reports, opposed the adoption of a dumping clause. Mr. W. A. Martin argued forcibly that "the system is liable to great abuse, and lends itself to the grant of additional protection to the local industry, often on grounds that are not justified"; that the consumers would lose the benefit of the lower prices, and that "a dumping clause is dangerous because it invites retaliation." Mr. (later Sir) Wm. Macintosh was not convinced that there had been consistent dumping, and argued that South Africa's own policy of dumping agricultural products was likely to continue, with a result that she "might find such a dumping clause lead to unpleasant retaliation." He disliked the rigidity of the Canadian clause, and expressed a preference for the Australian model, if any, on the ground that it was more elastic.

(7) ACTION TAKEN BY PARLIAMENT

In 1914 the first Dumping Clause, on the Canadian model, was introduced in the Customs Tariff Act (No. 20 of 1914). It was supplemented by further provisions in the Customs and Excise Amendment Act of 1922 (Act 35 of 1922) and superseded in part by the Customs and Excise Duties Amendment Act of 1923 (Act 23 of 1923); and finally the anti-dumping provisions were re-enacted as Chapter II of the Customs Tariff and Excise Duties Amendment Act of 1925 (Act 36 of 1925). In the following sections the provisions of these enactments will be examined from the point of view of their appropriateness for the economic purpose for which they were designed.

(8) COMPARISON OF DOMESTIC AND EXPORT PRICES

One problem in the drafting of an anti-dumping regulation is to determine which of the many records of domestic prices and export prices that are available for any commodity are to be compared for the purpose of ascertaining whether dumping is taking place. Theoretically, dumping is the acceptance by the seller of a lower net price for an identical transaction when made with a foreign instead of a domestic buyer. It is extraordinary how much confusion has existed, and how much thoroughly bad legislation has remained operative for many years, on account of failure to apply this definition consistently and logically.

(a) Time of the Comparison

It should first of all be perfectly clear that to be valid the comparison must be between the prices quoted by the seller for identical transactions at the moment of acceptance of the contract. No importance whatever attaches to the prices that may be ruling at any subsequent time when the goods happen to cross the customs barrier in transit to the importer. In the Canadian legislation, although the prices compared are those at the date of exportation, a regulation of 1904 clearly and properly provides for substituting the price at the date of purchase in the event of an increase in the domestic value in the interim.[1] The Natal Commission's proposal of 1906, based on Canadian regulations in force at that date, provides for the same adjustment. Yet for eleven years, that is, from 1914 to 1925, the South African anti-dumping legislation made this fundamental mistake. In section 8 (i) of the 1914 Act the prices of the goods to be compared are those "at the time of their exportation"; in section 12 (i) of the 1923 Act, "at the time of shipment," but in section 19 of Chapter II of the 1925 Act, for purposes of interpretation of the anti-dumping clauses "for the words 'time of exportation' shall be substituted the words 'date of purchase thereof by the importer.'" It is unnecessary to comment on the state of jeopardy in which all importers buying for forward delivery are compelled to transact their business, or the loss sustained by the South African community on account of fluctuations in supplies and prices, if importers are not permitted to derive profit from intelligent anticipation of future demand and supply.

In 1924, when world wheat prices rose and the price of bread in Durban increased by $33\frac{1}{3}$ per cent. between July and September, South African importers of Australian wheat who had brought forward in the early part of the year found that the dumping duty payable on some shipments "amounted to as much as 3s. 9d. and 4s. per 100 lb., owing to the fact that the flour was bought before the rise

[1] Viner, page 197, and J. W. Root, *Colonial Tariffs*, page 225.

or at the commencement of the rise in price to be shipped at a later date when the price of flour in Australia had risen by an equivalent amount."[1] It is not surprising that in these circumstances the importers preferred to take their profit by selling in Australia. South Africa was deprived of some of the anticipated arrivals and the dumping duty on those parcels was not paid. The advocates of anti-dumping regulations might well decide against attempts at practical application of their principles if considerations of administrative convenience can for eleven years permit so crude a travesty to masquerade as the embodiment of their proposal. The new Board of Trade appointed on the change in government in 1924 recommended the withdrawal of the dumping duties on wheat and flour (B.T.I. Ref. 644, 19th November 1924), but they were retained as a protective device. The 1925 Act, introducing the correct interpretation of dumping by substituting "date of purchase" for "time of exportation," actually makes provision (section 16 of Chapter II) whereby a special rate of dumping duty may be fixed arbitrarily by the Minister, if "the levying, in respect of wheat or wheaten flour, of the ordinary dumping duty . . . would, by reason of market fluctuations, be undesirable." The Board of Trade explains as the motive for this abandonment of the only legitimate measure of dumping an anxiety to ensure "that the wheat farmer does not lose any of his legitimate protection on account of fraud in respect of the date of sale" (B.O.T. Report 67, 27th April 1926). This can only mean that the administrative difficulties of ascertaining the domestic and export prices at the date of purchase were regarded as insuperable. The Report of the Board of Trade on Wheat Growing and Milling,[2] however, shows that the dumping duty was in fact being used to increase the rate of permanent protection to wheat farmers. The Board recommended that the existing dumping duties on Australian wheat and flour be

[1] Inquiry by the advisory Board of Trade into The Rise in the Price of Bread. (B.T.I. Ref. 644, dated 19th November 1924.)
[2] No. 67 of 27th April 1926.

withdrawn, that the average amount levied in dumping duty on imports from Australia be added to the ordinary protective tariff on imported wheat and flour (not simply from Australia), and that additional dumping duties be levied whenever "excess dumping of wheat and flour (*i.e.* dumping in excess of the amounts incorporated in the increased customs duties) is taking place. . . . It is of great benefit to all concerned to secure the certainty and stability consequent upon the imposition of fixed duties on wheat and flour." In 1926 the ordinary protective duties were accordingly raised by 5d. per 100 lbs. (£27,850 having been collected in dumping duty on Australian wheat alone (225,000,000 lbs.) imported between 1st July 1924, and 30th June 1925). Thus the excessive amount levied on the incorrectly calculated dumping duties was added to the permanent protective duty, and provision still made for the imposition of additional dumping duties on wheat and flour by as arbitrary a method as that employed hitherto. The whole episode, and this section of the report, must come as a shock to enthusiastic advocates of anti-dumping regulations.

(b) *What is the Domestic Price?*

To establish the fact of dumping, as defined, the domestic price which should be compared with the export price is the price at which the *same seller* makes identical sales in the domestic market. The South African legislation has undergone considerable modification since the 1914 Act was passed, but at no time has it made this fundamental stipulation. The 1914 Act refers, it is true, in the dumping section 8 (i), to the true current value "of the *same* goods when sold for home consumption in the usual and ordinary course," and the 1923 Act adds the phrase "in the principal markets" (cf. section 7 of the 1914 Act); but the 1925 Act in section 14 (3) gives a comprehensive definition of "domestic value" which greatly adds to the discretion of the administrating officer by permitting a comparison of prices with those of any goods that he may consider sufficiently "similar," although not necessarily either the same or sold by the same seller. These facts have opened the door for a much more extensive and dubious application of the legislation than could otherwise have been possible. All the Acts (section 9 of 1914 Act, and section 14 (4) of 1925 Act) give the Commissioner of Customs discretion in cases of special difficulty to assess the value for duty (subject to appeal). Nevertheless in a Board of Trade Report (No. 88 of 1928) on the dumping of wire nails from Germany and Belgium, although the dumping was held to be definitely established, the Board did not recommend a dumping duty "as considerable difficulty was experienced in ascertaining the true domestic value . . . owing to the existence of rings and cartels"; and an ordinary protective duty was actually recommended and imposed instead, although apparently not even asked for by the complainants. The difficulty of ascertaining the true domestic value still remained to be solved by the customs officials for the purposes of collection of the ordinary duty.

(c) Reduction of Prices to a Comparable Basis

It is clear that the export price of goods placed free on board ship at the port of export is not immediately comparable with the domestic price wherever it may be quoted. Thus for the purposes of the 1914 Act "the true current value for home consumption" is defined (section 7) as "including carriage to the port of shipment and the cost of packing and packages, but not including agents' commission when such commission does not exceed 5 per cent." The Customs Act of 1923 did not repeal this section with the dumping clauses (section 8), but stipulated that the dumping duty is leviable where the export selling price, free on board, is less than that for home consumption "plus the free on board charges." The wording of the Acts appears to have thoroughly confused the trading community, the manufacturers, the Customs Department, the legal advisers to the Government, and the advisers constituting the Board of

s   [273]

Trade and Industries.[1] The Customs Department appears to have interpreted section 7 as applying only to the levy of ordinary customs duty, and to have omitted the costs of placing goods on board from the "home consumption value" for purposes of applying the dumping duty; while under the 1923 Act the costs of packing for export were omitted, on the advice of the legal experts, in interpreting the phrase "free on board charges." Special difficulties arose in cases where packing in the domestic trade is returnable (*e.g.* cement bags), whereas export packing (cement casks) is included in the export price, since the appropriate adjustments were not possible under the wording of the Acts. The 1925 Act seems at last to have swept most of these difficulties away by stipulating that the comparison shall be between the export price free on board and the domestic value "plus the extra cost of packing and packages for export, carriage to the port of shipment, and all other expenses incidental to placing the goods on board ship ready for exportation to the Union."

The 1925 Act moreover dealt correctly for the first time with the question of drawbacks and excise. Where a drawback is granted on export the resultant difference in price between export and domestic prices is not regarded as dumping (section 19). Excise duties payable in the country whence the goods are exported are not included in the domestic value (section 14 (3)), since the net return to the seller is no less in the export sale than in the domestic sale in cases where the domestic price exceeds the export price by the amount of the excise duty payable.

(d) *Who shall ascertain Domestic Value?*

Finally, even if the domestic price had been correctly defined in the legislation, a judgment on the operation of the regulations must depend on the fitness of the machinery

---

[1] Cf. *Journal of Industries*, Vol. VII, pp. 315-25. Report by former member of the Board of Trade to the Minister of Finance. B.O.T. Report No. 42   18th November 1924.

for ascertaining the facts. Unless adequate provision is made to ensure that the true facts are established, the whole scheme is suspect. In South Africa it cannot be said that the machinery is yet adequate.

Under the original 1914 Act the normal method of ascertaining the domestic value was presumably to accept the declaration of the exporter, while under section 9 the Commissioner of Customs was empowered to determine the facts in difficult cases, subject always to the right of appeal to the Minister. The Customs Department was thus left with a large measure of discretionary power which could be arbitrarily or sporadically exercised. Without an adequate overseas investigating staff it was manifestly impossible to obtain prompt and regular advice of changing values. Dumping might therefore pass unnoticed or, having been detected, be subjected to rates of special duty which soon ceased to be appropriate to the facts. The prompt readjustments which are essential to the proper administration of anti-dumping regulations were barely obtainable. In fact, the Customs Department until 1923 normally required the complaining manufacturer in South Africa to establish to its satisfaction what was the domestic value of imported goods.

There was in consequence much discrepancy between the data adduced by the complainant, by the Department, and by the exporters' declaration. A report by a former member of the Board of Trade on cement dumping[1] well illustrates the range of divergence that existed. The complaining cement company in South Africa alleged that English domestic prices varied from 51s. to 58s. per ton less 2½ per cent.; the Customs Department gave the price as 42s. 9d. The author of the report, with commendable zeal, volunteered further prices, including a London firm's quotations ranging from 51s. to 58s. and 63s. 6d. less 2½ per cent., and the *Economist* and trade papers' quotations of 58s. to 63s. 6d. On the basis of these quotations he accepted the figure of 58s. and argued that dumping was taking place to an extent

[1] *Journal of Industries*, Union of South Africa, Vol. VII, 1924.

which justified a duty four times as high as that then in force. But it is clear that such evidence, especially prices quoted in trade papers, is not to be relied upon absolutely. With the exercise of still a little more zeal he could have ascertained, as we have done, that the cement quotations in the *Economist* "represent prices in the London area, including delivery charges from the works to the site, and are subject to discount or rebates depending upon the quantities taken by the consumer in a given period." They are not to be accepted in their crude state.

The 1923 Act made provision (section 13) for the acceptance by the Commissioner of Customs in cases of doubt of a certificate of domestic value signed by an investigating officer in the country of export. This method at least provided for more impartial evidence, but left too much arbitrary power in the hands of the officials, while providing no special machinery for appeal from decisions reached. The Board of Trade Report No. 48 (28th December 1924) on the case of Mozambique cement reveals much divergence in the evidence on which a dumping duty was actually applied. Before the proclamation of the duty the Commissioner of Customs apparently had no evidence of dumping beyond a quotation of a price for delivery of cement to Witbank in the Transvaal from Delagoa Bay. "There is no evidence that any actual transactions were put through on the basis of the quotation referred to." The Mozambique Company in its turn was apparently "invoicing its product to the local distributor and sole agent at a lower price" in Portuguese East Africa than the general public was paying, presumably with the object of concealing the true domestic value. Nevertheless, a duty was applied under the Act of 1923; and the Board of Trade produces singularly unconvincing evidence of prices in its report in support of its recommendation that the dumping duty should not be repealed.

Section 14 of the 1925 Act has partially rectified the position by providing for an appeal to the Minister; but it cannot be regarded as satisfactory that the investigations and report of a single investigating officer in the country of export shall constitute the evidence on which duties may or may not be imposed.

(9) LIMITATIONS ON THE AMOUNT OF DUTY

Limits are applied to both the minimum and maximum rates of *ad valorem* duty that can be levied. In view of the vagueness of the evidence concerning domestic value it is clearly desirable to fix a minimum limit of difference between the two prices before the regulations may be applied, if much vexatious dispute is to be avoided. In this matter it was not until 1925 that South African practice fell into line with the Canadian practice since 1904, of applying the dumping duty only where the difference exceeds 5 per cent. of the export price.

With more caution than logic, the legislation has throughout provided for an *ad valorem* maximum beyond which the dumping duty may not be increased. In the 1914 Act the maximum rate is 15 per cent. *ad valorem*; increased in 1923 to 25 per cent., and in 1925 to 50 per cent. ("one-half of the value of the goods for duty purposes"—section 15 (i).) Theoretically such limits are inadmissible if the general policy of penalising dumping is accepted; but it cannot be said that the fear of imperfect administration which has prompted the caution has been unwarranted.

(10) SPEED OF INVESTIGATION AND DATE OF APPLICATION

Unless a report that dumping is taking place is immediately investigated, and a duty applied before the consignment in question is cleared through the Customs, the regulations cannot be said to serve the purpose of preventing short-run dumping such as may result from the export of casual surplus stocks. Attempts to secure such promptitude have invariably aroused a strong protest from importers, who fear that an ordinary business transaction will be converted by unforeseen government interference into a certain loss. From 1914 to 1923 the South African legislation was innocuous against most sporadic or short-run dumping on account of a clause which required six weeks' notice of the intention to apply a dumping duty proclaimed in the *Gazette*. In six weeks it is possible to rush consignments at least ten thousand miles. The only possibility of using the legislation against sporadic shipments arose, therefore, in cases where they were likely to be intermittent and to re-occur at sufficiently short intervals to warrant keeping a proclamation in force, with all the administrative expense of checking the domestic values regularly throughout.

An effort has been made in the 1923 and 1925 Acts to increase the effectiveness of the legislation in connection with short-run dumping, by providing that the duties may be imposed from the date of publication of the proclamation in the *Gazette*. Unless the government officials have advance information of the impending arrival of "dumped" goods it is still impossible to apply the duty to what may be isolated consignments. As an example, a dumping duty was proclaimed against Mozambique cement on 2nd June 1924, but the Board of Trade, reporting in December 1924 (B.O.T. Report No. 48), admitted that "no dumping duty has been collected on Mozambique cement, except 13s. 9d. collected in June. . . . It should be explained that 30,200 lbs. of cement were imported in June, of which 28,200 were cleared on 2nd June before the dumping duty became operative."

(11) PERIOD OF OPERATION OF DUMPING DUTIES PROCLAIMED

There is no provision whereby anti-dumping regulations enforced against a particular trade cease to operate after a fixed term unless specifically renewed, nor does there appear to be any regular procedure in the matter. Such references to the withdrawal of proclamations as exist in official documents usually refer to the fact that no importations have taken place, or no duties been levied, for a considerable period. Much work is thrown on customs officials in the checking of prices where proclamations are allowed to continue in force without reason. It may be argued, on the other side, that the practice serves as a warning to importers, and prevents a renewal of dumping.

The community is prevented from ascertaining the importance of dumping duties in South Africa by the absence of any separate returns showing the amount of duties collected, the rate of duty charged on each consignment, and the extent of dumping taking place and actually penalised. It is consequently impossible to form any judgment on the effectiveness of the duties in force at any moment, or on the extent of the burden of additional taxation and higher prices which is being borne by the community in order to prevent detriment to a sectional manufacturing interest. It is only when other interests have been strong enough to secure the reversal of a decision and the removal of a dumping duty that evidence as to the effect of the dumping duties is forthcoming. It is distinctly regrettable that such information is not regularly placed before the community.

In addition to provisions against "ordinary" dumping by private traders, legislation has also been devised to combat dumping resulting not from deliberate discrimination by the seller, but from State action or the operation of other conditions which have resulted in lower prices for export.

(12) FREIGHT DUMPING

It is curious that the country which is probably more closely associated than any other with governmental attempts to frustrate monopoly control of shipping freight rates should at the same time place on its statute book legislation which seriously hinders the reduction of these rates to a competitive basis, in that it operates to prevent the South African consumer and importer from benefiting by accepting offers of shipping space at less than the ruling freight rates.

As early as 1911, Bloemfontein millers complained in

their evidence to the Union Commission on Trade and Industries "that flour was not only dumped by means of a cheaper export price, but also by means of freight when steamers require cargo to fill up." Legislation against so-called "freight dumping" was not introduced, however, till 1923. The Customs Act No. 23 of 1923 in section 12 (3) empowers the government "to determine a minimum rate of freight" and to levy "a special customs duty" equal to the difference between this rate and the net freight rate paid, whenever the goods are "carried to the Union at a rate of freight which, in the opinion of the Minister of Finance, is detrimental to the production or manufacture of those goods in the Union." The operation of the Act is restricted to goods whose value for duty purposes, together with marine insurance and freight charges, is less than £10 per ton.

The clause was applied in the same year on cement from seven European countries, the minimum rate of freight being fixed at 17s. 6d. per ton of 2000 lbs. Unfortunately, no statement was issued to the public, giving the reasons why the freight rate then ruling was objected to, but a Report (No. 60) of the Board of Trade in 1926 showed that over £8000 was collected in freight dumping duty during 1924 on cement from the United Kingdom, Belgium, Germany, and Norway, compared with only £30 in the first nine months of 1925. The freight rate on cement having been effectively prevented from falling, the duties were withdrawn in 1926.

In its Report on Dumping (No. 42) issued in 1924, the new Board of Trade rightly described this legislation as "a very arbitrary, unsatisfactory, and unsound method of assisting local industries. It is an essentially arbitrary procedure," the Board continued, "to vest in the Governor-General the fixing of a minimum rate of freight, since the determination of freight rates in general depends upon a variety of factors to be taken into consideration by shipping interests. It is also unsound in principle, because the fixing of minimum freight rates (already reprehensible in the case of shipping rings) by governmental authority is tantamount to placing a premium on high freight rates, whereas it is in the interest of the foreign trade of any country to secure the lowest possible shipping rates." If freight rates became so low as to endanger Union industries, the Board recommended an increase in the ordinary customs duty.

In view of such a display of economic insight on the part of the Government's advisers in 1924, a new freight dumping clause (section 15) in the 1925 Act provided another disappointment. The new method is to levy a duty equal to "the difference between the net freight paid . . . and that which would have been payable at the rate prevailing at the date of shipment for those classes of goods usually rated for shipping purposes on the same basis." The effect of such a plan is obviously to make the possibility of South Africa ever benefiting from the increase of competition in the provision of shipping services more remote than ever. In the absence of competition it is possible for transport enterprises to discriminate in their charges between different classes of goods, not merely on a basis of the difference in cost of conveying various types of cargo, but on a basis of "what the traffic can bear," *i.e.* what the elasticity of demand enables the monopolist to extort in each case without losing the traffic. The process by which competition brings down transport charges is not by offering lower rates on a class of traffic as a whole, but by singling out those commodities in each class which are classified on a basis, not of cost of transport, but of what the monopolist is able, in the absence of competition, to extort. It is precisely this healthy and beneficial process which the new freight dumping clause impedes.

The one instance of the application of this clause provides a classic example of the economic harm which it can inflict on the community. It was applied to superphosphates imported from Holland on 23rd December 1927, and from Belgium on 9th March 1928. Superphosphates are widely used as fertilisers by the farming community and are manufactured (from imported materials) in South Africa. In the second half of 1927 a new shipping line entered into sharp competition with the conference lines, and the freight rate on superphosphates (among other commodities) fell from 12s. 6d. per ton (it had been as high as 20s. a few years earlier) to 5s., fixed as from 30th September by the conferences lines. The imposition of the dumping duties resulted from an unpublished report by the Board of Trade to the Government that, "as a result of the current freight war, the local superphosphate industry was placed in a very serious and precarious position and was practically confronted with the necessity of ceasing operations entirely in the near future, unless steps were taken to counteract the effect of freight dumping" (as stated in B.O.T. Report No. 89, 15th March 1928). The only meaning that this statement can have is that the landed price of imported superphosphates had fallen on account of the freight dumping. The wheat farmers protested to the Minister that the duty had raised the prices of superphosphates, and the Board of Trade was instructed to investigate a second time. The published report No. 89 will bewilder students of economics. It maintains that the freight rate was to be raised on 1st April 1928 to 10s. a ton as the result of the dumping duties, that "the local manufacturers will no doubt be able to carry on under the 10s. freight," and recommends that the dumping duties be withdrawn when the 10s. rate is reimposed: but it then proceeds to state that the orders for superphosphates were placed on c.i.f. quotations before the freight rate fell, with the consequence that the landed price was *not* lower (despite their previous report), although the overseas exporters themselves secured the benefit of the lower freight. The importers had to pay dumping duty because the superphosphates were shipped at the lower freight rate, but the price they paid was not lower, being fixed by contract, and the price to the farmers was raised by the amount of the duty. "These farmers have been detrimentally affected without the local industry deriving any commensurate benefit" (from the duty). As a result, at the recommendation of the Board, the importers have actually been repaid the amount of dumping duty

[282]

levied, on condition that they reimburse their customers. But, although no dumping duty is at present being levied (so far as can be ascertained without published returns), the proclamations have not been withdrawn, and the importers may at any time find themselves taxed because their suppliers have secured a favourable freight contract.

Finally, it should be noticed that freight dumping as defined in South Africa is not dumping at all, on the basis of the ordinary definition, since it does not imply that the seller is accepting a lower price for export than for identical domestic sales.

(13) "SALES" DUMPING

Where the importer in the receiving country is financially linked to the exporting business, or is an agent receiving goods "on consignment," the export price assumes the significance of a book-keeping entry in a branch accounting system, and the domestic price must then be compared, after suitable adjustment, with the selling price charged in identical transactions by the importer. South African legislation has dealt with cases of this description under Art. 35 of 1922 (section 6), and since 1925 under section 15 of the 1925 Act.

For the purposes of the 1922 Act the price in South Africa is compared with "the price at which similar goods are sold wholesale in the principal markets of the country of their manufacture for consumption therein, added to the cost of packing and packages, the free on board charges and the cost of the freight from the port of shipment," and the difference is levied as a special duty. It will be noticed that no mention is made of ordinary customs duty. If the ordinary duty levied were paid in whole or in part by the exporter, the consignment was not on that account liable to dumping duty, although the net price received on export sales would then be lower than on domestic business.

Since 1925 the definition of sales dumping has been amended in a most significant way, for if the price at which imported goods are sold in South Africa does not include the full duty to which they are subject under the ordinary customs tariff, a dumping duty may be imposed. The comparison of the price in South Africa is now made with "the domestic value thereof plus the extra cost of packing and packages for export, inland carriage, sea freight, insurance and all the charges to that port, including landing and delivery charges and any duty (other than a dumping duty) payable under this Act or any amendment thereof." No longer will it be possible, if this Act is systematically enforced, for protectionists in South Africa to argue that customs tariffs do not raise prices! The duty has been applied to rubber heels and rubber hose from Canada and the United States.

(14) EXCHANGE DUMPING

The stimulation to exports caused by the steady and continuing depreciation of European currencies during the post-War years produced a curious result in that, in spite of selling policies on the part of exporting manufacturers in the countries concerned which were in all probability the very reverse of "dumping," the customs policy of the South African Governments since 1922 has been to describe the phenomenon as dumping, and to levy special duties calculated in most arbitrary fashion. The increase in export trade as the currency of the countries in question depreciated was of course due to the fact that the external value of the currency fell more rapidly than its internal value, *i.e.* that the price of goods in the country did not rise sufficiently to offset completely the fall in the exchange. Manufacturers found that although they charged much higher prices in their own currency for the goods for export than they did for sale in the home market—*i.e.* that although "reverse dumping" took place—their export trade boomed. In consequence the term "exchange dumping" is probably in almost all cases a misnomer.

The Act of 1922 contained the first provision against

[284]

exchange dumping, which remained in force until super-seded by the Act of 1925. The first method used (section 5) was as arbitrary as the first provision against so-called freight dumping, which has already been examined: a rate of exchange was to be determined from time to time by the Governor-General and the goods revalued on that basis, the difference between that value and the value actually charged to be levied as "a special or exchange duty." Differences of less than 10 per cent. from the price of similar commodities from countries with an exchange rate which had not depreciated were not to be charged (section 5 (1)), and the exchange duty was limited to 50 per cent. of the value of the goods. The unsatisfactory features of such a scheme need not be dwelt upon: six weeks' notice of intention to levy the duty had to be given, the arbitrarily selected rate of ex-change was consequently out of date before it was applied, the rate was not altered to keep pace with changing condi-tions, and as the exporting countries gradually succeeded in stabilising their currencies at a new parity and prices adjusted themselves to it, the rates of duties became simply prohibitive. Such duties were enforced against Italian and Belgian asbestos-cement sheets from 1924 till 1929, against Belgian cement and superphosphates from 1924 to 1926, and against asbestos-cement sheets from Jugoslavia and France from 1925 to 1929. Without information as to the amount of duty collected it is not possible to hazard a guess at the extent of the arbitrary interference with trade that must have resulted.

The Act of 1925, which embodied the suggestion of the new Board of Trade, defines exchange dumping in a manner which is not much more satisfactory. The dumping duty to be levied is now "the difference between the export price of the goods in question and the export price of goods of the same class or kind imported into the Union, from countries, the exchange value of whose currency in relation to Union currency is not depreciated by more than 5 per centum, and from which such goods on importation are not otherwise liable to any dumping duty in terms of this section." The maximum limit of 50 per cent. of the value of the goods is retained, but the minimum difference below which a dumping duty may not be levied has disappeared. The theoretical objections to a policy of assessing the value of the products of one country, which may possess very special advantages for that trade, by comparison with the value of those from other countries, are not great in themselves if we assume a free market, absolutely comparable goods produced on an appreciable scale in several countries, and conditions which will secure one market price, but the application is another matter. In South Africa it has at times been difficult to find a country without a depreciated currency, but with a current export business to the Union in the commodity concerned and against which no dumping duty was at the time in existence. For example, when an attempt was made to calculate the amount of exchange dumping of cement from Belgium in 1926 (B.O.T. Report No. 60), the only country against which no dumping duties were already in force was the United States. The Board of Trade secured a cabled quotation from New York for delivery of cement to South Africa, compared with which the amount of Belgian dumping worked out at 83 per cent. of the value, as the result of which a new exchange dumping duty was proclaimed as from 1926, the maximum rate of 50 per cent. apparently operating. A similar duty was levied against Jugoslavia. It is not stated whether the United States was actually selling cement to South Africa at the price quoted; but the method of assessing the duty is clearly most unsatisfactory and arbitrary. It is to be hoped that no further need will arise to apply this particular provision.

(15) ANTI-BOUNTY DUTIES

The countervailing duties against bounties for which provision has been made in South African legislation since 1914, under section 8 (2) of Act 26 of 1914 and subsequently under section 15 of Act 36 of 1925, require no elucidation here, for the provisions have never yet been applied. But the theoretical position should be briefly considered. The fact that an exporter secures a bounty, bonus, rebate or subsidy on exports does not necessarily imply that the amount received is used to lower his export price as compared with his domestic price, and unless that is established dumping is not proven. The manufacturer may utilise the bounty to reduce all his prices equally, to effect improvements, or pay extra dividends, or for any purpose. The bounty is in fact only one instance of unequal benefit by different producers from national expenditure. A better quality road than the average is as much a bounty as a grant of money from the State exchequer, but its value cannot easily be assessed for purposes of duty! If dumping is alleged as the result of a bounty, the facts should be ascertainable in the ordinary way, and the ordinary dumping legislation can be applied to the extent to which dumping is proven. There can be no need or justification for special anti-bounty duties in addition.

(16) CONDITIONS FOR APPLYING ANTI-DUMPING LEGISLATION

It must surely have always been clear to legislators that the acceptance of goods from sellers in other countries at prices lower than those charged in the country of origin is not always to be condemned as either immoral or uneconomic. Legislation in South Africa has defined conditions under which alone the anti-dumping regulations may be applied. In the 1914 Act it is only necessary that the goods should be "of a class or kind made or produced in the Union." In consequence the whole South African community might be deprived of the benefits of lower prices simply because someone in the Union was producing the same class of goods on any scale, irrespective of whether even his interests were being injured. Tremendous power to injure the community was in this way entrusted to the administrators of the legislation. The later legislation restricted the discretion a little further: under the 1922 Act

[287]

the importations must be "at prices which are detrimental to South African industries" and "an industry in the Union . . . (must be) . . . likely to be seriously affected," and the 1923 Act may be applied where "detriment may, . . . in the opinion of the Minister of Finance, result to a Union industry."

From all these conditions applied before 1925 the most fundamental economic safeguard is missing. The investigators and administrators are nowhere charged to consider whether the importations are detrimental to the South African community as a whole. It is sufficient that the importation is likely to be detrimental to a sectional interest —a Union industry—a principle which if consistently applied might prove sufficient to prevent any further economic progress. The possibility is ignored that the sectional interest of a manufacturer may not coincide with that of the consumer. A change was made in 1925 which aroused great hopes: under section 15 a prior investigation and report is to be made by the Board of Trade before a duty can be applied, and the Minister must be satisfied not only that detriment may result to a Union industry but also "that it would be in the public interest" to impose a duty. But actual results have not confirmed expectations.

That this general criticism has weight is evident from several examples of the application of the dumping duties, in which, judging from official reports, the authorities have concerned themselves solely with such questions as the size to which the local industry might expand if all competition were withdrawn, the possibility of its satisfying the whole demand of the country, irrespective of whether the cost of production would remain at the competitive level or the problem of ensuring that selling prices would continue to bear the same relation to costs. Wrapping paper, cement, superphosphates, and wire nails are outstanding examples. In the case of an article in as universal and continuous demand as wrapping paper (B.O.T. Report No. 41), a dumping duty was applied against Canadian and Swedish supplies on 12th September 1924, when the only factory in the Union, near Johannesburg and one thousand miles from Cape Town, employed normally only fourteen white men (three when the report was written), possessed unsuitable plant, which could not be reconstructed in less than six months after new capital had been found, and at best was designed to produce only 150 tons per month maximum production, at a time when the Union requirements were estimated (without reference to price) at 400 tons per month. The factory already enjoyed a protective tariff of $\frac{5}{8}$d. per lb., and the effect of the dumping duty as reported "will be to divert the trade from these countries to other competitors, chiefly Germany, Norway, and Finland."

The case of cement has greater importance and illustrates different economic conditions (see B.O.T. Reports No. 48 and 60). Cement and asbestos-cement sheets have been the subject of ordinary, exchange, and freight dumping duties imposed against importations from thirteen different countries. With the exception of one factory at De Hoek in Cape Province, the Union cement works are all in the interior. The Board of Trade reports that "even if the whole of the importations ceased, the local industry would be able to supply the Union's demands" (but no reference is made to elasticity of demand with falling price). The importance of low-priced cement in a country where building costs are high and immense constructional schemes must be undertaken, in connection with irrigation dam and railway development, need not be emphasised. The customs duty is 1s. minimum per 400 lbs. on cement, and 20 per cent. minimum on asbestos-cement manufactures. There has always been keen competition from overseas in the coastal markets, and the internal factories have been able to compete by virtue of three conditions:

(1) the freight charges from European and North American ports, and the customs tariff;

(2) favourable railway rates from their factories to the coast;

(3) the monopoly hold they have over the internal

T [289]

markets, on account of higher railway rates on imported cement to the interior, which have enabled them to charge high prices in the internal South African markets, and consequently to "dump" at the coast. After the War a company secured the monopoly of the right to manufacture cement in Mozambique, behind a high tariff, and came to the relief of the Rand apparently by utilising their monopoly power to charge high prices in Mozambique and "dump" supplies in the Transvaal market at lower prices than the South African producers were charging. The Board of Trade, having satisfied themselves that the Mozambique cement was being dumped, a dumping duty was imposed, without any consideration having been given (judging by Report No. 48) to the fundamental questions:

(1) whether the policy of discriminating charging adopted by the Union producers of cement, possessing as they did a large degree of monopoly control, was in the general interest;

(2) whether the detriment to the internal users of cement, caused by the higher prices, does not outweigh the detriment to the cement industry caused by the loss of its power to discriminate.

It seems incredible that on a weighing-up of the situation the sectional interests of the few persons engaged in producing cement can be reasonably regarded as of greater national importance than the provision of such a commodity at the lowest possible prices.

The conclusion must be that in the administration of this legislation the interests of the South African community as a whole have not been sufficiently before the investigators, whose duty it is to make recommendations. Alfred Marshall might indeed have foreseen South African experience when he wrote of dumping duties: "Neither experience nor general reasoning afford any good ground for supposing that such special taxes would be so managed as to effect their purpose well" (*Money, Credit and Commerce*, p. 209).

In all its investigations the Board of Trade ought to have access to, and should utilise, the special experience of all sections of the community. When an investigation is to be made, ample notice should be given in the Press and evidence invited from the general public. Evidence should be taken in public and reports should, without exception, be published. The *procedure* of the Canadian Tariff Advisory Board might in fact be followed. It does not, however, appeal to the South African Board of Trade. "In South Africa the Board takes all evidence *in camera*, but, whenever supplementary evidence appears to be desirable, enquiries are addressed to parties who may be affected by the favourable consideration of any particular application. On the whole, this method appears to have given generally satisfactory results." If this paper has shown anything, it is that the results have been far from "generally satisfactory." The investigating Board cannot be relied upon to suspect the existence of, and to seek out, the additional evidence which may cause it to vary its conclusions.

An opportunity also exists for improving the efficiency of actual administration by taking more complete advantage of membership of the British Commonwealth. Governmental relations between the sister nations of the Commonwealth are characterised by greater intimacy than is unfortunately yet attainable by the governments of independent foreign countries. Where similar legislation is being administered in more than one part of the Commonwealth much could be gained by schemes for pooling systematically the experience acquired in each for the benefit of all. The seconding of technical officers from one administration to another is a possibility which has much to commend it where administrative procedure need not be concealed, but where the opportunities for securing mutual benefit are great.

(17) IS ALL DUMPING HARMFUL?

Subject to the conditions explained in the last section, the South African legislation may be applied against all

T* [291]

instances of dumping. Yet it is generally recognised that long-run dumping, either continuous or recurring with such regular periodicity that it can be relied upon to continue, benefits the community receiving the dumped goods; while the administrative difficulties in the way of arresting in time isolated consignments of casual surplus stocks which may be dumped are almost always too great to make the attempt worth while. Every producing business is faced from time to time with sales of surplus stocks by its home competitors, and has to weigh up the case for buying them up or letting the public secure them.

There remains the class of intermittent dumping which does not recur with sufficient regularity to enable the community to rearrange its production on the basis of allowing for it, and which consequently causes temporary dislocation to local production. It may result simply from the desire of producers in times of depression in foreign countries, where prices are maintained above the competitive rate (as for instance behind a tariff), to sell abroad, at the best price they can get, such of their output as cannot be disposed of at home without "spoiling the market." On the other hand it may have behind it the predatory motive of maintaining a hold on the foreign market in the face of new competition, or of cutting out existing manufacturers in the foreign market with the object of raising prices after the competition has been killed.

Three observations can be made about such dumping. In the first place, the existence of "predatory" dumping is very greatly exaggerated. Very few, if any, groups of producers have so complete a monopoly of world supplies that they would be able after dumping to raise the price at which an importing country can cover its requirements. This is particularly true of a country like South Africa, so situated that no one large exporting group in one country has the advantage of proximity over other competitors in the South African market. Secondly, it is not the motive of the dumper, but the economic effect of the dumping, which may be harmful, and attempts to avoid the harm must apply equally against all forms of dumping which have these ill-effects, whether predatory in intent or not; just as, on the other hand, they should leave untouched all dumping which is not harmful to the community as a whole.

(18) THE PROBLEM NOT SIMPLY INTERNATIONAL

This leads one to the third point. If, as we have seen, the harm caused by dumping consists entirely in the dislocation and loss that it may cause to producers, and if interference to prevent it is desirable in those cases where the gain to the community from lower prices cannot be regarded as adequate compensation, then any measures adopted should cover such cases of dumping by manufacturers and sellers within the national boundary as well as those from outside. The harm caused is identical. The Port Elizabeth jeweller who gave evidence in 1908 was concerned with stopping dumping as much from Cape Town as from overseas. One of the criticisms that can perhaps be made against Professor Viner's work on this subject is that he treats dumping almost entirely as an international problem, and consequently does not so effectively eradicate the popular impression that it is only when foreign sellers are concerned that harm results and interference is desirable. Alfred Marshall wrote wisely: "It is obvious that international dumping is more likely when once detected, to be proclaimed aloud: it seems probable, therefore, that domestic dumping is at least as large in the aggregate as international, though opinions differ greatly as to the extent of each: and it is certain that the main incentives to dumping, and the technical problems raised by it, are substantially the same in domestic and international trade."[1] Certainly predatory dumping occurs much more frequently inside a tariff wall than in international trade, for a protective tariff enormously simplifies the formation by sellers of rings for the purpose of raising prices, and the monopolist group which wishes to fix prices will concentrate on removing local competitors, local

[1] Marshall, *Money, Credit and Commerce*, page 209.

dumping being one method of achieving that object. The country which applies anti-dumping legislation against international dumping without making equally strenuous efforts to restrain its own nationals from indulging in the same objectionable practices lays itself open to the charge of pursuing a crude protectionist policy in the interest of a favoured section of its population, or of permitting evil deeds against the community only when its own nationals are the miscreants! The United States of America, for example, has at least passed legislation in the form of section 2 of the Clayton Act of 1914 to make discriminating charging illegal within the United States. The wording, though perhaps questionable, is:

"That it shall be unlawful for any person engaged in commerce, in the course of such commerce, either directly or indirectly to discriminate in price between different purchasers of commodities, which commodities are sold for use, consumption, or re-sale within the United States, or any territory thereof, or the district of Columbia or any insular possession or other place under the jurisdiction of the United States, where the effect of such discrimination may be to substantially lessen competition or tend to create a monopoly in any line of commerce: Provided, that nothing herein contained shall prevent discrimination in price between purchasers of commodities on account of differences in the grade, quality, or quantity of the commodity sold, or that makes only due allowance for difference in the cost of selling or transportation, or discrimination in price in the same or different communities made in good faith to meet competition: And provided further, that nothing herein contained shall prevent persons engaged in selling goods, wares, or merchandise in commerce from selecting their own customers in *bona fide* transactions and not in restraint of trade."

It would seem to be only reasonable to expect of a community that insists on checking the evils of international dumping that it should at least consent to similar regulation of its own business conduct. The South African Board of Trade, in its Report No. 73 of 1926 on *Business Practices and Public Regulation*, made no recommendations in this connection.

(19) DUMPING BY SOUTH AFRICA

It should not be overlooked that dumping is also an established policy of South African producers, to a large extent on account of special government assistance. The most clear case of dumping, in the ordinary sense of the term, is by the sugar industry; but elaborate discrimination in railway rates for export consignments operates as a bounty on the export of agricultural produce of all kinds, and special legislation has provided for bounties on meat exports, all of which might on investigation reveal price discrimination between home and export markets.

The case of sugar deserves special mention. The industry enjoyed in 1929 a protective duty of 8s. per 100 lbs. on sugar other than candy, loaf, castor, icing, and cube sugar, on which the duty is 9s. per 100 lbs. Production has grown from 82,000 tons in 1910 to 242,000 tons in 1926-7 and nearly 300,000 tons in 1928-9, and well over a quarter of the product is exported. The industry has a virtual monopoly of the South African market, imports during the last few years averaging less than 2 per cent. of the production. The distribution of the crop is arranged by a Crops Disposal Committee for the whole industry. The price received by the producers has been fixed by the Board of Trade in 1926 on domestic sales at £25 per ton for first refined sugar, and maximum retail prices have also been fixed at the ports. The exported sugar is sold at world prices, and below average cost of production, the average price realised in 1925-6 for refined sugar being £14 per ton and for cargo sugar under £11. The industry finds itself in consequence exposed to attack from two sources; on the one hand overseas producers of sugar occasionally find it possible to dump surplus stocks over the tariff into the South African market, so that the sugar industry actually petitions for a dumping duty in addition to its protection, and on the other hand the South African public is becoming more and more alive to the existence of a monopolistic control of supply, which fixes the selling price to South Africans high above the price at which South African sugar is sold for export. It is not even certain that the quantity allocated for sale on the South African market is fixed at the point which brings the maximum monopoly profit. The elasticity of demand is possibly such that a larger allocation of the total production to the home market would produce a greater aggregate revenue.

From the point of view of the domestic consumer, as Professor Viner has shown, the dumping of produce by a monopolist group of producers is not necessarily harmful in that he may not be worse off than he would otherwise be *under the same monopoly conditions*. The producers fix the amount which will be offered for sale on the domestic market at the point which will yield maximum net return, and if the industry is subject to decreasing costs as output rises it may be profitable to dump the surplus overseas, even at prices below average cost of production, provided that the reduction in aggregate costs at least covers the apparent loss on the export sales. Prohibition of dumping would not benefit the home consumer unless it then paid the producing group to sell a larger output at home at a lower price and smaller aggregate return, rather than reduce output to the previously fixed amount for sale in the domestic market and incur the higher productive costs per unit. A mathematical investigation by T. O. Yntema into the influence of dumping on monopoly price (*Journal of Political Economy*, December 1928), apparently yields the interesting conclusion that, while the dumping of casual surpluses will always mean the maintenance of higher prices to domestic consumers, in the case of permanent dumping there is, given the continuance of the monopoly, a probability that under decreasing marginal costs domestic consumers may tend to benefit by lower prices. The obvious conclusion is that the monopoly conditions should be removed wherever possible, particularly where created by a customs tariff. Thus, although there may be little benefit from prohibiting dumping and forcing export prices up to the domestic level, there is a strong case when the power to dump presents itself for attempting to remove the monopoly conditions at home by reducing the import tariff and encouraging competition generally, in order that domestic prices may be reduced gradually to the world level. To illustrate from a particular case, if a sugar industry pursues a selling policy of dumping part of its output in the export market, the interests of the community as a whole require, not the imposition of dumping duties, but the gradual withdrawal of part of the protection which makes dumping possible.

Professor Viner[1] himself, in maintaining his proposition that dumping may not injure the domestic consumer where marginal costs are decreasing, treats as an important exception what is in fact only the most obvious case of the harm that a sectional monopoly does to the rest of the community. He refers with approval to the policy practised by dumping industries of supplying other manufacturers, who utilise the dumped product as a raw material in their

[1] *Memorandum on Dumping* (publications of League of Nations; II, Economic and Financial; 1926, II, 63, pp. 7-8). " It is often alleged that dumping results in higher prices to domestic buyers, but, with the unimportant exception of casual sales at dumping prices of over-stocks of goods already produced, there is little probability that such can ordinarily occur to any significant degree *if* the producers charge to domestic buyers, whether dumping is practised or not, the price which will yield them the maximum net return. . . . To the proposition just stated, however, there is one important exception. Where raw materials or half-manufactured products are exported at dumping prices, there may be serious injury from the dumping to more advanced domestic industries, which, though they pay the full domestic prices for their materials, must nevertheless compete in foreign markets with the products of foreign rivals manufactured from materials purchased at the dumping prices." In such cases Professor Viner would prohibit dumping unless domestic buyers using the product as a raw material in manufactures for export receive supplies at the lower price.

own export industry (*e.g.* sugar used by manufacturers of jams and preserves for export), with consignments at the export price, in order that overseas competitors may not secure an advantage. To the extent to which such concessions are made, the monopolist seller foregoes his monopoly profit on the sales that would have taken place at the full domestic price. Against this loss he may set off the increase in his share of the world market for his type of product which arises from the increased use of it as a raw material in an export. But the possibilities of expanding his sales at world prices are not confined to the making of concessions to those export industries that happen to utilise his product as a raw material *at first hand*. The price that he charges for his product enters indirectly into the production costs of many other constituent raw materials of other export industries, and the case for selling at the world price may be no less strong in each of these. Probably the concessions which are made can be attributed to two main facts: the seller thereby makes sure of part of the highly competitive world market, and secondly he avoids the popular indignation which his differential prices would be almost certain to arouse in such cases, the burden of the higher domestic charges being more obvious than usual to the general public.

(20) EFFECT OF ANTI-DUMPING REGULATIONS ON FOREIGN RELATIONS

One other aspect deserves mention. The fact that South Africa (against the interests of her own population) allows (and encourages by Protection and other State intervention) the monopoly conditions to continue in which dumping is profitable to her own producers undoubtedly encourages foreign governments to apply counter-measures and to retaliate: and retaliation makes the position worse generally for the South African community as a whole.

The question assumes added importance in the case of a country whose government is desirous of entering into most-favoured-nation agreements with foreign governments. The form of anti-dumping regulations requires that the countries against which the regulation applies be specifically named in the proclamation, and the question arises whether the grant of most-favoured-nation treatment to a country does not prevent discrimination against that country in the event of proof of dumping by its exporters. The question must be left to the international jurists and those responsible for the negotiation of trade agreements to decide, but the implications to South Africa cannot be neglected.

INDEX

A

Agriculture—
 advantages of territorial division of labour in, 157
 available supplies of agricultural products in Great Britain (Table), 163
 depression in, causes of, 150
  in U.S.A., Canada, Australia and Argentine, 149
 Protection for, arguments against, 157–158
  arguments for, non-economic balance between urban and rural population, 166–167
  security in case of war, 162
 effects of, 153 ff.
  ondistribution, 154–155
  on prices, 165
  on production, 155 ff.
 proposed forms of, 152–153
 wages in, 188
Amery, Rt. Hon. L. S., 10–11, 47, 48, 53–56, 61
Anti-bounty duties in South Africa, 273–274
Anti-dumping—
 criticism of South African measures, 290–291
 conditions of application for duties in South Africa, 287–291
 difficulties of imposition of duties, 129
 legislation in Australia and Canada, 129
 limits on in South Africa, 277
 measures, 263–264
 provisions in South Africa, 269
 regulations, effect on foreign relations, 298–299

Australia—
 anti-dumping legislation in, 129
 effect of tariff on scale of production in, 96
 Tariff Board, 195–196, 201–205

B

Balance of Trade—
 meaning of, 245–247
 under a free exchange-rate, 253–259
 of United Kingdom, 1929, 1930, 1931, 260
Baldwin, Rt. Hon. S., 38, 42, 53, 111, 168, 186, 188, 192–193, 199, 203, 207, 214
Balfour, A. J., 111, 232
Banks—
 and the balance of trade, 247
 effects of movement of bank rate, 76, 249
 functions of Central Banks under gold standard, 78
Beaverbrook, Lord, 28, 182
Bennett, Rt. Hon., 140, 142, 219
Beveridge, Sir William, 62, 69, 241
Bounties on export, 132
British Empire—
 export surplus of gold, wheat, wool, diamonds, jute and ground nuts, 143–144
 export surplus of wheat, 139–141
British Tariff, revenue from, 170
Burton, Mr. T. E., 64

C

Canada—
 anti-dumping legislation in, 129
 effects on import of capital into, 1910–1914, 23.
 Tariff Advisory Board, 200, 206

[300]